Chairing the Academic Department

Leadership among Peers

By Allan Tucker

AMERICAN COUNCIL ON EDUCATION
Washington, D.C.

Library of Congress Cataloging in Publication Data

Tucker, Allan, 1921-
    Chairing the academic department.

    Includes bibliographies.
    1. Departmental chairmen (Universities)—United
States. I. Title.
LB2341.T78   378′.111   81-1774
ISBN 0-8268-1424-4   AACR2

9   8   7   6   5   4   3   2   1
Printed in the United States of America

To the memory of Robert O. Lawton

Contents

Figures and Tables

Tables

Foreword

An institution can run for a long time with an inept president but not for long with inept chairpersons. Given the importance of the chairperson's position, the lack of published material about it is surprising. Occasional studies and compendia of journal articles about the position have appeared but have usually been of little immediate help to those struggling to be good chairpersons. Practitioners have not been well served by this literature, since it is written for students of the position and directed to theoretical rather than practical dimensions. In an attempt to correct this situation, the American Council on Education is publishing this book and sponsoring the Departmental Leadership Institute workshops, of which the author is the director.

Three characteristics of the position of department chairperson have become increasingly clear in the last decade. First, as institutions have grown more complex, more decisions are being made by chairpersons. As the basic academic unit, the department is the place where colleges and universities actually conduct the majority of their activities. Decisions made here are very difficult to undo elsewhere. Effective leadership and competent administration of the department, therefore, are essential to the sound operation of the institution.

Second, the selection of chairpersons is often based more on academic considerations or the person's reputation as a scholar than on his or her management qualifications. Traditionally selected from faculty ranks, chairpersons are now called on to exercise a variety of administrative skills not usually acquired as faculty members. Fresh to the office, many chairpersons find themselves facing a bewildering array of issues with little to guide them.

Third, the position of department chairperson is frequently the first rung of the academic administrative ladder. While some chairpersons will return to their faculty positions, others will aspire to further administrative challenges. Solid grounding in administrative style and technique early in one's career can pay lasting dividends, allowing one to assume additional and more complicated responsibilities.

This book focuses on precisely the kinds of concerns that new chairpersons have. Moreover, it is sufficiently comprehensive that even old hands can profit from reading it. The Council welcomes this opportunity to help chairpersons fulfill their responsibilities, for sound management at the department level can only further higher education's goals.

J. W. PELTASON, *President*
American Council on Education

Preface

A key position in the hierarchy of college and university administration is that of department chairperson, for it is the chairperson who must supervise the translation of institutional goals and policies into academic practice. Yet most chairpersons are drawn from faculty ranks and assume the position having had little administrative experience. Moreover, few opportunities for orientation and training are available to them.

This paradox became more and more apparent to me during the eleven years I served as academic vice chancellor of the State University System of Florida. Subsequently, after joining the faculty of Florida State University as professor of higher education, I submitted to the W. K. Kellogg Foundation a proposal requesting funds to design and test a model for enhancing the planning, management, and leadership competencies of department chairpersons. In 1977 the Kellogg Foundation awarded a major grant to Florida State University for this purpose.

To help define the primary issues confronting departments, chairpersons in the nine state universities of the Florida university system were questioned about their own experiences. In addition, information was gathered from their counterparts in many institutions of higher learning outside Florida. Materials were developed to address the topics suggested by the initial inquiry, and these materials were presented and tested in a series of seminars and workshops for chairpersons in Florida's state universities. This book reflects further revisions of these materials.

The fourteen chapters deal with common problems that chairpersons encounter. Departments vary considerably in size, age, and level of maturity. Modes of department governance also vary greatly, as do chairpersons' personalities and leadership styles. To develop a set of absolute prescriptions that would provide every chairperson with solutions to every problem would be an almost impossible task; no such attempt has been made here. The book does, however, present examples of common department problems and shows how some of these were solved. It suggests ways to recognize and approach these problems, but it is not intended to be a definitive document that must be slavishly followed if a department is to be effective. Rather, the book will, I hope, spur chairpersons to analyze their own departments and to compare them with those described here. The cases discussed may or may not be directly applicable to each department, but the process of comparison may help generate solutions to similar problems.

ALLAN TUCKER

Acknowledgments

I wish to thank the W. K. Kellogg Foundation for its generous support of the department leadership program, from which this book has evolved. I am particularly grateful to Dr. Arlon E. Elser, a program director of the Kellogg Foundation, for his valuable suggestions concerning the design and development of the project and for participating in many of the workshops. Dr. E. T. York, former chancellor of the State University System of Florida, Dr. Bernard F. Sliger, president of Florida State University, and Dr. Jack Gant, dean of the college of education, Florida State University, provided vital encouragement and moral support during the design and testing of the project materials. Dr. Robert O. Lawton, former academic vice president of Florida State University, deserves special recognition not only for his enthusiastic encouragement but also for attending and participating in many of the workshops. Many other persons—including presidents, vice presidents, deans, and chairpersons within and outside Florida—also provided assistance in the form of suggestions and critiques. In addition, I wish to express my appreciation to Dr. Jerry Miller, director of the division of academic affairs and institutional relations, American Council on Education, for his continuing interest and support.

The responsibility for determining the order, content, and style of each chapter has been mine. At least four persons, including myself, were involved over a period of three years in the writing, revising, editing, and rewriting of each chapter. Following is a list of the contributors who, under my direction, participated in the preparation of the manuscript:

George F. Aker, professor of adult education, Florida State University

Neil B. Betten, professor of history, Florida State University

John R. Bolte, associate vice president for academic affairs, University of Central Florida

Robert A. Bryan, vice president for academic affairs, University of Florida

Gary W. Peterson, associate professor of educational technology, Florida State University

Emanuel I. Shargel, associate professor of educational research, development, and foundations, Florida State University

Ilona Turrisi, director of budget analysis, Florida State University

John S. Waggaman, associate professor of higher education, Florida State University

I also wish to acknowledge Mary Miller, Linda Thompson, and Kathleen Bishop for their patient and tireless efforts in typing and retyping the many revised versions of each chapter. Special thanks are due Gretchen Smith, American Council on Education, who edited the manuscript and made many valuable suggestions concerning the shape of the book.

I accept full responsibility for any of the book's errors and inadequacies, and I share with my colleagues any credit for its contribution to the well-being of academic department chairpersons.

1

The Chairperson's Roles, Powers, and Responsibilities

||||| ||||||||| ||||||||||||||||||||||||||| |||||||||||||||||||||||||||||||||||||||||||||||||||||||||||||||||||||||||||||||||||||||||||||||||||||||||||||||||||||||||||||||||||||||||

The present economic crisis in higher education raises a fundamental question concerning the ability of colleges and universities to fulfill their traditional functions. Specifically, can institutions of higher learning maintain flexibility and viability, preserve quality, remain accountable, and respond effectively to the changing needs of society within the context of continuing inflation and steady-state or even declining resources? Academic departments are the organizational units within an institution that are most severely affected by steady-state or declining resources, and those who chair these departments can have considerable influence in resolving this problem.

Paradoxically, most department chairpersons are drawn from faculty ranks and have had, at best, very little administrative experience. A 1977 survey of 400 department chairpersons in the State University System of Florida found that 68 percent had no prior administrative experience, the turnover rate was 15 to 20 percent per year, and the chairpersons' term of service was usually six years. Forty-one percent of these chairpersons were elected by their colleagues, and another 44 percent were appointed by their deans with faculty consultation.[1]

While specially designed national and regional workshops are conducted for new presidents, vice presidents, and deans to help prepare them for their new responsibilities, few such opportunities are available to department chairpersons, who outnumber all other types of university administrators combined. The increasing complexities of operating institutions of higher education, along with shrunken budgets, have led deans and other university administrators to delegate more and more tasks to department chairpersons. Thus, it is in the best interests of colleges and

1. Survey conducted by Allan Tucker, unpublished.

1

universities to ensure that department chairpersons become as knowledgeable as possible about planning, management, and leadership techniques. The following list shows, by category, the astonishing variety of tasks and duties that face the department chairperson:

Department governance
Conduct department meetings
Establish department committees
Use committees effectively
Develop long-range department programs, plans, and goals
Determine what services the department should provide to the university, community, and state
Implement long-range department programs, plans, goals, and policies
Prepare the department for accreditation and evaluation
Serve as an advocate for the department
Monitor library acquisitions
Delegate some department administrative responsibilities to individuals and committees
Encourage faculty members to communicate ideas for improving the department

Instruction
Schedule classes
Supervise off-campus programs
Monitor dissertations, prospectuses, and programs of study for graduate students
Supervise, schedule, monitor, and grade department examinations
Update department curriculum, courses, and programs

Faculty affairs
Recruit and select faculty members
Assign faculty responsibilities, such as teaching, research, committee work, and so forth
Monitor faculty service contributions
Evaluate faculty performance
Initiate promotion and tenure recommendations
Participate in grievance hearings
Make merit recommendations
Deal with unsatisfactory faculty and staff performance
Initiate termination of a faculty member
Keep faculty members informed of department, college, and institutional plans, activities, and expectations
Maintain morale

Reduce, resolve, and prevent conflict among faculty members

Encourage faculty participation

Student affairs

Recruit and select students

Advise and counsel students

Work with student government

External communication

Communicate department needs to the dean and interact with upper-level administrators

Improve and maintain the department's image and reputation

Coordinate activities with outside groups

Process department correspondence and requests for information

Complete forms and surveys

Initiate and maintain liaison with external agencies and institutions

Budget and resources

Encourage faculty members to submit proposals for contracts and grants to government agencies and private foundations

Prepare and propose department budgets

Seek outside funding

Administer the department budget

Set priorities for use of travel funds

Prepare annual reports

Office management

Manage department facilities and equipment, including maintenance and control of inventory

Monitor building security and maintenance

Supervise and evaluate the clerical and technical staff in the department

Maintain essential department records, including student records

Professional development

Foster the development of each faculty member's special talents and interests

Foster good teaching in the department

Stimulate faculty research and publications

Promote affirmative action

Encourage faculty members to participate in regional and national professional meetings

Represent the department at meetings of learned and professional societies

The chairperson's job, obviously, is difficult and complex. A brilliant university or college administration with inept chairpersons cannot survive; an inept administration, with the help of a group of brilliant chairpersons, usually can. The position of department chairperson, then, is an important one. The discussion that follows is an attempt to describe and, to some degree, define the role of the chairperson.

The Paradoxical Nature of the Role

One distinctive characteristic of the chairperson's role is its paradoxical nature. The chairperson is a leader, yet is seldom given the scepter of undisputed authority. He or she is first among equals, but any strong coalition of those equals can severely restrict the chairperson's ability to lead. Deans and vice presidents look to chairpersons as those primarily responsible for shaping the department's future, yet faculty members regard themselves as the primary agents of change in department policies and procedures. The chairperson, then, is both a manager and a faculty colleague, an advisor and advisee, a soldier and a captain, a drudge and a boss.

Chairpersons are the only academic managers who must live with their decisions every day. The dean and the vice president make many important administrative decisions, such as which colleges or departments will get the lion's share of the year's operating budget. The dean and the vice president, however, do not have to say good morning—every morning—to their colleagues in the department; they do not have to teach several times a week alongside their colleagues; they do not have to maintain a family relationship with their faculty members. The department chairperson, on the other hand, does. He or she must be acutely aware of the vital statistics of each family member—births, deaths, marriages, divorces, illnesses, and even private financial woes.

This intimate relationship is not duplicated anywhere else in the college or university because no other academic unit takes on the ambience of a family, with its personal interaction, its daily sharing of common goals and interests (with frequent contention over how those goals are to be pursued), and its concern for each member. No matter how large the department, no matter how deeply divided over pedagogical and philosophical issues it may be, its members are bound together in many ways: they have all had the same general preparation in graduate school; their fortunes generally rise or fall with the fortunes of the discipline to which they all belong; and they share the same general value system of their profession. Working alongside the members of this "family" is the chairperson, a manager who is sometimes managed, a leader who is sometimes led, a parent who continually strives to keep peace for the sake of mutual benefit and progress.

These conditions are not the only ones that make the department chairperson's role paradoxical. He or she must deal with the expectations and desires of the students in the department, the personal and professional hopes and fears of the department faculty members, the goals and priorities of the college dean, the often perplexing and—from the department's perspective—sometimes shadowy priorities of the central administration, the sometimes naïve and sometimes jaundiced views of the alumni, and the bureaucratic procedures of accrediting agencies. Few administrators can, by themselves, face these conflicting constituencies and find solutions to all problems. Yet the chairperson must induce these constituencies to work together to help solve the problems they themselves generate.

A department chairperson's constituencies, in addition to department faculty members, include students and alumni. Students often seem to want less work and more entertainment. Undergraduates generally want the department to reduce the number of required courses for the major or to abolish certain degree requirements, such as specific courses in foreign languages, statistics, mathematics, humanities, or laboratory science. Graduate students generally want the scope of the qualifying examinations reduced and the language requirement modified or abolished; graduate assistants often want their teaching and research duties reduced. Students, until they become alumni, want "interesting" lecturers who give "fair" tests and don't require much outside reading or problem solving. Alumni want almost the opposite. Faculty members often want to increase the requirements for the department major to equal the number of credits necessary for the baccalaureate degree; they also are inclined to double the duties of the teaching and research assistants.

An astute chairperson will strive to establish a creative tension among these three constituencies—students, alumni, and faculty members—to reach a rational compromise on these particular issues. The compromise should not revolutionize higher education, fragment the already delicately balanced undergraduate curriculum, or increase the cost of the graduate program to the point that it drives the department into bankruptcy.

College deans, the central administration, and professional accrediting agencies pose other problems. The first two groups are seldom at odds with each other over department priorities, and only a powerful and supremely confident department chairperson should attempt to generate creative tension between them. The professional accrediting agencies, with their seemingly narrow interests and excessive demands, are seldom concerned with the institution's general academic welfare. Occasionally the chairperson can persuade the college dean and the central administration to join with the department against the accrediting agency. He or she could also enlist the aid of the agency and the dean to educate the idealists in the central administration about the hard realities of life in the department trenches. Or, in a daring maneuver, the chairperson could, in a pincer movement, catch the college dean between the central administration and the accrediting agency and, for example, make the dean surrender more resources to the department. Whatever the alignment of forces and whatever the issues at hand, the department chairperson almost always becomes the fulcrum in the balancing act of allocating institutional resources.

Power and Authority

To be a leader, a person must start with a modicum of power and authority. Leadership, especially in the collegial environment, has seldom been simply a function of personal charisma. Charisma can help one amass power and authority, but charisma alone will not get the job done. The department chairperson begins with a good deal of power and authority, most of which is not readily discernible to the casual observer. It is best for all concerned if he or she uses the levers of power and authority unobtrusively. In this way, he or she can become an invisible leader, which, most will agree, is the best kind, especially in an institution of higher education.

In most colleges and universities the chairperson's power is manifested by the exercise of certain roles. Following are examples of roles that can provide the chairperson with power and authority: the bearer of news—good and bad—to department faculty members; the defender of the department; the primary contact for the department faculty members with regard to external professional assignments and consulting; the appointer of committees and committee members; the sometime initiator and constant arbitrator of curriculum development and reform; the allocator of department resources; the maker, even if by proxy, of the schedule of course offerings; the final arbiter for assigning courses and teaching loads to individual faculty members; one of the most influential voices in tenure and promotion cases; in most institutions, the official evaluator of faculty members; and the person who usually sets or recommends salaries for the department faculty members.

Even some of the most onerous tasks that a department chairperson must undertake can bestow a power and authority that, if used consciously and carefully, help enhance his or her leadership role. Consider three relatively minor aspects of the chairperson's professional administrative life: bearing good and bad news; defending the department; and being the primary contact for outside organizations seeking to enlist department members for various professional activities and consulting.

We all know that knowledge is power, and the chairperson generally is the first department faculty member to know what the institution's budget for the next year will be or what programmatic priorities the board of trustees, the board of regents, the central administration, or the college dean have decreed for the future. It is the chairperson who must make this news, good or bad, known to the faculty members. If, in sharing bad news, the chairperson is quick to blame the dean, the central administration, the institution's control agency, or specific individuals among those groups, he or she is probably unhappy or insecure in the job. Sometimes, of course, specific persons are to be blamed for bad news, but within the complex social structure of a college or university, there is seldom one villain responsible for the setbacks suffered by a department faculty. The same can be said for good news: rarely is one person in an institution responsible for a department's good fortune. In imparting information, however, the chairperson can shape the faculty members' opinion about that news and, in the process, establish an ambience—a set of attitudes, a good psychology—that can last for a year or perhaps longer. It is important, then, that chairpersons learn how to share information with colleagues.

The first lesson for chairpersons is that knowledge must be shared. A department that is kept in relative ignorance about budget, programs, and personnel development is a department mismanaged and unable to defend itself against decisions made about its destiny by those outside it.

The chairperson generally is the first line of defense for the department and the spokesman for the department in budget fights with the dean's office and the central administration offices. The faculty members expect their leader to be a vigorous advocate of the department's programmatic and philosophical positions, and the proper exercise of this role confers a degree of authority. A wise chairperson, of course, makes sure that his or her advocacy of a certain issue reflects the department faculty's consensus or at least has the support of the senior faculty members, who are often responsible for the chairperson's appointment. If the chairperson's aspirations for the department are continuously inconsistent with the faculty's, one of two things can be safely assumed: the department will soon have a new leader, or the department has been in such serious trouble that the dean or the central administration has appointed the chairperson to act as a troubleshooter and to implement drastic change.

The chairperson is also responsible for the department's external communications. Outsiders flood the department chairperson's desk with requests for help and advice. An alumnus wants a speaker for a luncheon or a dinner; a high school principal wants a commencement speaker; a professional organization wants a consultant; a newspaper feature writer wants to write a story on what is going on in the department. Other requests come from the dean's office or the central administration. The president wants expert advice on an issue he or she is writing or talking about; the vice president is establishing yet another university-wide committee, council, or task force and wants "some good people who will make constructive contributions"; a new visiting trustee or regent must be entertained or educated.

That the chairperson must respond to these requests is in itself a sign of authority and power. But more important, these requests generally represent golden opportunities for advancing the cause of the department and its members. These requests, in their innocent form, are also acid tests of the chairperson's judgment, for the wrong responses can turn the opportunities from gold to brass, damage the department's reputation, and ensure a brief term of office for the chairperson.

Yet another seemingly innocent duty, that of appointing committees and committee members, turns out, on close examination, to be a source of power and authority, especially in medium-sized and large departments. An academic department can be led—but not run—by one person. It is too familial in character to be organized along the lines of a military hierarchy. Authority must be dispersed, so that the collegial nature of this important academic unit can flourish. Hence the necessity for committees.

The department chairperson has the power to establish new committees and, although not always without a fight, dispense with old ones. Through this influence on committee structure, the chairperson's strength of purpose is tested. At least three important functions are assigned to committees: tenure and promotion recommendations, salary matters, and curriculum development. In small departments the entire faculty may serve as the committee that deals with each of these tasks. In larger departments separate committees are formed for each function. Sometimes the department faculty elects committee members, sometimes not.

Generally, institutional policy limits membership on the tenure and promotion committee to senior faculty, although some institutions make a point of including junior faculty. The policy of including junior faculty seems democratic and laudable, but the junior members of tenure and promotion committees almost always suffer from the conflicts within these committees. If the members of the promotion and tenure committee are elected, the chairperson must act as a precinct captain and get out the vote—the right vote—or risk losing a large measure of control over the department's future. The salary committee is usually shunned by the wiser faculty members, for much unhappiness results from its deliberations. But a department should have such a committee, even though it, like all other committees, is advisory. With the advice and, indeed, the protection of such a committee, the chairperson is able to face the faculty each fall when classes begin. Prudent appointments to the curriculum committee can help maintain a delicate balance of firebrands and wary old conservatives. A department must avoid the extremes of a silly, faddish curriculum that earns the derision of faculty members outside the department and of an obsolescent curriculum that arouses the contempt of funding agencies, the profession itself, and the students.

A department may have other committees, including a search committee, a library committee, an equipment committee, and a social committee. The only one that possesses any real leverage is the faculty appointments or search committee, which recommends the hiring of new faculty members. This committee, like the tenure and promotion committee, makes recommendations to the chairperson (and sometimes to the department faculty) about scholars who may eventually become part of the family. It is of utmost importance, therefore, that the members of this committee be of one mind with the chairperson. The chairperson, moreover, must see to it that the committee conducts its business in a manner that ensures the future health of the department.

Although administrators may be the least likely agents of curriculum development and reform, the chairperson can—and should—have a strong influence on such activities within the department. Most faculties are exceedingly conservative about curriculum development and reform unless faced with such harsh realities as dramatically declining enrollments. The advent of such realities usually causes an unnatural burst of creativity among the faculty; new courses, programs, and proposals for reduced prerequisites bloom like flowers in May. In such cases it is the chairperson's responsibility to protect the discipline and the profession that the department represents and to see that the department's curriculum and degree programs maintain their integrity.

At the same time, the chairperson must be the conscience of the faculty members. He or she must continually prompt them on many matters: the dangers of a rigid curriculum; new developments in the profession; the dire consequences of sliding into obsolescence; new teaching techniques; the services available to them through the institution's office of instructional resources (or other similar agency); the condition of the department's library holdings, its laboratories, and its research and teaching equipment. This concern, visibly and continually expressed, automatically confers the power that goes with conscientious leadership. The performance of these duties, as routine as many of them may seem, gives the chairperson what he or she most needs—the trust and respect of the faculty.

In most departments, a key role of the chairperson is the allocation of resources within the department. Resources are always limited; there are never enough for everyone. And someone must be the final arbiter in the allocation of these resources. Rarely can a group of single-minded, aggressive individuals reach a rational compromise on the distribution of limited resources. Such things may happen in utopian novels but seldom in the real world. Hence the chairperson must preside over this important task. The authority to allocate resources is the most visible of the chairperson's levers of power; consequently, it must be used with great tact and courage. Decisions about resource allocation will never be enthusiastically received by all concerned, but such decisions must be made. Furthermore, the rationale for these decisions should be logical and openly stated.

One great temptation that any chairperson faces is the urge to spread the department resources as evenly as possible. Such a procedure gives everyone a little piece of the action and avoids arguments over that *bête noir* of all academic administrators—enforcing program or personnel priorities. The problem with spreading resources evenly is that this practice inevitably pleases no one and irritates everyone. Departments, like colleges and universities, must have priorities and must follow them. If a college or university has no priorities, department chairpersons are usually the first to argue that the institution lacks leadership, that it is rudderless, and that no one knows where it is going. The same observations apply to departments in which certain programs and certain faculty members get more resources than others.

One way to get the department faculty to agree on a priority system for resource allocation is to reach a consensus that strength must be built on strength. Nearly every department has its strengths, and the faculty is well aware of these strengths. For example, the senior professor in organic chemistry may have the best teachers and researchers and the best laboratory in the department; the three young associate professors in European history may be the best teachers and researchers and may have the best library holdings; the microelectronics group may have the greatest national visibility and the most contract and grant work. Certain programs and faculty members are the obvious choices for receiving the biggest share of the department resources, and few in the department (and virtually no one outside the department) will long contest a decision to allocate these programs and professors a goodly share of the budgeted operating resources for the year.

The rub comes when the department chairperson must, with the support of at least part of the faculty, decide whether to let a weak program die, whether to keep a weak program alive at the expense of stronger programs, or whether to start a new program that, because of new developments in the field, will aid in attracting students and federal or private financial assistance. Sometimes department members cannot be persuaded to let a weak program die with dignity; sometimes such a program has a life of its own, usually because those involved in it are incapable of working on another program or because of tradition, sentiment, or nostalgia or any combination of these factors. Clearly, the chairperson has the duty to assess the program's weakness and then act on the assessment and cut the program's resources. If the chairperson keeps alive a weak program, he or she has a further duty to point out to department colleagues that the program survives at the expense of resources that could go to stronger programs.

Establishing and implementing a new program is almost always a risky business, and leadership plays a crucial role. Almost any chairperson, regardless of leadership style or personal authority, can impede and usually stifle the establishment and growth of a new program. Department faculty members generally recognize this fact; consequently, the chairperson is apt to be heavily lobbied in these affairs. There is no sure formula for success in such an undertaking, but certain caveats are relevant.

- Woe to the chairperson who tries to establish a new program without the support of an influential segment of the department faculty.
- Woe also to the chairperson who, at the behest of a starry-eyed dean or a zealot in the central administration, tries to start a program without the consent or advice of the department's best faculty members.
- Woe to the chairperson who starts a program, for whatever reason, without consulting others in the discipline outside the university, outside the state, and outside the region.
- Woe to the chairperson who does not inform the faculty that the financial consequences of starting a new program will affect the entire department.

Another somewhat obscure but real source of the chairperson's power is his or her jurisdiction over assigning courses and teaching loads to faculty members. Clearly this task is not as visible, glamorous, or influential an activity as resource allocation, but it affects the emotional and intellectual life of every faculty member.

The heart's and mind's desire of most faculty members is to teach the subject that is, to them, the most important thing in their life. A person does not become a professor to make money or to acquire power, although these latent yet thoroughly natural motivations can burst into bloom in a sometimes alarming manner after a few years of teaching and research. Most professors can lead a happy and useful life if they are allowed to teach courses they *want* to teach to those students who will profit most from that teaching. Nothing—except salary—so concerns a professor as much as what he or she is scheduled to teach. (Younger faculty members who are building a knowledge of their subjects and the platform for their professional careers are especially concerned with course assignments.) Nothing—again, except a low salary—so dispirits a faculty member as to be relegated to teach three sections of a Western civilization survey, three sections of trigonometry and algebra, or four sections of the principles of physics. Most faculty members live to teach their subject specialty to superior students. This happy state is the Edenic vision, the academic Shangri-la, that lurks in every professor's mind and is often the prime motivation for his or her work. Consequently, the chairperson, by means of the authority to assign courses, can shape the careers and professional destinies of most of the department members and, in essence, make the majority of them basically happy or unhappy.

The responsibility for assigning courses plays such a crucial role in the life of the department that its power is generally shared by department committees that recommend who should teach what courses and when they should be taught. The task is delegated to a committee not because it is drudgery, but because the function itself is so important to all faculty members. Yet, as in resource allocation, there must be a final arbiter, and that arbiter is the department chairperson. Hence, like it or not, the authority to assign courses and teaching loads becomes a source of power that may be used to reward deserving faculty members.

Obviously, the department chairperson plays an extraordinarily influential role in matters of promotion and tenure. At many universities and colleges the chairperson can override the vote of the faculty in promotion and tenure decisions; at others, the vote of the faculty must be sent to the dean, whether or not the chairperson agrees with that vote. But at virtually all institutions, the chairperson must make his or her recommendation to the dean regarding every tenure and promotion case. This recommendation is almost always heavily weighed by the dean, the central administration, and whatever institution-wide review board or committee may exist. Last but not least, the institution's president or chancellor takes seriously the recommendation of the department chairperson; consequently, his or her views on a particular candidate for tenure or promotion are critical.

As in the case of resource allocation, the decisions on promotion and tenure are not going to please everyone. It is impossible for the chairperson to avoid facing at least one difficult promotion or tenure decision every two or three years. Those who try to avoid making a difficult decision are apt to find themselves in the same predicament that results when available resources are spread evenly across all programs. Such nonactions—which, in fact, *are* actions—please no one and irritate everyone. Chairpersons who stand before the department faculty or the dean and wash their hands of the matter fool no one; furthermore, they lose the respect of the faculty, the dean, and the central administration. Chairpersons who ask a higher level of review to make a hard tenure or promotion decision that they failed to make are evading responsibility. They may succeed in escaping the pain once—or maybe even twice in a very tolerant administration—but a third attempt usually leads to a request from the dean for a change in department leadership. The chairperson's role in promotion and tenure decisions, as in resource allocation decisions, is an important and highly visible one. Here again, power must be used with tact and prudence.

The act of evaluation—at most universities an annual occurrence—is clearly linked to promotion and tenure, and at almost all institutions the responsibility for this spring ritual falls to the chairperson. But woe to those who regard it *only* as a ritual, because each evaluation will become a plank in the platform upon which rests other crucial decisions regarding promotion and tenure. Furthermore, evaluation is another of the chairperson's highly visible levers of power, and a merely ritualistic observance of the evaluation process might erode its effectiveness. This particular function is very important and will be discussed later at greater length.

The final and most visible of all the chairperson's powers is the responsibility to set or recommend annual salaries for each faculty member in the department. At some institutions the chairperson has sole authority for setting salaries (within his or her budget, of course); at other institutions he or she merely makes recommendations about salaries to the college dean. Whatever the institution's procedure, the chairperson, through this power, establishes the value system by which the department lives and operates. As noted earlier, a faculty salary committee usually assists the chairperson in this responsibility. The chairperson's interaction with this committee is probably unique, for, having done the annual evaluation of all the faculty members, the chairperson can better judge the relative value of each of them. Of course, the committee members are in the awkward position of having to consult with the chairperson, at least in an indirect way, about their own salaries. Setting salaries and recommending the setting of salaries is a job no one wants, and the committee is usually less than zealous in its recommendations. Inevitably, the basic decisions turn out to be the chairperson's, and with this painful task comes the final and most important source of his or her power.

In connection with the power and authority that a department chairperson possesses and that are used to fulfill the responsibilities and tasks of the role, it is appropriate to consider "authority" and "power" from a more formal perspective.

Authority may be defined as the power, granted officially from a higher level, to command resources or to enforce policies and regulations. The permission to use power comes from a higher level of the institutional hierarchy and is used by the chairperson to make firm commitments for his or her department. In the case of a state university or university system, the board of regents or board of trustees is empowered by the state legislature to operate and control the state university or university system. The board, in turn, delegates authority and responsibility to the university presidents for the operation of the individual institutions. The presidents delegate authority to vice presidents and deans. Whatever official authority chairpersons have has been delegated to them by their deans; the dean can delegate no more authority than he or she has been delegated.

An examination of the term *authority* leads to an examination of the term *power*. Persons in authority generally have power, which may be defined as the ability to change or influence behavior. In many cases, power is acquired by having access to or actually possessing certain resources that others desire. These resources may be physical, personal, economic, or psychological. The power that has been discussed here is the kind that comes with the position of chairperson and may be called "position power." A chairperson's position power presumably depends on how much authority is delegated by the dean.

In providing leadership to their faculty members, chairpersons also utilize whatever personal power they may have. Personal power derives from peers' respect for and commitment to the chairperson. Personal power is informally granted to the chairperson by the faculty members and depends on how they perceive him or her as an individual and as a professional. A chairperson with a great amount of personal power is usually perceived as possessing one or more of the following characteristics: fairness and even-handedness in dealing with people; good interpersonal skills; national or international reputation in the discipline; expertise in some area of knowledge; influence with the dean; respect in the academic community; ability to help faculty members develop professionally. Personal power is not a power that can be formally delegated; it is a power that a chairperson must earn.

Special Responsibilities and Functions

In the discussion of the chairperson's general power, authority, and functions, a constant note has been sounded about his or her role in shaping the department's future. Many of the chairperson's standard functions, functions through which power and authority are derived, automatically make him or her the department's chief planner. This role is an almost imperceptible one, because seldom does any of these standard functions appear to be solely a planning function. The sum of these standard functions, pursued almost on a daily basis, makes the chairperson the chief architect of the department's future.

Consider once again how the chairperson's actions affect the department's future. The appointment of the curriculum committee members helps shape the department's enrollment patterns, its degree programs, its standing in the institution and in the profession. The appointment or selection of promotion and tenure committee members helps shape the character of the department, as well as its programmatic strengths and weaknesses and its standing in the institution and the profession. The allocation of department resources down to the smallest detail—who gets the new line item for a secretary, for example—has obvious implications for the department's future. Assigning courses and teaching loads profoundly affects the lives of the faculty members. The way in which the chairperson conducts the annual faculty evaluations and renders these judgments also affects the lives of individual faculty members. And, finally, recommending or setting salaries will stimulate a series of behavior patterns that, for better or worse, will deeply affect the department's future.

The chairperson is the department's chief planner, whether we choose to recognize this fact or not. Some departments may have a committee on the future that reports at reasonable intervals to the faculty at large, and this committee—and the department, as well—may believe that it controls the department's destiny. In the largest sense of the term *planning*, the committee may in fact effect some changes. For example, departments can consciously decide to deemphasize analytical chemistry and build up organic chemistry, junk the international program in political science and concentrate on public administration, or starve the power grid group in electrical engineering and fatten up the photovoltaic group. None of these planning decisions, however, can come to fruition if the day-to-day decisions of the chairperson and his or her committees run counter to such plans.

Some additional examples may illustrate how difficult it is for plans to be realized unless the chairperson is conscious of his or her role as planner. The chemistry department knows that all the agency funding will be concentrated in organic chemistry, yet the enrollment in analytical chemistry, particularly the graduate enrollment, keeps going up. In addition, the best candidate for the assistant professor position in the department, who was interviewed at the November national meetings, is an analytical chemist. Why did the department even interview an analytical chemist? Because the senior professor in the department—who is also an analytical chemist, a member of the promotion and tenure committee, and a member of the appointments committee—asked the chairperson to interview the young chemist as a courtesy because "some of the fellows in the Society thought we ought to have a look at him."

Another example: The political science department, during the October national meetings, couldn't find just the right person for its public administration position. Lo and behold, the appointments committee chairperson, a black, puts on the chairperson's desk the stunning resumé of a young black political scientist who states that she would like to begin her professional career in that department but whose specialty is international relations. The chairperson shifts uneasily in his seat as he reads the resumé, remembering last month's tongue-lashing from the dean and the provost about the department's lack of minorities and women.

And another example: Several members of the state's society of professional engineers, on their way home from lobbying the governor for a new building for the engineering college, stop off to talk to the chairperson of the electrical engineering department. They remind him that little work is being done on increasing the efficient transmission of electricity in power lines and that all this nonsense about photovoltaics is simply a way of avoiding thinking about real-life power grid problems. The chairperson, unable to enlighten this group and depressed about the recent editorial in the local newspaper about the eroded influence of the department's once-favored power grid group, stares out the window wondering, "Just where is photovoltaics going?"

The point of each example is this: There are two kinds of planning—both necessary. One is the abstract generalized planning that establishes goals and priorities without much regard for the realities of an ever-changing existence. The other is the kind of planning that is not perceived as planning at all but as a routine activity. The "routine" kind of planning, however, can have more effect on the department's future than all the position papers a committee on the future could write in any given year. The chairperson should establish or help establish a rational plan for the department's future, a plan that clearly includes a system of priorities yet that is realistic. At times the priorities must be reversed; at other times the system must be defended and upheld no matter how withering the opposition may be. In planning, perhaps more than in any other activity, the metaphor of the chairperson as hybrid is apt—he or she must be both a lion and a fox.

In any organization with the ambience of a family, someone must be the magister, the trainer of tyros; and in the academic department, this duty generally falls to the chairperson. The chairperson—initially, at least—is perceived by the new faculty members as the leader, for he or she knows about the local folkways, the institutional pitfalls, and the way in which a faculty member may succeed professionally. If graduate advisors had done their job properly, their students, upon becoming faculty members, would not need so much coaching from a department chairperson, and the chairperson's chore would be considerably lightened.

The majority of the nation's graduate schools successfully educate and train their doctoral candidates in the mastery of a subject, but few new Ph.D.'s are well versed in how to conduct themselves as teachers and as department members. The chairperson must remember that although many new faculty members have had experience as teaching assistants, that experience may have been poorly monitored and generally unstructured. Often graduate teaching assistants, through the neglect of their superiors, have picked up bad teaching habits and have brought them along to their first full-time faculty job. One of the worst habits new teachers can bring to the classroom is an attitude that implies that students somehow hinder the faculty's serious work. Although this attitude is seldom ingrained, many new faculty members have assimilated it while working on their dissertation or preparing for doctoral qualifying examinations. Under those circumstances, they come to the mistaken opinion that teaching is only of secondary importance.

The chairperson, then, must see to it that the new faculty members learn how to conduct themselves in a classroom. The attitude that students are hindrances is easy to overcome, for it is not a natural attitude; otherwise faculty members would not be faculty members but would be pursuing other goals in industry or government. But someone must tell newcomers about the department's traditions, its goals, and its place in the college and in the institution. Someone has to tell them about the feuds within the department, the idiosyncracies of its members, the whole rhythm and flow of department life. In short, someone has to socialize the new members, else they are likely to have a bruising first year or two. In some quarters, this bruising experience may be viewed as a necessary rite of passage, but it is nonetheless an inefficient use of time and resources and can be a seriously damaging experience. The chairperson or a trusted faculty member must conscientiously train new members. The chairperson cannot ignore these matters; for the general welfare of the department, he or she must take a personal interest in new faculty members.

Earlier, the paradoxical nature of the chairperson's job was noted and the role of advocate briefly discussed. That role should be examined more closely, because it is no simple matter. Clearly, the chairperson must be an advocate for the department. He or she must be an advocate in budget negotiations with the college dean and the central administration. Success in these negotiations depends on how carefully data are prepared to support the needs of the department, how clearly and honestly the data are presented, and how relevant the data are to regional and national priorities of the profession or discipline represented by the department. For example, the chairperson of the English department should never march into the dean's office and invidiously compare the budget of the English department with that of the chemistry department. A dean who knows something about cost analysis and who has the priority system of the institution's departments firmly in mind can easily ignore internal comparisons. Most deans, provosts, and vice presidents hate to be told that one department gets better budget treatment than another, and these administrators are generally well armed with elaborate defenses built around cost analyses and priority systems. In a budget fight, for example, the best way to be a successful advocate for the department is to shame the dean into concessions by comparing the department's budget and its professional standing with other departments of the same discipline in competitive institutions in the state, region, or nation. This tactic, however, can be successful only if the department has a good record of performance and, in the uncomfortable language of budgeteering, has been "productive."

The chairperson must at times be an advocate for one or more faculty members. These kinds of situations generally arise from salary allocations and promotion and tenure cases. Again, rhetoric seldom wins the day in salary allocation disputes. The presentation of simple, compelling, honest data is the chairperson's best instrument as advocate. Sometimes the dean, the institutional review board, or even the president will not agree with a department recommendation on tenure or promotion. Immediately, all concerned are treading on dangerous ground. If the department has insisted on sending forward a promotion or tenure recommendation with which the department chairperson disagrees, if the institution's policies and procedures allow the recommendation to go to the next highest level, and if, at that and subsequently higher levels, the recommendation is turned down, the chairperson should not fight the case. The chairperson, however, must tell the department at the outset what his or her recommendation is going to be and inform the department that he or she will not fight. In this difficult situation, to state one's intention is a more honest way to conduct oneself than to yield to the temptation to be a hero and "fight for the department."

Although fighting for the department has great possibilities for high drama—or comedy—it is not good for one's self-esteem or intellectual integrity. If the chairperson and the department are fully united in a promotion or tenure case, however, then they should fight for it all the way. If they lose, the loss is an honorable one, and at least they gain markers that can be called in at the next confrontation with the higher administration, whether it be over budget, curriculum, space, or personnel.

But turnabout, as college deans are fond of saying, is fair play, and sometimes the chairperson must be the advocate of the dean or the central administration. Just as departments must have priorities, so too must colleges and institutions. Not every department can always be designated a high-priority department. Indeed, some, because of the character of the institution, can never attain prominent status. (One such example might be a humanities department in a technological university.) When resources are allocated for each year's operating budget, the chairperson must report as fully and as honestly as possible not only on the resources allocated to the department, but also on the reasons for those allocations. When decisions that adversely affect the department are handed down, the chairperson must be able to share the institution's perspective and try to implement even an unfavorable decision with some grace and style. If the chairperson is strongly opposed to a decision and, consequently, his or her relationship with the faculty and the dean deteriorates, he or she should consider resigning. The matter is as simple and as cold as that. The chairperson who cannot accept the decisions of the higher administration in resource allocation or other institutional matters does no one a service by staying on; all that results is the embitterment of everyone concerned. The chairperson can always devote his or her energies to changing those institutional or collegiate priorities—and even have fun mounting such a challenge—but once the decisions are made for the year, the only thing to do is to put those decisions to work for the good of the institution and wait until next year.

Perhaps the most important of the chairperson's special responsibilities is that of faculty evaluator. Here he or she becomes the judge on the bench, the dispassionate, if possible, evaluator of each faculty member's performance. In an increasing number of institutions around the country, the process of evaluation has been formalized as a legal requirement that must be fulfilled each year. But even in those institutions in which the evaluation process is not formalized, chairpersons cannot escape the role of evaluator. Wittingly or unwittingly, they enact this role in all their functions: appointing committees, assigning courses, allocating resources, recommending promotion and tenure, and setting or recommending annual salaries. Hence, the annual evaluation meeting between chairperson and faculty member, even if not required, is a good way of fulfilling the evaluation responsibility. The meeting should have a specific agendum, or an external frame of reference, to give each participant a sense of purpose; otherwise, the meeting is likely to become a social visit or the discussion is apt to turn to more agreeable business than the awkward matter of how one has performed one's job during the past year.

The agendum should be related to department priorities, resource allocation, or the department's plans for itself. It is easier for the chairperson and the faculty member to discuss job performance if the department has established certain goals for itself and its members. How did the faculty member help fulfill the department's objectives during the past year? If there were problems, what were they and what caused them? Not all faculty members are team players, nor should they be. Some persons cannot be judged by what they contribute toward achieving the department's stated goals for the year or the next five years. Too much emphasis on team playing can inhibit or even stifle a faculty member's creativity.

If certain members of the department have not overtly contributed to the department's goals and are not likely to, however, then it becomes necessary for the chairperson to establish, year by year, a set of individual goals for these persons. The goals should not be too specific, or else both the chairperson and the faculty member may find themselves trapped by undue specificity. For example, to suggest that the faculty member should, in the next year, publish three articles in learned journals is probably too bureaucratic, but both chairperson and faculty member can comfortably agree that a reasonable goal for next year would be the publication of some research in a reputable journal. Sometimes, however, the chairperson must be specific, both for the good of the faculty and the reputation of the department. The associate professor who has spent three years writing a book may have to be told that for only one more year will he receive special resources (clerical help, graduate assistants, and so forth) to help bring the book to completion. Or the bright young assistant professor may have to be told that she has conducted enough experiments to validate a hypothesis; next year she must send off a research grant proposal to a funding agency and free up some department resources so that others in the department can begin to write research proposals. All these matters are relative and depend on the chairperson's good judgment and personal knowledge of each faculty member's capabilities.

The important point is that evaluation must be viewed as a constructive, not a destructive, act. For it to be constructive, the chairperson must establish goals against which yearly job performance can be measured. If no goals have been set, then the evaluation inevitably becomes either too personalized or so vague as to be worthless or insulting. The chairperson must realize that most faculty members *want* to be evaluated; they want their performance judged and, of course, praised. But no faculty member can walk into an annual evaluation conference expecting to be praised if he or she knows that the goals agreed upon last year have not been met. And even if they have not been met, the faculty member will usually welcome the opportunity to explain why not.

The annual evaluation conference, then, should not be viewed by the chairperson or the faculty as a painful or awkward ordeal. It can and should be a chance for colleagues to examine together what the year's work has produced, what went right, what went wrong, and why it went wrong. But this useful and constructive experience is possible only if chairpersons set goals for colleagues—with, of course, their help—and address those goals each year, no matter how painful it may be at times to keep the evaluation process focused on those goals.

As we have seen, the department chairperson assumes many roles, and some of these roles may, at times, conflict with others. The dean may have certain expectations about the chairperson's role, the faculty may have others, and the chairperson may have yet others that do not correspond to those of the dean or the faculty. Such a dilemma may have no easy or satisfactory solution. The chairperson must become accustomed to being in an atmosphere beset by contradiction.

The various kinds of power that chairpersons exercise daily have also been discussed. Few of these powers are based on formally delegated authority. Instead, these powers may depend, to a large degree, on precisely how they are perceived by the chairperson as well as by the faculty members. Chairpersons who perceive that they have no power usually have none; chairpersons who perceive that they have power usually do. In any event, the exercise of this power must be tempered with sound judgment.

Questions and Exercises

The Chairperson's Roles

In dealing with various kinds of persons, the chairperson assumes those roles most appropriate to accomplish his or her objectives. The role indicates how or in what capacity the chairperson relates to an individual or a group in performing an activity. Following is a list of twenty-eight possible roles that chairpersons assume to some degree at one time or another:

teacher	representer	decision maker
mentor	communicator	problem solver
researcher	evaluator	recommender
leader	motivator	implementor

planner	supervisor	facilitator
manager	coordinator	entrepreneur
advisor-counselor	anticipator	recruiter
mediator-negotiator	innovator	peer-colleague
delegator	peacemaker	
advocator	organizer	

1. What roles do you think your faculty expects you to assume as chairperson?
2. What roles do you think your dean expects you to assume as chairperson?
3. What roles would you most like to assume as chairperson?
4. Which of these roles seem to conflict? Why and how do they conflict? What problems do conflicting roles pose for the chairperson? How may chairpersons resolve these problems?
5. What are your personal visions or goals toward which you would like to move your department during your time as chairperson?
6. Some chairpersons are elected to the position by faculty members; others are appointed by the dean with or without faculty consultation. What are the similarities and differences between these two kinds of chairpersons in terms of (1) the tasks for which the chairperson is responsible; (2) how the chairperson relates to his or her faculty and dean; and (3) strategies used in getting the job done? What are the reasons for these similarities or differences?
7. In universities that have collective bargaining, some chairpersons are members of the bargaining unit, whereas others are considered part of management. What are the similarities and differences between these two kinds of chairpersons in terms of (1) the tasks for which the chairperson is responsible; (2) how the chairperson relates to his or her faculty and dean; and (3) strategies used in getting the job done? What are the reasons for these similarities or differences?

The Chairperson's Powers

The functions and responsibilities inherent in the position of department chairperson cannot be executed without power and authority. By virtue of holding the position, the chairperson has certain powers. A list of selected powers available to some chairpersons is given below. Carefully consider each power in terms of (1) the extent to which it is available to you, (2) the extent to which you exercise it, and (3) the extent to which you have the capacity to exercise it more frequently.

- *Academic contacts*—power to assist in developing professional acquaintances
- *Additional teaching*—power to control summer teaching assignments
- *Clerical support*—power to secure adequate clerical assistance for faculty members
- *Colloquia*—power to develop stimulating academic environment through seminars, visiting lecturers, and so forth
- *Committees*—power to form department committees and make committee assignments; power to recommend persons for important college or university committees
- *Community*—power to maintain good contacts with community; publicity
- *Consulting*—power to assist in making contacts leading to paid consulting jobs for faculty members
- *Counseling*—power to counsel faculty members about teaching and research
- *Course assignment, teaching loads, scheduling*—power to control number of courses, contact hours, and meeting times of classes
- *Curriculum*—power to influence curriculum development
- *Evaluation*—power to evaluate overall faculty performance; power to evaluate for promotion, tenure, salary raises, and so forth
- *Goal determination*—power to influence setting department goals
- *Influence*—power to establish contacts with higher administrators, to deal with the dean, and so forth
- *Information*—power to use advance knowledge of what is going on around the college
- *Inspiration*—power to exercise professional leadership and stimulation
- *Interdepartment relations*—power to sustain liaison with other departments
- *Paid extra teaching*—power to control extension teaching appointments
- *Paid extra work*—power to affect the acquisition of paid short courses
- *Professional affiliations*—power to recommend faculty members for assignments and responsibilities in regional and national activities
- *Promotion*—power to influence promotion decisions for department members

- *Recruitment*—power to recruit qualified faculty members
- *Research*—power to assist faculty members in acquiring research funds
- *Research*—power to secure research time for faculty members
- *Research assistance*—power to help obtain research assistants, supplies, and so forth
- *Sabbaticals*—power to influence awards of sabbatical leaves
- *Salary increases*—power to influence raises (step, merit)
- *Speaking and consulting*—power to assign unpaid community service activities to professors
- *Student assistants*—power to control amount of student help supplied to professors
- *Supplies*—power to help secure adequate equipment and supplies
- *Tenure*—power to influence award of tenure to department members
- *Travel funds*—power to assign funds for travel to professional meetings

The Chairperson's Authority

Authority is defined as the permission that a chairperson receives from a higher level of the institutional hierarchy to make firm commitments for his or her unit. Authority is the power delegated from above to command resources or to enforce policies and regulations.

1. Is it conceivable that a dean may delegate more authority to one chairperson than to another on a formal basis? On an informal basis? Give some examples.
2. What factors determine the amount of informal authority that deans delegate to their chairpersons?
3. Many department chairpersons say they do not have enough formal authority to do all the things they have to do; that is, if they had more authority, they could be more effective chairpersons. What authority would you as chairperson wish to have? (Remember that the dean cannot delegate any authority that he or she does not have.)
4. To what extent do most chairpersons exercise the power available to them in carrying out their responsibilities?
5. In addition to being able to recommend promotion, tenure, and salary, what other powers are available to a chairperson

for rewarding faculty members who perform well?
6. Other than being able to recommend dismissal, no promotion, or no merit increases, what powers are available to a chairperson for penalizing faculty members who continue to perform in an unsatisfactory manner?
7. Compare formal authority and personal power as they relate to the chairperson's effectiveness.

References

Booth, David B. "Institutional and Disciplinary Ideas for Development." *Educational Record*, Winter 1977, pp. 85–90.

Brann, James, and Emmet, Thomas A., eds. *The Academic Department or Division Chairman: A Complex Role*. Detroit: Balamp, 1972.

Brown, J. Douglas. "Departmental and University Leadership." In *Academic Departments*, edited by Dean E. McHenry, pp. 188–94. San Francisco: Jossey-Bass, 1977.

Dressel, Paul L.; Johnson, F. Craig; and Marcus, Philip M. *The Confidence Crisis*. San Francisco: Jossey-Bass, 1971.

Ehrle, Elwood B. "Selection and Evaluation of Department Chairmen." *Educational Record*, Winter 1975, pp. 29–38.

Heimler, Charles H. "The College Departmental Chairman." *Educational Record*, Spring 1967, pp. 158–63.

Hersey, Paul, and Blanchard, Kenneth H. *Management of Organizational Behavior: Utilizing Human Resources*. 3rd ed. Englewood Cliffs, N.J.: Prentice-Hall, 1977.

Heyns, Roger W. "Leadership Lessons from Watergate." *Educational Record*, Summer 1973, pp. 172–74.

Heywood, Stanley J. "The Department Chairman—An Essential Leader." Paper presented at Western Interstate Commission on Higher Education Administrative Leadership Conference, 14 November 1969.

Hill, Winston W., and French, Wendell L. "Perceptions of the Power of Department Chairmen by Professors." *Administrative Science Quarterly*, March 1967, pp. 548–74.

Leslie, David W. "The Status of the Department Chairmanship in University Organization." *AAUP Bulletin*, December 1973, pp. 419–26.

McKeachie, Wilbert J. "Memo to New Department Chairmen." *Educational Record*, Spring 1968, pp. 221–27.

Newman, Frank. "Taking the Helm." In *The Third Century: Twenty-six Prominent Americans Speculate on the Educational Future*. New Rochelle, N.Y.: Change Magazine Press, 1976.

Roach, James H. L. "The Academic Department Chairperson: Functions and Responsibilities." *Educational Record*, Winter 1976, pp. 13–23.

2

Types of Departments
and Leadership Styles

||||||| |||||||||||||||||||||||||||||||||||||||||||||||||||||||||||||||||||||||||||||||||||||||||||||||||||||||||||||||||||||||||||||| |||||||||||||||||||

Departments

Because of the variety of postsecondary institutions in this country, it may not be possible to develop one model for all departments. But some attempt should be made to do so, if only to give the department chairperson a framework of sorts.

For the sake of analysis, departments may be divided into four categories: small, large, immature, and mature. Overlappings among these categories do occur, of course, but the categories can serve as benchmarks for our discussion of departments. We shall define a "small" department as one that has up to nine full-time faculty members, including the chairperson. Departments with four or fewer members are not really departments but programs that have achieved department status because of their excellence or because of tradition, sentiment, nostalgia, or tolerance on the part of the central administration. We shall define a "medium-sized" department as one that has between ten and nineteen full-time faculty members, and a "large" department as one that has twenty or more full-time faculty members.

Hersey and Blanchard define *maturity* as "the capacity to set high but attainable goals . . ., willingness and ability to take responsibility, and education and/or experience of an individual or group. *These variables of maturity should be considered only in relation to a specific task to be performed.*"[1] According to this definition, a mature academic department is one in which the faculty members have the experience and capacity *as a group* to work together, set high but attainable goals, reach group decisions, and readily accept responsibility for their decisions and as-

---

1. Paul Hersey and Kenneth H. Blanchard, *Management of Organizational Behavior: Utilizing Human Resources*, 3rd ed. (Englewood Cliffs, N.J.: Prentice-Hall, 1977), p. 161. Italics in original.

signments. Not only are some departments more mature than others, but a department may display more maturity in one situation than another, depending on the problem or task with which it is dealing. An immature department is one that has great difficulty in reaching consensus or in developing and implementing a plan of action; its members are either unable or unwilling to work together effectively. Generally, mature departments are those that have been in existence for a long time, say fifteen years or more. Of course, age does not guarantee maturity; in fact, a mature department can regress to immaturity. Generally, however, a young department, whether small or large, is an immature department, according to our definition, simply because the process of learning to work cooperatively takes time and effort.

Let us first discuss small departments, both immature and mature. The members of an immature small department are usually highly self-conscious and defensive about its existence in the college or the institution. Repeatedly, the department is called on to justify its own existence, to defend its intellectual premises and its place in the great chain of academic being, and to resist budget raids by older, more powerful departments. In the formation and development of its curriculum, such a department often tends toward polarization; it may become faddish or wildly eclectic in its course offerings and degree programs, or it may hunker down behind a stodgy, traditional program in an attempt to gain instant respectability and acceptance from the rest of the institution. Its value system for promotion and tenure is undeveloped, although guided by institutional policy. Often it either rebels against such policy by claiming the virtues of innovation and uniqueness, or it interprets institutional policy as rigidly and conservatively as possible in an attempt, once again, to gain acceptance and credibility within the institution.

These polarities of behavior tend to follow disciplinary lines. The new, small science department—particularly the chemistry department—is likely to be more traditional and conventional than its mature counterparts in other institutions. The new social science department—especially the sociology department, which is itself a newcomer to the pantheon of academic disciplines—is likely to be innovative, eclectic, and chaotic as it struggles to establish itself.

The extreme behavioral patterns exhibited by immature small departments often lead the dean or central administration to appoint as chairperson a faculty member with a dominant personality who will try to run the department like a platoon. This response is only a natural one and usually quite necessary.

Leaders of immature small departments must continually remind themselves and their faculty members that they are going through a necessary stage of development and that life will not always be so difficult. The curriculum established now will have an effect on the department's future, as will promotions, tenure awards, and resource allocations. This phase of a department's existence is the stormiest, and all department members should try to remember that since things will inevitably change, they should not commit themselves to decisions that will make change more difficult to realize.

In the mature small department, conditions are entirely different. This type of department has long since lived through the development stage and often takes on the relaxed air of a country club as it goes about its business. Since all its members know each other, they usually share a unity of purpose and a sense of group cooperation seldom found in any other kind of department. Of course, there may be personality clashes or grave philosophical differences among the members, but the strife is genteel, as it is in a country club. Seldom is the chairperson of such a department a hard-driving platoon leader. Usually he or she comes from the faculty ranks. Often the position in such a department becomes, intentionally or not, a rotating position, institutional policies to the contrary notwithstanding.

Yet beneath this serene surface, danger abounds. The department's very strength, its close-knit unity, and its lack of visible strife may be its undoing. Decisions tend to be made in town-hall fashion; the whole department may decide, with the chairperson as presiding officer, on resource allocations, curriculum development and reform, course assignments and teaching loads, and, if institutional policy permits, promotion and tenure.

The problem with this kind of democratic activity is that it makes establishing and implementing priority systems extremely difficult, although not impossible. Everyone defers to everyone else, and even the chairperson may follow the path of least resistance—spreading the resources evenly, giving each faculty member's courses and programs equal billing in the catalog and in the schedule of courses, promoting everyone's friend, tenuring all newcomers as soon as possible, and trying to give everyone the same salary (prorated, of course). In five years—at the most—such a department will be in serious trouble with its faculty members, the dean, and the central administration.

Chairpersons of mature small departments must be perhaps more strong-willed than those of other kinds of departments. Not only must they be strong-willed; they must also be the most graceful and patient diplomats of them all. The chairperson's position in the mature small department may offer a severe test, and anyone who takes the job should not be deceived by the surface calm, for he or she will have to work continually to keep the department from sliding into senility.

The preceding examples represent the extremes of maturity ranges of small departments. Real departments may lie anywhere between these extremes.

Immature large departments tend to have the same sorts of problems as their smaller counterparts. If anything, such departments more compellingly invite the implementation of the department-as-platoon concept than do smaller departments. To state it simply, a strong will and steel nerves are necessary requisites for leading an immature large department. Again, in every decision made with colleagues, the chairperson's best course of action is to remind them continually that present decisions affect the department's future. An immature large department should be almost wholly concerned with the future, not with the present. An immature large department is often the result of a merger of several more mature, smaller ones. The new organization makes it imperative that the members learn to work with their new colleagues to overcome the tribulations of immaturity.

Mature large departments have a tendency to organize themselves either into feudal territories or into assembly lines. In the last thirty years department organization has tended toward internal atomization or fragmentation. This tendency is a natural one, for as knowledge increases and becomes ever more specialized, units within academic disciplines begin growing apart from the parent discipline.

The classic example of this kind of fragmentation is found in the psychology department, typically a mature large department. It often has so many subunits that it can be considered a school. In psychology, the experimentalists are a breed apart, as are the clinical psychologists. Indeed, there appears to be a trend in some institutions to set up the clinical psychology subunit as a separate department. Add to these subunits such groups as the social psychologists, the school psychologists, and the consumer behavior psychologists—to name a few—and the problems of a psychology department chairperson are easy to understand. Chemistry departments also tend to become atomized. The larger and more mature the chemistry department, the greater the differences among the organic, inorganic, theoretical or quantum, and analytical groups. In such departments, the chairperson's major challenge lies, of course, in resource allocation. Each territorial group, powerful in itself, presents its case to the chairperson, and consensus-based decisions are extremely difficult to achieve.

In the mature large department, promotion and tenure issues are generally easier to resolve than resource allocation problems, for the competing units develop a sense of pride and *esprit de corps* and seldom recommend weak cases to the entire department. The best course of action for the chairperson is to encourage, not discourage, competition among subunits. Fostering open competition is better than stifling initiative and innovation or attempting to administer these warring units according to the principle of sharing the wealth. But competition means that in the resource allocation process there will be some winners and some losers, and departments that adopt this mode of operation should be prepared to make and to accept decisions that recognize firmly established priorities.

In addition to the tendency towards fragmentation, mature large departments also exhibit a tendency to adopt the assembly-line concept of operation. This approach is almost inevitable. Large numbers of freshmen must be run through the introductory courses in such departments as chemistry, English, mathematics, economics, and speech. At the same time, there are large numbers of graduate students who must be taught, whose theses and dissertations must be approved, and whose teaching assistantships must be supervised. Under these circumstances the chairperson and the faculty have a difficult time maintaining the necessary collegial mode of operation, and the family ambience of a small or medium-sized department begins to dissolve under these pressures. The administrative hierarchy begins to grow under the pressures of numbers: the chairperson has to appoint an associate or vice chairperson, a director of freshman English, a director of the undergraduate chemistry labs, and a director of introductory speech courses. With its increasing variety of assistant and associate chairpersons, the department's internal structure begins to resemble the hierarchy of the institution's central administration.

These developments may be inevitable, but they tend to isolate the chairperson. To resist this isolation, the chairperson must continually seek ways to improve communication with faculty members; he or she must continually "get out among 'em" and not succumb, for example, to the tempting argument that because the department is so large, department faculty meetings are useless.

Department meetings in mature large departments are almost always stressful for the chairperson, and it is only natural to wish to avoid stress. Such meetings must be held regularly with agenda posted in advance.

The chairperson must spend time with heads of department divisions and, above all else, communicate to each division head the needs and goals of the other divisions. Only in this way can a spirit of teamwork and department unity be maintained. This approach is time-consuming and requires hard work, but if the chairperson of a mature large department is to avoid becoming just another academic bureaucrat, he or she must bend every effort to the goal of personal communication and interaction with faculty members.

Academic departments can be classified in other ways, of course. In fact, this kind of analysis could easily become an art. All chairpersons, however, no matter what category their department falls into, must remember that most faculty members still cling, consciously or subconsciously, to the Platonic ideal, even with regard to the academic department. This eternal absolute undergirds the premises of many an argument voiced in department faculty meetings when such issues as resource allocation, course assignments, course and program development or revision, and promotion and tenure cases arise. The ideal department is one in which every professor is a superstar and every course and program is vital to the welfare of the department, the college, the institution, the nation, and the whole human community. The ideal department is well funded, and its members' salaries are generous. The chairperson serves only as the clerk of the court, duly recording the faculty's judgments and seeking always to implement those judgments.

The Platonic ideal is, like all ideals, unattainable, but it nevertheless exists in the minds of the faculty members. Although most faculty members are hardheaded enough to recognize that the ideal is, after all, only an ideal, this perception of academic life led most of them to join the profession in the first place. A wise department chairperson never forgets the Platonic ideal; if resourceful, he or she can use it to help the department grow in unity and maturity.

Leadership Styles

Just as there are many kinds of departments, so there are many kinds of department chairpersons; their variety is as infinite as the variety of human nature. It is possible, however, to generalize about human nature and to categorize the types of chairpersons according to their leadership styles.

Michael Maccoby, in *The Gamesman*, describes four types of leadership styles of corporation executives: the spectator, the technician, the jungle fighter, and the gamesman. Maccoby assigns to each type characteristics that, while especially appropriate in the context of corporate affairs, are not exactly applicable to academic affairs. We use Maccoby's terminology because it is interesting and provocative, but we have altered his definitions to fit realities in the academic department. Chairpersons may be interested in seeing how closely these types resemble their colleagues or themselves. The terminology should not be taken too seriously or too literally, but rather in a light-hearted though inquiring spirit.

The spectator chairperson is a passive and acquiescent manager who flourishes in mature departments, either small or large. In the small department, the chairperson leaves the faculty alone; in the large department, the administrative hierarchy is so well developed that the faculty is generally unaware of the chairperson's presence. The spectator does very little except make sure that the department's business is conducted on time; seldom does he or she become an advocate for anything except a trouble-free life for the department. All power and authority are turned over to department committees, and generally compromises are sought on such troubling matters as curriculum reform, resource allocation, and promotion and tenure cases.

This role closely approaches the ideal of a chairperson, who serves as clerk of the court. It is often a useful role, for departments, like nations, have their cyclical movements of reform and orthodoxy, of strife and peace. The spectator chairperson functions best in a department that has just experienced a stormy period of reforms, leaving an exhausted faculty that needs serenity in order once again to focus its attention on the cardinal functions of teaching, research, and service. The spectator should not, however, be left in place too long, lest the department slide into stagnation, and decline. A chairperson who assumes this role in an immature department, whether small or large, may be ineffective unless he or she has been picked deliberately by the dean or the central administration to preside over the dissolution of a unit that should never have been made a department.

The technician chairperson is a superb bureaucrat. He or she always submits staff reports on time, follows to the letter the directions given by the college, knows all the rules and regulations of the institution, the state, and the federal government, and knows how to follow those regulations to keep everyone out of trouble. The technician chairperson has read all the literature on management techniques and assiduously follows the best advice given there; even so, he or she often appears to lack vision, imagination, and courage. Such a chairperson can function well in any kind of department and has the great virtue of being able to bring order out of chaos. By virtue of knowing the rules and regulations, the technician chairperson can inhibit the zealots and pilgrims among the faculty; by the same token, he or she can use that knowledge to prod a sluggish, lazy department.

The technician chairperson is seldom the head of a high-priority department, which requires relentless pursuit of excellence. He or she is content to ensure that the department functions well in accordance with commonly accepted procedures and policies. Being able to maintain the status quo is no mean virtue, however, and many departments in transition from immaturity to maturity or from nonpriority status to priority status are often well served by the technician. Unlike the spectator, the technician does not turn over all power and authority to committees—he or she knows the rules and regulations too well to do that—but generally conducts affairs in a democratic fashion. The style of the technician is one step further removed from the Platonic ideal of the chairperson.

The jungle fighter chairperson has taken the position for two reasons: to make the department better and perhaps someday to become dean. He or she is unabashedly ambitious and understands that a strong, successful department is the best self-advertisement. Such a chairperson is sometimes brilliant, possibly dangerous, and during his or her term department life is never dull. Next to personal success, the jungle fighter chairperson wants nothing more than the department's complete victory in all major issues; he or she becomes its forceful advocate for all its positions. If this ambition were only for the department, the college dean or the central administration would find it extremely difficult to negotiate with the jungle fighter. The either-you-give-me-what-I-want-or-I'll-resign attitude in confrontation with the upper-level administration, however, seldom results in the chair-

person's resignation; this approach is likely to be a brinksman-
ship approach, with the jungle fighter usually pulling back before
superior forces.

The jungle fighter flourishes in large departments, both immature and mature, and is most successful in large, mature, high-
priority departments. Such a person is capable of making truly
significant—even brilliant—contributions to the department, but
his or her value to the rest of the university or college depends
on what priority level the department has been assigned. Although not a team player, the jungle fighter is probably the best
agent of change among all types of chairpersons. He or she tends
to be less democratic than the technician and plays a heavy hand
in the affairs of department committees, consequently relinquishing little power or authority. Indeed, such a chairperson
pretends to speak and act for the faculty at times when he or she
is speaking or acting only for personal aims or for the goals of a
few department members. But jungle fighters get their way more
often than not. They can make a weak department strong and
lay the foundation for a great department. This role is yet one
step further removed from the Platonic ideal.

The gamesman chairperson is one who takes the job in order
to improve the department, the college, and the institution. While
not above ambition for higher office, the gamesman is not necessarily devoted to a future in academic administration. The
gamesman plays life like a game and is interested in both strategy and tactics. Such a chairperson is cool and dedicated. He or
she likes to win, as much for the pleasure of winning as for any
other reason, but remains a sportsman and knows how to accept
defeat.

The gamesman's leadership style embodies all the paradoxes
inherent in the chairperson's difficult and perplexing job. He or
she is strong but flexible, a manager who is sometimes managed,
a leader who is sometimes led, a Janus-like advocate who can
defend, at different times, the interests of the department faculty
as well as the interests of the whole institution. He or she tries to
reduce the number of occasions when the department's goals are
perceived to be at odds with the institution's goals by convincing
others that everyone's interests are best served by keeping the
department strong. The gamesman is intelligent and courageous
and probably has a highly developed sense of humor.

Although the terms *spectator*, *technician*, *jungle fighter*, and
gamesman refer to an overall leadership style, a chairperson may
combine in varying proportions characteristics of two or more

of these types. A gamesman may become so carried away with the game that he or she becomes a jungle fighter. A spectator, confronted with a dilemma, may be forced to learn to use rules and regulations as a technician does. A jungle fighter who has been bruised in combat or who has mellowed with age may decide to forsake ambition and try being a gamesman. A real chairperson generally does not exhibit only one type of behavior; rather, his or her personality more likely reflects a melding of all these types.

Leadership styles may be viewed from other perspectives as well. Leadership styles may be categorized, for example, as directive or supportive. "Directive" behavior consists primarily of one-way communication from the chairperson to faculty members, in which he or she explains what is to be done when, where, and how. The chairperson's main concern here is to see that the task or assignment is accomplished. "Supportive" behavior, on the other hand, consists of two-way communication between the chairperson and the faculty members. Here the chairperson provides personal or psychological support, including encouragement, praise, and general concern for the personal and professional welfare of each faculty member.

A chairperson's behavior is neither exclusively directive nor supportive; leadership style consists of a mix of both. Leadership behavior varies, however, according to the particular mix of these behavior patterns. The proportion of directive behavior to supportive behavior indicates the chairperson's leadership style.

We can visualize four different mixes of behavior patterns by plotting directive behavior on a horizontal axis and supportive behavior on an intersecting vertical axis. The result is a graph with four quadrants, with each quadrant representing a different mix of directive and supportive behavior (see figure 2.1):

Quadrant 1—High directive and low supportive (a great deal of direction to the faculty members, not much personal and psychological support)

Quadrant 2—High directive and high supportive (a great deal of direction to the faculty members, a great deal of personal and psychological support)

Quadrant 3—Low directive and high supportive (not much direction to the faculty members, a great deal of personal and psychological support)

Quadrant 4—Low directive and low supportive (not much direction to the faculty members, not much personal or psychological support)

Fig. 2.1. Leadership style graph

Four Basic Leadership Styles

The four quadrants in figure 2.1 represent four leadership styles. It can be argued that quadrant 1 exemplifies the best approach for dealing with an immature department, while quadrants 2, 3, and 4 exemplify the styles appropriate to a department as it progresses toward a high degree of maturity. Remember that "department maturity" has been defined as the members' experience and capacity to cooperate in setting high, attainable goals and in reaching group decisions and the group's willingness and ability to accept responsibility.

This conception of leadership styles is different from the one derived from Maccoby's terminology. The notion of directive and supportive behaviors can be applied more easily to specific situations and assumes, as we shall see in some detail, that a chairperson can adjust his or her personal style to meet different situations. In this case, the chairperson changes behavior according to the department's level of maturity. If the department is immature, the chairperson spends a lot of time being directive, assigning tasks, and monitoring them. As the department matures, the chairperson continues to be directive but also becomes supportive. A department's progression toward maturity can be conceived of as a continuum, and the chairperson must be able to estimate the level of maturity with which he or she is dealing at any given time. When the department approaches the highest level of maturity, the chairperson, according to this model, becomes nondirective and nonsupportive. The assumption here is that a productive, established department needs neither direction nor support in many situations.

This model may be compared with the spectator chairperson model, which is also nondirective and nonsupportive. In both cases the absence of active leadership might allow a department to slip into stagnation. The leadership model that designates chairpersons as spectators, technicians, jungle fighters, and gamesmen, however, refers to overall style and does not assume the chairperson's ability to change leadership style readily to fit the situation.

Not only are some departments more mature than others, but the same department may display more maturity at one time than another, depending on the problem or task with which it is dealing. Once a chairperson determines the department's level of maturity with regard to any specific task, he or she should apply the most appropriate leadership style to the situation at hand. As the department matures, the wise chairperson provides less direction and more support. When the department attains a high level of maturity, the chairperson may adopt the fourth leadership style—less support and less direction. This leadership style is appropriate, however, only if the department has achieved a high level of maturity with regard to the particular task or problem at hand.

When a department begins to display less maturity than it has in the past, the chairperson may need to make a regressive intervention. This tactic entails adopting a leadership style more appropriate to the present level of maturity rather than the one used when the department was at a higher level of maturity. Once the department is again able to cope with the task at hand, the department chairperson may return to the former leadership style. Keep in mind that, according to this model, no one leadership style is always most appropriate. Effective leadership style will vary according to departments and issues. Some academic departments may be best served by one leadership style at any particular time; other departments, or even the same departments under different circumstances, may be better served by another style.

Robert K. Murray, in his article "On Departmental Development: A Theory," describes a model tracing five stages of growth and evolution in a typical department. A department in the first stage of growth—especially a department in a small, undistinguished institution—has only a few members and is ruled autocratically and arbitrarily. The second stage, frequently coinciding with an increase in department size, is characterized by turmoil and power struggles, during which faculty members fight for a greater voice in decision making. This infighting often leads to the chairperson's resignation; faculty morale is low, and the department atmosphere is antagonistic. The third stage of a department's evolution is marked by "rampant democracy." A department in this stage spends an inordinate amount of time making democratic decisions and having committee meetings. Such a department is characterized by a rotating chairmanship and a sense of drift; the chairperson simply rubber-stamps the decisions of the faculty. The fourth stage is characterized by the department's large size and a split between nontenured junior professors and tenured senior professors, who make the important governance and policy decisions. The chairperson has a good deal of power but knows that his or her authority comes from the peer group of senior professors. The fifth stage, occurring in some very large distinguished departments and in a few small ones, leaves ordinary governance matters to competent secretaries and specially selected academic bureaucrats. A department in this stage of development is at the peak of prestige and influence but is beginning to collapse because of lack of organization.

A department need not evolve consecutively through all five stages. In a given institution at any given time, departments may be in different stages, and the progression from stage to stage is not necessarily smooth nor inevitable. Murray's theory does, however, provide an interesting conceptual scheme that can be used to explain the organizational problems of some departments.

A chairperson's leadership style may range from autocratic to democratic. As departments evolve, mature, grow, and perhaps even decline, the chairperson's style must change to suit the department's changing needs. Leadership style is a matter of personal choice or preference, but an autocratic style may be most appropriate for a young and relatively immature department. At this point in a department's life, an autocratic chairperson can set a course for the department and give it direction. For example, a prominent department in a large university, when first established, was headed by an extremely autocratic and authoritarian chairperson who personally molded it. He was succeeded by a less autocratic chairperson who continued to follow his general plan for the department, but who encouraged greater faculty participation in policy-making decisions. The department now has a national reputation, elects its chairpersons on a rotating basis, and arrives at crucial decisions in a democratic manner.

If the evolution of a department follows the expected pattern, autocratic rule during the formative years may be desirable. Autocratic rule may also be necessary even when a new department is made up of mature scholars or when an older department is strife-torn and divided. As the department matures, however, the faculty members may expect to become more involved in the governing process. The chairperson may then adopt a less autocratic and more participatory leadership style. Unfortunately, some chairpersons choose an autocratic style because it suits their personalities rather than because it suits the department's needs. Such persons are frequently too rigid to allow faculty members to become involved in policy decisions. If a chairperson cannot become less authoritarian as the department matures, he or she may have to be replaced. The chairperson's term of service, which averages six years,[2] may be related to the cycle of change in a department's evolution.

Characteristics and Skills of an Effective Chairperson

The roles of the department chairperson, as we have noted, may vary considerably. Not the least important role is that which the chairperson develops for himself or herself. A chairperson who is both an effective leader and an efficient facilitator often possesses many of the following characteristics:
  - good interpersonal skills; ability to work well with faculty members, staff, students, deans, and other chairpersons
  - ability to identify problems and resolve them in a manner acceptable to faculty members
  - ability to adapt leadership styles to fit different situations
  - ability to set department goals and to make satisfactory progress in moving their departments toward those goals
  - ability to search for and discover the optimum power available to them as chairpersons; ability to maximize that power in motivating faculty members to achieve department goals and objectives
  - active participation in their professions; respect of their professional colleagues

The job of chairperson varies so much from department to department that a detailed standard job description is difficult to compose. Each chairperson, to a large degree, creates the role according to his or her own talents and skills within a framework that is consistent with institutional, department, and personal goals, both academic and administrative.

Chairpersons must determine what goals they can realistically set for themselves and for their departments during the period

2. Survey conducted in 1977 by Allan Tucker, unpublished.

of their leadership. They must ultimately decide what roles they must and want to play, and how best to play them. Chairpersons must decide whether they want to provide leadership to their faculty members or act in the capacity of executive secretary, whose prime responsibility is to implement the faculty's wishes. Chairpersons must be sufficiently perceptive to judge the extent to which their faculty members and deans will permit them to be the kind of leaders they want to be, and they must be able to satisfy these expectations, as well as follow their own goals. Their effectiveness as chairpersons will depend on their being able to judge which roles to fulfill under any given set of circumstances and then to fulfill them.

A job description will not relieve chairpersons of the necessity or the responsibility for making such judgments; they themselves must decide the nature of the position. The elements that make the chairperson's job ambiguous and frustrating are the same elements that also make it challenging and interesting. When the position becomes only frustrating and loses its interest and challenge, it is time for the chairperson to consider seriously whether he or she can continue as an effective leader.

A Justification for Departments

Enough has been written about the role of the chairperson and the kinds of departments to raise the question, If the job is all that complex, if departments are that difficult to manage, why have departments? Surely, some will argue, there's a better way to provide instruction, conduct research, and offer service to citizens. To date, however, there has been no better way to organize colleges and universities than through academic departments based on recognized disciplines. Almost all efforts to organize colleges and universities differently have failed, particularly those efforts in public institutions, which must account for the disbursement of tax-levied funds used to support them. To be sure, a few successful institutions of higher education in this country do not have academic departments stemming from recognized academic disciplines. These innovative organizations, some of them still in the experimental stage, are almost all privately funded, highly specialized schools with a strong liberal or fine arts emphasis. But the Goliaths of both public and private higher education are orthodox in their organization of knowledge-dispensing and knowledge-creating units.

The idea of organizing universities and colleges by departments derives from the medieval university's system of organization, which still heavily influences higher education in America and in Europe. Departments are the descendants of the medieval *trivium* and *quadrivium*, and over history universities have clung to this kind of organization of human knowledge. In Europe, the institute is often more important than the academic department, but on closer examination, the institute turns out to be an old— or new—subunit of an academic department, a subunit that has declared its independence and has prospered. Perhaps American chemists and psychologists should study the European institute, learn how it functions, and apply their findings to their own situation.

Certainly, the academic department is a comprehensible way to organize knowledge—if not to administer the teaching of it— and it must also be a fairly efficient and cost-effective form of organization. If it were not, it probably would have perished long ago. Perhaps the debate about whether academic departments are good or bad instruments of education can best be settled by paraphrasing Winston Churchill's famous comment about parliamentary government: the academic department may be the worst way to organize knowledge, to administer its disbursement, and to create new knowledge, but it is better than any other way we have thus far devised.

Questions and Exercises

Maturity

In considering maturity (see Hersey and Blanchard's definition on page 28), we can divide groups into four main categories: (1) those who are neither able nor willing to take responsibility; (2) those who are willing but not able to take responsibility; (3) those who are able but not willing to take responsibility, and (4) those who are able and willing to take responsibility. The highest level of maturity is category 4; the lowest level is category 1.

1. *a)* On the basis of the above definition, how would you rate the maturity of your department on most issues—low, moderate, or high?
   b) How many years has your department been in existence?
   c) How many faculty members does your department have?
2. *a)* On the basis of the maturity level rating you have given your department and using the concept relating maturity to leadership style, which quadrant represents the optimum amount of direction or support that you as chairperson should provide?

b) Which quadrant represents the most ineffective leadership style for your department?

Determining Your Leadership Style

Although there are many definitions of leadership, one important definition is the process of influencing the behavior of a person or a group in order to achieve some goal under a specific set of circumstances. The implication here is that no single leadership style is equally effective or ineffective for every department in every situation.

Following is a list of questions that ask you to evaluate yourself in terms of how directive and supportive you are in providing leadership to your faculty members. By answering the questions and following the instructions, you will be able to place yourself in one of the quadrants on the leadership style graph. This questionnaire has not been validated, nor is there any intention to try to validate it. The results, therefore, should not be taken too seriously. However, working through the exercise will help clarify the concept of leadership style and give you a general idea of your style.

How directive are you? (Circle the response that best describes your situation.)

1. How often do you review the department's goals and missions with at least one-third of your faculty members?
   - 1 Hardly ever
   - 2 Occasionally but not too often (1 or 2 times a year)
   - 3 Fairly often (3 to 5 times a year)
   - 4 Quite often (more than 5 times a year)

2. When you give an assignment to a faculty member or a committee, how much detail do you give the individual or committee on how to carry out the assignment?
   - 1 Hardly any detail
   - 2 Some but not much detail
   - 3 A fair amount of detail
   - 4 Lots of detail

3. During the period that the faculty member or committee is carrying out the assignment, how much monitoring do you do of the progress being made?
   - 1 Hardly any monitoring
   - 2 Occasional but not much monitoring
   - 3 A fair amount of monitoring
   - 4 Lots of monitoring

4. In meeting with individual faculty members to discuss their assignments, how specifically do you discuss the assignments?

    1 Not specifically at all   3 Somewhat specifically

    2 Not too specifically   4 Very specifically

Add the four numbers that you have circled for the four questions and divide by 4 to obtain the average. If the number after the decimal point is 0.25, round off to the next lowest whole number. If the number after the decimal point is 0.50 or 0.75, round off to the next highest whole number.

On the leadership style graph, place an *X* above the horizontal dotted line in the space that corresponds to your number. This number represents, on a scale of 1 to 4, the extent to which you are directive.

| Quadrant 1 | High directive
Low supportive | Quadrant 3 | Low directive
High supportive |
| Quadrant 2 | High directive
High supportive | Quadrant 4 | Low directive
Low supportive |

How supportive are you? (Circle the response that best describes your situation.)

1. How many of your faculty members have come to you to relate personal accomplishments or problems during the past year?

    1 Hardly any   3 Between 25 and 50 percent

    2 Less than 25 percent   4 More than 50 percent

2. With how many of your faculty members have you made a point of meeting socially during the past year?

   1 Hardly any   3 Between 25 and 50 percent

   2 Less than 25 percent   4 More than 50 percent

3. To how many of your faculty members have you made a point of giving personal encouragement during the past year?

   1 Hardly any   3 Between 25 and 50 percent

   2 Less than 25 percent   4 More than 50 percent

4. To how many of your deserving faculty members have you written unsolicited informal or formal notes commending them for special achievement during the past year?

   1 Hardly any   3 Between 25 and 50 percent

   2 Less than 25 percent   4 More than 50 percent

Add the four numbers that you have circled for the four questions and divide by 4 to obtain the average. If the number after the decimal point is 0.25, round off to the next lowest whole number. If the number after the decimal point is 0.50 or 0.75, round off to the next highest whole number.

On the leadership style graph, place an X to the right of the dotted vertical line in the space that corresponds to your number. This number represents, on a scale of 1 to 4, the extent to which you are supportive.

Find the place on the graph where the two numbers intersect. The point of intersection will fall in one of the sixteen squares in the graph. The square will be in one of the four quadrants of the graph. For example: Suppose your "directive" score (on the horizontal dotted line) was 2 and your "supportive" score (on the vertical line) was 3. The two numbers would intersect in square *j*, which is in quadrant 3. Your leadership style, according to this simple and nonvalidated test, is low directive and high supportive.

Now that you have determined your leadership style, compare it to the leadership style that would be most effective for your department, given your estimation of its level of maturity.

References

Baldridge, J. Victor, et al. *Policy Making and Effective Leadership: A National Study of Academic Management.* San Francisco: Jossey-Bass, 1978.

Blake, Robert R., and Mouton, Jane S. *The Managerial Grid.* Houston: Gulf, 1964.

Bogue, E. Grady. "Administrative Malpractice: The Limits of Common Sense." *Educational Record*, Winter 1978, pp. 77–86.

Cohen, Michael D., and March, James G., eds. *Leadership and Ambiguity: The American College President.* Carnegie Commission on Higher Education. New York: McGraw-Hill, 1974.

Corson, John J. *The Governance of Colleges and Universities.* New York: McGraw-Hill, 1960.

Hersey, Paul, and Blanchard, Kenneth H. *Management of Organizational Behavior: Utilizing Human Resources.* 3rd ed. Englewood Cliffs, N.J.: Prentice-Hall, 1977.

Johnson, F. Craig. "Data Requirements for Academic Departments." In *New Directions for Institutional Research: Examining Departmental Management*, no. 10, edited by John C. Smart and James R. Montgomery. San Francisco: Jossey-Bass, 1976.

Maccoby, Michael. *The Gamesman.* New York: Simon & Schuster, 1977.

Millett, John D. *New Structures of Campus Power: Success and Failures of Emerging Forms of Institutional Governance.* San Francisco: Jossey-Bass, 1978.

Murray, Robert K. "On Departmental Development: A Theory." *The Journal of General Education*, October 1964, pp. 227–36.

National Training Laboratories Institute for Applied Behavior Science. *Reading Book: Laboratories in Human Relations Training.* Washington, D.C.: National Education Association, 1969.

Richman, Barry M., and Farmer, Richard N. *Leadership, Goals, and Power in Higher Education: A Contingency and Open-Systems Approach to Effective Management.* San Francisco: Jossey-Bass, 1974.

Smart, John C., and Elton, Charles F. "Administrative Roles of Department Chairmen." In *New Directions for Institutional Research: Examining Departmental Management*, no. 10, edited by John C. Smart and James R. Montgomery. San Francisco: Jossey-Bass, 1976.

3

Delegation and
Department Committees

||||||||||||||||||||||||||||||||||||||||||||||||||||||||||||||||||||||||||||||||||||||||||||||||||||||||||||||||||||||||||||||||||||||||||||||

Delegating Responsibility

One of the first questions that a newly appointed department chairperson asks is, How can I effectively fulfill all my responsibilities as chairperson and at the same time not reduce my teaching, research, and service activities? Chairpersons who single-handedly try to carry out all their administrative tasks and simultaneously maintain their previous levels of professional activity are bound to find that the workload is impossible to manage. At some point they must decide to what extent they wish to retain their commitment to teaching, research, and professional activities. Some chairpersons give up most or all of their teaching and research in order to fulfill their administrative and leadership tasks. Others, by carefully delegating many administrative tasks to faculty members and department committees, manage to schedule sufficient time for some teaching and research. Then there are those chairpersons who continue to carry out all their customary teaching, research, and service activities, paying attention to administrative tasks only when absolutely necessary. Chairpersons usually choose the model most suited to their talents, abilities, and professional objectives.

Academic vice presidents and deans are not seriously concerned with the extent to which the chairperson personally carries out the department's administrative activities—so long as the tasks are carried out. Nor do deans and academic vice presidents apply pressure on department chairpersons to conduct research. Faculty members, however, often expect chairpersons to continue their research and scholarly activities even while administering the department. Some chairpersons who are no longer actively engaged in research complain openly about the difficulties and frustrations of the chairperson's job and indicate repeatedly to their colleagues that they can hardly wait to return to the classroom or laboratory. The sincerity with which these statements are made cannot be overlooked. In the 1977 survey of department chairpersons, however, 90 percent responded that they would serve an additional term in the position if invited to do so. For those who envision a career in the area of university administration, the relinquishing of research activity may simply mark the beginning of a new career interest. On the other hand, many chairpersons try to maintain their ealier activities simply for love of their discipline or in anticipation of returning to their former roles when their time as chairperson is over.

Some chairpersons are appointed by the dean and serve at the dean's pleasure; others are appointed by the dean from a list of candidates recommended by a faculty search committee; and still others are elected by their colleagues to serve for one or more terms. In some departments, the position of chairperson rotates among its members. In many cases, chairpersons receive extra compensation and other perquisites, such as full-time summer appointments and more luxurious office space. The material and psychological rewards of the position are intended to compensate for frustrations encountered in the job, such as abrasive incidents with both deans and faculty members, longer hours, and reduced time for teaching and research. Occasionally the frustrations cause chairpersons to resign, especially when the dissatisfactions outweigh the benefits. The department whose chairperson serves a fixed term, usually two or three years, gives the chairperson an option to exit gracefully after a full cycle or two of experience.

Clearly the role of chairperson involves many tasks that are quite time-consuming. In their study of chairpersons at one state university, Gerald W. McLaughlin, James R. Montgomery, and L. F. Malpass found that chairpersons considered the following tasks most demanding: providing informal leadership for faculty members; representing the department to the central administration; allocating financial resources; maintaining faculty morale; encouraging organizational improvement; managing academic programs; planning for the long term; advising students; and encouraging faculty members' professional development.

Even though these tasks were considered most demanding, they provided some satisfaction. Still other tasks were perceived as providing no satisfaction at all. These included maintaining student records, serving on college and university committees, managing facilities, and preparing and presenting budgets. Especially onerous were tasks governed by federal, state, and university laws and administrative rules and requiring much detail work.

Incidentally, chairpersons in the study cited above reported that they worked an average of fifty-five hours per week. They spent an average of twenty-six hours on department leadership and administrative tasks, ten hours on teaching and student counseling, nine hours on research and professional development, and four hours on college and university activities. Several of the chairpersons polled had been in office for five years, and their schedules indicated the extent to which they had adapted their professional lives to their administrative role.

A national survey of chairpersons of medium-sized to large university departments, conducted by John C. Smart and Charles F. Elton and reported in their article "Administrative Roles of Department Chairmen," revealed that the types of roles that the chairperson assumed were related to the department's academic discipline. For example, chairpersons in the basic disciplines, whether the sciences or the humanities, spent more time in the "faculty role" than did those in applied sciences departments. They spent relatively more time recruiting, selecting, and evaluating department faculty members; encouraging their professional development and research and publication efforts; maintaining a healthy department climate by reducing conflicts among the faculty members; and providing informal leadership for the faculty members.

Chairpersons of social science departments—such as anthropology, political science, psychology, and sociology—spent more time in the "instructional role." They spent more time than others teaching and advising students; managing clerical and technical personnel in the department; and maintaining accurate student and department records.

Chairpersons of departments of pure and applied science—such as biology and agriculture departments—spent more time in the "research role" than did chairpersons of the nonscience departments, such as English, history, and communications. They spent relatively more time obtaining and managing grants, gifts, and contracts; recruiting, selecting, and supervising graduate students; and managing department finances, equipment, and grants. Chairpersons in this group also showed low commitment to the instructional role.

The "coordinator role" was not predominant among chairpersons of any particular discipline but was most often associated with chairpersons of education departments. Those in the co-ordinator role spent more time than their colleagues soliciting ideas to improve the department, planning and reviewing the curriculum, and assigning teaching, research, and other duties to faculty members. They also spent more time coordinating department activities with external groups, representing the department at professional meetings, participating in college and university committee work, and interacting with university administrators on behalf of the department. Education chairpersons also spent less time in the faculty role. Perhaps this emphasis on coordinating is related to the fact that education professors spend a great deal of time supervising practical teaching and working with public school personnel; this coordinator role may be carried over when the professor becomes a chairperson.

Whatever the reasons for favoring one of the roles described above, the chairperson must still attend to those tasks that are part of other roles. These tasks may be secondary, but they cannot be totally neglected. To chairpersons who complain of having insufficient time for filling all their roles, university administrators often respond by suggesting that they learn better time management skills. In fact, administrators often suggest that the busiest faculty member be chosen chairperson because busy people manage their time successfully. Many books offer valuable techniques for organizing and managing one's time, and these are helpful for those who are not skillful at getting tasks scheduled and accomplished. Effective time management, however, will not significantly reduce a chairperson's work; such a reduction is possible only if the chairperson learns to delegate tasks. The extent to which chairpersons learn to delegate tasks will determine the amount of time they will have available for teaching, research, and other activities of their choice.

Some chairpersons, as we have noted, continue to carry out all their customary teaching, research, and service activities, but they do this at the expense of administrative tasks; in effect, the administrative tasks are assumed only when absolutely necessary. The attitude that characterizes this kind of administration is that nothing deserves attention until a crisis erupts. The chairperson sees the job as a chore and never bothers to learn about either the intricacies of leadership or the techniques of organization and delegation.

The crisis-fighting approach to department administration leads to an accumulation of unopened mail, unsubmitted reports, missed deadlines, and unattended faculty concerns. The result is a department with low morale and an unfavorable work environment. Often, in the face of faculty disapproval or even rebellion, the chairperson assigns more and more responsibility to the clerical staff. The staff, then, may take on airs of administrative authority, thus further antagonizing faculty members. In such a case, the department chairperson is not really fulfilling his or her responsibility. If a chairperson wants to have time for teaching and research and still effectively lead the department, he or she must learn to practice the art of delegation.

How, then, does a chairperson become an organizer and coordinator of tasks and activities? By delegating tasks and responsibilities to staff members, to faculty members, or to committees. The ability to delegate functions, tasks, and responsibilities requires a trust and confidence in peers and staff members, a trust that occurs when there is consensus within the department about goals, objectives, policies, programs, and priorities. Delegation also requires a willingness to accept the results of the delegated effort, even if these results are not as extraordinary as those the chairperson might have achieved working alone. A chairperson who is compelled to oversee every detail and to operate with "zero defect" standards is often unable to tolerate the work of those who seem less competent.

The chairperson's responsibilities for the completion of a certain task do not end once the task has been delegated. The work of others must be evaluated, checked, and occasionally endorsed. To evaluate something, however, usually takes less time than to do it. The chairperson, by careful delegation, can save between 60 to 90 percent of the time he or she might devote to a single task, especially if the instructions are clear and precise and if those delegated are in tune with the chairperson's style and thinking. Although not every task can be assigned to any person, many detailed but routine tasks can be easily relegated to secretaries, graduate student assistants, and staff associates.

Often, the chairperson can find faculty members who will willingly perform some administrative chores. Department tasks that provide growth and development opportunities are useful governance training for junior faculty members, and they should be given credit for service to the department. For example, these tasks could be made a part of the assigned workload, or the faculty members could be rewarded with some perquisite or a special title. A chairperson must be careful not to overload the unpromoted, untenured junior faculty member to the point that his or her career is threatened.

Senior faculty members who are having difficulty adjusting to the department's changing teaching or research goals or who are in an unproductive phase of their career might also welcome the opportunity to contribute to the department by assuming some delegated responsibility. In delegating tasks to senior faculty members, the chairperson must be sure that these persons are both willing to accept and competent to perform the assignment. Great tact and delicacy may be required in enlisting the efforts of senior faculty members.

Committee Structure

Department committees are useful to the chairperson because he or she can delegate certain tasks to them. They also help provide a logical order to the department decision-making process. Moreover, the faculty is more likely to accept decisions that are made or recommended by a committee, especially if the process for selecting committee members has been approved by the faculty. Much of a department's work is accomplished through committees, and the chairperson should understand how they work and the various ways in which they can be organized.

In a survey of fifteen selected academic departments at Ohio State University, reported in her article "The Internal Organization of Academic Departments," Doris Ryan found that the number of committees per department ranged from sixteen to none, with an average of seven.[1] The larger the department, the more committees it had; small departments often operated, in their entirety, as a single committee.

The size of a committee is clearly related to the tasks that it is assigned, as well as to the department structure. Large committees frequently occur in large departments that have formal subgroups, especially when each subgroup desires representation on those committees. For example, in a large psychology department, the clinical psychologists, who were not represented on the admissions committee, argued that the experimental psychologists, who dominated the selection process, were rejecting many good applicants. Generally, committees consisting of three to nine members seem to be more productive than larger committees. An odd number of members eliminates ties when voting.

There are two general types of committees—standing and ad hoc. A standing committee operates on a permanent basis. Al-

1. Doris W. Ryan, "The Internal Organization of Academic Departments," *Journal of Higher Education* (June 1972): 467.

though its membership may change, it continues to operate from year to year unless some administrative decree terminates its activities. Two examples of standing committees that operate on a permanent basis are admissions committees and faculty evaluation committees. Ad hoc committees, on the other hand, are formed for specific tasks and cease operation when their tasks are completed. Ad hoc committees may include search committees and others that respond to immediate needs. The frequency with which committees meet depends on the tasks assigned to them; some meet on a regular schedule, others on call.

Committee functions may logically be divided into three categories: developing policies, performing administrative activities, and providing technical advice. The policy-making function consists of developing rules, regulations, and criteria for governing certain department activities, such as evaluating faculty performance, admitting students, determining equitable workloads for faculty, assigning space, and so forth. The administrative function consists of making decisions on specific issues or recommending positions to the department chairperson. These administrative functions, all based on predetermined policies and criteria, include reviewing the applications of persons seeking admission to a program and making a decision as to whether they should be admitted; evaluating the performance of faculty members; recommending equitable workloads for specific faculty members; and assigning space to faculty members.

A committee may be established for the sole purpose of developing policies and criteria to govern a single activity, and a second committee may be appointed to implement those policies. In some instances, a single committee is charged not only with developing such policies, procedures, and criteria, but also with implementing them. For example, a faculty evaluation committee may be required not only to develop department policies and criteria for evaluating the faculty but also to evaluate individual faculty members. Similarly, an admissions committee may be required not only to develop policies, procedures, and criteria for admitting students, but also to act on applications for admission.

Committees that provide technical advice are usually composed of faculty members with special expertise for addressing particular problems. These committees are usually ad hoc and are given assignments such as designing and planning new facilities, deciding what types of equipment should be purchased, developing core and specialized curricula for specified programs, and so forth.

Members of these committees may be appointed by the department chairperson, elected by the department, or chosen by a combination of both methods. Similarly, the committee chairperson may be appointed by the department chairperson, elected by the committee members, or elected by the department. In some cases, the department chairperson may also be the committee chairperson, a voting member of the committee, or an ex officio member, or he or she may not be a member at all. How these matters are handled depends on the department's nature and size and the tasks that must be accomplished.

The department chairperson must provide sufficient guidance and direction for the committee. The committee's charge should be clear and precise, and the committee should be apprised of its responsibilities, including what criteria must be followed, under what constraints it must operate, what its members can and cannot do, and what deadlines must be met. Most committees operate in an advisory capacity to the chairperson or to the department. Some advisory committees, however, are perceived as having a decision-making responsibility. One example is the admissions committee, whose task is so important that wise chairpersons rarely overrule its recommendations. In any event, an advisory committee should know that it operates in an advisory function. For committee members to work hard on some problem and then have their work ignored or rejected is disheartening, especially if they think that they are part of a decision-making rather than an advisory committee.

Sometimes chairpersons do not give clear guidance to committees. When a committee is not given a specific charge, criteria to follow, or deadlines to be met, it often accomplishes little or nothing at all. Possibly this result is just what the chairperson desired. Occasionally, a chairperson is pressured to do something that he or she is reluctant to do. Leaving the matter to a committee without giving it guidance, direction, or deadlines—especially if the committee members are at odds with each other—will give the chairperson time to let things simmer.

Some department administrative tasks can easily be delegated to committees, especially when the chairperson is willing to accept a decision that is arrived at fairly. Sometimes, however, the chairperson wants the department to take a certain course of action, which, if he or she proposed it, would arouse some opposition. In such a case, a chairperson could form a committee to recommend to the department that particular course of action.

Can there be any degree of certainty that a committee's conclusions will coincide with the chairperson's ideas? Some administrators use the following strategy. First, they discuss their ideas informally with individual faculty members to identify those who are or who might be sympathetic to the plan. These chairpersons do not use hard-sell tactics and are careful not to show undue eagerness to implement the action. Second, they select a committee of faculty members who are sympathetic to the plan and who also enjoy the respect of their colleagues. An appointed committee of this kind, properly instructed and charged, will usually come up with conclusions and recommendations that are consistent with the chairperson's original plan. If committee members or other faculty members suspect the Machiavellian nature of the chairperson's procedures, they may firmly resist adopting the intended action, regardless of its merits. Many faculty members consider machinations of this sort questionable; nevertheless, many chairpersons have been known to use such tactics. Our description of these tactics, however, is not intended to be an endorsement of them.

An elected committee may not be as predictable in terms of the recommendations it will make. If the chairperson wants an elected committee to recommend a certain course of action, he or she should talk to the committee members individually to gauge their feelings and attempt to persuade them to his or her way of thinking. If the chairperson cannot obtain the support of the committee, he or she might temporarily abandon the issue. Some chairpersons have been known to appoint two committees to work independently on the same problem in order to have a choice of recommendations. Faculty committees and departments as a whole almost always react negatively to a fresh proposal when it is introduced at a formal meeting, especially if the chairperson introduces it without having done any groundwork or having issued previous warning. And a negative reaction is not easily changed. A wise chairperson, therefore, will informally prepare committee members or department members before presenting a new concept at a formal meeting.

The work of department committees may be summarized as follows:
- Committees may function in policy-making, administrative, or technical roles.
- Committee members may be appointed, elected, or both.
- Committees may function in an advisory or decision-making capacity.
- Committees may meet regularly or on call.

- Committees may be permanent or ad hoc.
- The department chairperson may be the committee chairperson, a voting member of the committee, or an ex officio member, or not serve on the committee at all.
- The optimum number of members should be an odd number between three and nine.
- The charge to the committee should be clear and precise.

A department should, on occasion, examine the number and functions of its committees. Their value has been emphasized, but to overburden the faculty with a plethora of committees is counterproductive; only those committees that are necessary should be formed. Some large departments even have a committee to control the tendency of committees to multiply needlessly.

Following is a representative, though far from inclusive, list of department committees and a brief summary of the main functions of each. Few departments have all these committees, and some may not have any.

- *Admissions committee*—usually reviews applications of students for admission to the department and makes recommendations to admit or to deny admission
- *Graduate policy and programs committee*—determines admission and graduation requirements and standards; monitors quality of graduate programs
- *Student recruitment committee*—develops and implements methods of publicizing to prospective students the department's program and professional opportunities within the field
- *Seminars and symposia committee*—arranges and publicizes lectures, seminars, and symposia for faculty members and students within and outside the department
- *Governance committee*—at request of chairperson, considers the structure and functions of department committees; makes recommendations or advises chairperson concerning a broad range of department business
- *Field liaison committee*—establishes and maintains relationships with outside agencies and organizations; coordinates service activities of department faculty
- *Curriculum committee*—develops and monitors curriculum, including core and required courses
- *Promotion and tenure committee*—reviews the records of faculty members eligible for promotion or tenure and recommends appropriate action; in some departments, establishes the standards and criteria for these decisions

- *Faculty evaluation committee*—reviews records of faculty members for purposes of annual evaluation and merit increases; in some cases, establishes criteria for these reviews
- *Faculty development committee*—develops, implements, and monitors procedures that contribute to the professional advancement of faculty members
- *International students committee*—develops and implements procedures for meeting special needs of foreign students
- *Faculty assignment committee*—schedules classes; develops and implements procedures for ensuring that the department's work is equitably divided
- *Student advisory committee*—a student-directed and student-run committee, concerned with student welfare; nominates student members to certain faculty committees
- *Search committee*—develops and implements procedures for recruiting new faculty members and recommends appropriate appointments
- *Examination and grading committee*—sets standards for and reviews the grading system; administers qualifying and comprehensive examinations for graduate students
- *Off-campus program committee*—recommends and supervises courses and programs offered off campus
- *Placement committee*—develops and implements procedures for placing graduates of the program
- *Planning committee*—assesses the department's future needs and develops short- and long-range plans for consideration by the chairperson and the department; sometimes plans new buildings and facilities

Well-organized departments sometimes develop rules and guidelines for the operation of their committees; other committees operate on the basis of unwritten rules. More energy is sometimes spent in developing bylaws for committees than in dealing with the issues. Following is an example of committee guidelines that were adopted by a large department in a large university. This example is not offered as a model but only as an illustration for chairpersons interested in formalizing their department's committee structure. Note that the guidelines stipulate the committee's purposes and duties, describe how members are selected, outline operating procedures, and provide for a periodic evaluation of the committee's activities.

Appropriate guidelines could be drawn up for each committee within the department. The guidelines need not be lengthy or complex, but the charge should be clear.

GUIDELINES FOR THE FACULTY EVALUATION COMMITTEE

Purposes and Duties

1. To design faculty evaluation criteria and procedures for use within the department.
2. To communicate the evaluation criteria procedures to the faculty in a timely fashion.
3. To implement the evaluation procedures for department promotion and tenure, annual evaluation, and merit, and for master's and doctoral directive status.
4. To advocate review and monitor procedures that contribute to professional advancement of untenured and junior members (e.g., to establish conditions suitable for research, writing, and publishing).

Committee Memberships

1. Each of the three degree programs in the department will elect three faculty members as representatives on the committee to serve for a one-year term.
2. The committee chairperson will be named by the department chairperson from among those elected.

Committee Procedures

1. The committee will meet as frequently as may be required to do its work.
2. All candidates for promotion, tenure, and merit, as well as candidates for master's and doctoral directive status within the department shall be reviewed by the committee.
3. The committee will make a brief report of its work to the faculty at the end of the winter quarter.
4. The department chairperson will explain and discuss with the committee the reasons for any action that is contrary to the committee's recommendations. The committee members will inform the faculty of such instances.

Review

The committee will be responsible for conducting a yearly review of its procedures. If necessary, the committee will propose recommended changes to the governance committee.

The many tasks that confront department chairpersons can be extremely time-consuming. To avoid being totally consumed by these tasks and to find sufficient time for desired scholarly activities, chairpersons must learn to delegate some of their tasks. Some chairpersons cannot bear the thought of sharing their responsibilities with colleagues; they fear that other persons are unable to do the job as well as they themselves. Delegation, however, is the only solution to the chairperson's problem of finding time to do all that he or she must do or wants to do. Chairpersons who recognize this fact are continually looking for the right person or committee to whom some department tasks can be entrusted.

Questions and Exercises

List the ten most time-consuming activities that you personally performed during the past year in your capacity as department chairperson (refer to the list of the chairperson's tasks and responsibilities on pages 2–4). Beside each activity that you list, indicate which of these tasks must be performed only by you; which could be delegated to a person in the department, such as a student assistant, secretary, or faculty member; and which could be delegated to a committee. If you think the task could be delegated, write the title of the person or the name of the committee to whom it could be delegated.

1. *a*) How many time-consuming tasks did you list?
   b) How many of these tasks could you delegate to a person or to a committee?
   c) How many could you not delegate to a person or a committee? Explain why not.
2. How many committees does your department have?
3. Which ones help you most with your administrative responsibilities?
4. Do you believe that your department has the right number of committees? Too many? Too few?
5. Which committees would you add, eliminate, or change? Give reasons.

References

American Society of Association Executives. "So You're on a Committee." Washington, D.C.: ASAE, 1976.

Anderson, G. Lester. "Organizational Diversity." In *New Directions for Institutional Research: Examining Departmental Management*, no. 10, edited by John C. Smart and James R. Montgomery. San Francisco: Jossey-Bass, 1976.

Baldridge, J. Victor, et al. *Policy Making and Effective Leadership: A National Study of Academic Management*. San Francisco: Jossey-Bass, 1978.

Cohen, Michael D., and March, James G., eds. *Leadership and Ambiguity: The American College President*. Carnegie Commission on Higher Education. New York: McGraw-Hill, 1974.

Dressel, Paul L., and Simon, L. A. "Allocating Resources among Departments." *New Directions for Institutional Research*, no. 11. San Francisco: Jossey-Bass, 1976.

Johnson, F. Craig. "Data Requirements for Academic Departments." In *New Directions for Institutional Research: Examining Departmental Management*, no. 10, edited by John C. Smart and James R. Montgomery. San Francisco: Jossey-Bass, 1976.

McLaughlin, Gerald W.; Montgomery, James R.; and Malpass, L. F. "An Investigation of Department Heads at a State University." Paper presented at the 1973 American Educational Research Association Conference, New Orleans, Louisiana.

Millett, John D. *New Structures of Campus Power: Success and Failures of Emerging Forms of Institutional Governance.* San Francisco: Jossey-Bass, 1978.

Richman, Barry M., and Farmer, Richard N. *Leadership, Goals, and Power in Higher Education: A Contingency and Open-Systems Approach to Effective Management.* San Francisco: Jossey-Bass, 1974.

Ryan, Doris W. "The Internal Organization of Academic Departments." *Journal of Higher Education*, June 1972, pp. 464–82.

Smart, John C., and Elton, Charles F. "Administrative Roles of Department Chairmen." In *New Directions for Institutional Research: Examining Departmental Management*, no. 10, edited by John C. Smart and James R. Montgomery. San Francisco: Jossey-Bass, 1976.

4

Department Decision Making and Bringing about Change

||||| ||||||||||| |||||||||||| |||||||||||||||||||||||||||||||||||||| |||||||||||||||||||||||||||||||||||||| ||||||||||||||||||||||||||||||||||| |

Every department, at some time or another, has to make decisions. The matters to be decided vary considerably, ranging from issues of great import to more transient ones. Departments must make decisions about larger issues—such as priorities, goals, and the allocation of department resources—as well as smaller issues, including the extent to which the department should become active in off-campus programs, the allocation of travel funds, and the teaching load of department faculty members.

The examples listed above are familiar ones. The list could be expanded to include decisions about personnel problems, budgetary problems, interpersonal problems, organizational problems, and so on. A study of the decision-making process reveals that most decisions are based on the use of a simple problem-solving model. Ordinarily when a person becomes aware that a problems exists, the first step is to identify and clarify the nature of the problem. Then a list of possible solutions can be formulated. (The possibility of doing nothing is frequently the first item on the list.) Thinking about solutions generally leads to a consideration of the possible consequences of each alternative. A person decides which solution seems most likely to produce the desired results and then proceeds to carry it out.

In the academic department, there are times when several decisions must be made simultaneously and other times when only a single, though difficult, decision must be made. Within this context, some chairpersons come to think of themselves as firemen, rushing about trying to extinguish small fires before they become conflagrations. Others fail to see the first signs of impending difficulties and react only after a crisis has occurred. Although the chairperson's personality greatly influences his or her approach to decision making, he or she can consciously adopt methods that seem best suited to the problem.

The chairperson must take the lead in deciding if things are to change or stay the same in the face of the exigencies of academic life. The questions of how to decide and who is to be involved in the decision-making process are difficult and perplexing. Most administrators recognize the desirability of involving faculty members and students in the problem-solving and decision-making processes. Nevertheless, many problems do not permit a great deal of faculty or student participation, simply because they must be dealt with swiftly. In any event, the question of the degree of faculty and student involvement in department decision making is one that most chairpersons must address.

The degree of faculty and student involvement in department decision making is often related to the chairperson's attitude and style. (A chairperson's mode of operation is probably also related to personality variables that need not be discussed here.) The chairperson's style of department leadership can range across a broad continuum, from extremely authoritarian or autocratic to extremely democratic.

The variety of styles within these extremes has been described by Robert Tannenbaum and Warren H. Schmidt in their article "How to Choose a Leadership Pattern." Summarized below is their list of leadership styles. Notice that the styles become more democratic and less autocratic, more relationship-oriented and less task- or directive-oriented, as we proceed down the list.

1. *The chairperson makes the decision and announces it.* The chairperson identifies the problem, evaluates alternative solutions, chooses one of them, and announces to the faculty which solution will be implemented. Little faculty participation is encouraged.

2. *The chairperson makes the decision and tries to sell it.* The chairperson recognizes that his or her decision may not be accepted outright by all concerned. He or she seeks to reduce any resistance by indicating what the faculty will gain.

3. *The chairperson makes the decision and invites questions.* The chairperson seeks acceptance of his or her decision by helping the faculty understand it by means of a question-and-answer session.

4. *The chairperson presents a tentative decision subject to change.* This style permits the faculty to exert some influence on the decision.

5. *The chairperson presents the problem, gets suggestions, and makes the decision.* The chairperson comes to the faculty with a problem that he or she has identified and analyzed but has not

solved. He or she asks the faculty for suggestions; however, all understand that the final decision is the chairperson's.

6. *The chairperson defines the limits and asks the faculty to make the decision within these limits.* The chairperson delegates to the faculty (including himself or herself) the freedom to make the final decision. Before doing so, however, the chairperson states the problem as he or she sees it and sets the boundaries, or areas of freedom, within which the decision can be made.

7. *The chairperson permits the faculty to make the decision within broadly defined limits.* This situation occurs when problems are vague and require a high degree of freedom of exploration if creative solutions are to be found. Only broad limits are imposed and the chairperson, if he or she participates at all, participates as an equal.

Criteria for Degree of Faculty Involvement

The continuum of leadership styles suggests that chairpersons can perform their functions in a variety of ways. Although many believe, as a matter of principle, that faculty and student involvement in decision making should be maximized, the truth of the matter is that not all faculty members and students can be, should be, or should even wish to be involved in every decision a chairperson makes. Do any guidelines or rules exist that suggest when faculty members and students should be asked to participate in the decision-making process?

When problems confront a department and decisions must be made, the chairperson might ask himself or herself several basic questions that can help determine the degree to which the faculty should be involved. These questions are based on three relevant criteria:

- *Expertise*—Who knows how to solve the problem? The chairperson alone? A particular faculty member or group within the department? The whole department?
- *Acceptance*—Is faculty acceptance of the decision crucial for effective implementation? Will implementation fail if the faculty refuses to go along with the decision?
- *Time*—Is there enough time to get the faculty involved in the process of decision making? Is the issue so crucial that an immediate decision is necessary?

While these criteria are logically independent of one another, they should all be considered when an important problem or issue arises. It would be possible to construct a matrix of hypothetical issues, with different values for each criterion, but instead we will discuss each criterion separately.

Expertise. Some decisions require expertise in specific areas. If the chairperson possesses such expertise, he or she is perfectly capable of making a decision alone. Lacking that expertise, the chairperson may seek it from faculty members in the department and should not hesitate to call on those who have experience and interests in areas connected with the problems to be addressed. Frequently the expertise needed for rational decision making may be found outside the department, within the institution, and is available for the asking. Sometimes simple pride or fear of asking for help can prevent a chairperson from using staff resources wisely and advantageously.

Acceptance. Some decisions, important or not, require that the department faculty accept them if they are to be carried out. Important decisions that affect the well-being or survival of the department will require the faculty's acceptance if they are to be implemented. Some decisions that are seen as unimportant are readily accepted by the faculty, who is grateful not to have been bothered with them. In such instances, the chairperson can make the decision alone or delegate the matter to a staff member. On the other hand, some seemingly unimportant decisions may require faculty involvement in order to gain acceptance. The chairperson must rely on his or her judgment to evaluate the faculty members' mood.

People willingly participate in an activity when they can see the benefits that accrue from a common endeavor, when they see the department's success as synonymous with their own. On the other hand, the most benign and rational decision can be resisted, subverted, or diverted by a group if it feels that it had no share in making the decision. What better way is there to encourage faculty members to accept and implement decisions than to have them participate in the process of making decisions?

Time. Occasionally problems arise and decisions must be made with great speed. In the context of modern bureaucratic organizations, opportunities arise that must be seized without hesitation or they will be lost. The chairperson must judge whether an immediate decision is better than no decision at all.

Implementing Change

The three criteria we have been discussing—expertise, acceptance, and time—vary in importance according to circumstance.

Considering these criteria when the question of faculty involvement arises will help a chairperson decide whether, in those particular circumstances, the faculty ought to be involved. A related problem is *how* faculty members can be encouraged to participate in the decision-making process. Some are ready and eager to be involved in department problem solving, while others show little interest in sharing in the hard work that is a part of intelligent decision making. No single method of involving faculty members in the decision-making process is best. Departments vary considerably in size, tradition, role and mission, and the personalities and skills of their members. Each chairperson's decisions about the methods and techniques of faculty involvement must take into account the special, often idiosyncratic, characteristics of the department. Nevertheless, each chairperson must determine whether a matter should be brought to a meeting of the full faculty, referred to a committee, discussed informally with faculty members, or acted upon according to his or her own best judgment. These determinations depend partly on how the chairperson views his or her role and partly on his or her experience in working with each option.

Most department chairpersons, on the basis of their past experience, choose to share the decision-making process with their faculty members for the following reasons. First, faculty members will have to implement almost any decision the chairperson makes and are therefore more likely to be cooperative if they are involved in making the decision. Second, as mentioned earlier, individual faculty members often have expertise or experience to contribute to the decision-making process. Third, when conflicts do occur, resolving them in the context of open discussion is less disruptive than neglecting them altogether and possibly causing them to multiply unnecessarily. Finally, department decisions take place within the broader contexts of academe and a democratic society. The university, as an institution, has a long tradition of collegiality; the idea of a community of scholars is compatible with processes of shared decision making by equals.

Some department decisions can be implemented only by first changing a specific policy or procedure. Change, it has been said, is society's only constant. Certainly a huge number of changes have taken place in colleges and universities in recent years, and these changes reflect changes in society as a whole.

In most social groups, a creative tension exists between forces that operate to bring about change and forces that operate to resist change. Although the American education system in general and institutions of higher education in particular are conservative and resistive of change, the continuous pressures of political and social events demand responses, and these responses result in a good deal of change. During the turbulent sixties, it seemed as if the pressures for a thorough democratization of educational curriculum and governance would revolutionize the structure of higher education. The seventies showed a great decline in student unrest, and many predictions of the preceding decade failed to materialize. Nevertheless, there is now a good deal more student participation in academic affairs than occurred in the fifties and sixties—for example, students now sit on boards of regents and on many academic committees.

Economic uncertainties and declining enrollments have combined to threaten the optimistic predictions of unlimited growth in the power, size, and influence of academic institutions. In fact, in many instances, programs and institutions are themselves threatened. The demands of minorities, particularly blacks and women, have led to numerous changes in school policy and procedure. The rise of teacher militancy at the elementary and secondary level has been followed by increasing unionization in many colleges and university systems. Changes in technology have led to changes in instructional techniques; educational television and computer-assisted instruction are becoming more common. These are but a few of the many pressures toward change that come from within and outside the college. Therefore, to ask what changes will be required is more realistic than to ask whether change will be required.

Departments have been and are subjected to many pressures for change from within and without the institution. The discussion of decision making is related to the kinds of change departments will be required to make. The chairperson's role in bringing about needed change can be central in determining whether change is indeed desirable, in planning for change, and in providing leadership in the process of implementing change.

While the question of change and the problems of implementing it can be easily discussed and the need for change readily acknowledged, the actual processes of bringing about change are quite perplexing. The results of some social science research suggests that many methods used to effect changes in human behavior are quiet inefficient.

Amitai Etzioni, who has investigated problems of change, argues that attempts to effect behavioral change in humans through educational and advertising methods may not be successful unless there are accompanying changes in the environment. In his article "Human Beings Are Not Very Easy to Change, After All," he cites failures in antismoking campaigns, alcohol and drug abuse programs, and traffic safety programs that depended primarily on advertising and propagandizing. He then contrasts these failures with efforts that succeeded in altering behavior when persons were removed from situations or environments that contributed to the problem in the first place. In discussing the dismal failures of the intensive educational campaigns to help disadvantaged children, Etzioni concludes that educational programs will continue to fail as long as the children's total environments are unchanged. Change has been implemented successfully when persons *willingly* enter a new social community. Etzioni suggests that the total change approach, exemplified by people who join a kibbutz or an organization like Alcoholics Anonymous, is often successful. While total change appeals to a radical perspective, it obviously works only with volunteers, and many persons will simply not volunteer for a radical revision of their social environment.

Although Etzioni's research is not primarily concerned with change in academic organizations, some of his findings are applicable to this discussion. For example, a department chairperson, the sole representative of her institution, participates in a regional or national workshop for academic administrators. She returns with enthusiasm and many ideas for implementing change, only to encounter a resistive and unyielding environment. In this case, motivating the department chairperson to desire change was in itself not sufficient to bring it about.

Etzioni's research also suggests that finding new persons to implement decisions for change may be easier than obtaining cooperation from those whose ways are set. Unless positions are available for new faculty members, chairpersons of some departments must wait for recalcitrants to retire before attempting any change. In those instances when the chairperson is the obstruction to changes necessary for the department's survival, the dean must seek ways of changing the chairperson's behavior or perhaps of changing the chairperson.

In his article "Hauling Academic Trunks," J. B. Lon Hefferlin notes that few institutions change spontaneously and suggests that the most important factor influencing change is the market conditions under which educational institutions operate. Colleges and universities and their departments must attract resources or fail in their mission. Departments compete, within and without the institution, for scarce resources. If they fail to compete, they are liable to wither away. A department's curricular offerings must attract students, and the working conditions must attract faculty members, or mediocrity and stagnation will result. Many, if not most, departments closely watch what departments at other institutions are doing and try to do the same sorts of things—i.e., they sail with the wind rather than trying to go against it.

The second most powerful factor influencing academic change, according to Hefferlin, is the institution's ethos toward change. Each college or university and its departments have their own historic orientation toward change. This orientation, whatever it is, tends to be self-perpetuating, since those in power usually choose persons like themselves to succeed them. Yet choosing innovative successors often results in meaningful change. It is easier to replace persons than to change their attitudes, and frequently curricular or structural changes in universities or colleges must take place at the time when old professors retire or leave and new ones replace them. Dwight Ladd's study *Change in Educational Policy* indicates that changes in colleges and universities do not take place unless the faculty is convinced of the desirability of change.

A third factor that influences change in higher education is the institutional structure, which can be an aid or a barrier to change. The same is true of department structure as well. The department's decision-making process may be facilitated by clear procedures, by the nature of committees within the department, and by the rules that govern curricular issues and personnel policies. Some departments have written bylaws that outline the structure, while others have a structure based on higher authority. Departments that have no formal rules or procedures often have informal rules based on precedent or tradition. A problem in most large institutions is the rigidity of the bureaucracy. Strict, bureaucratic rules and procedures certainly operate against policies that are flexible, adaptive, and responsive.

In certain areas within departments, the need for change seems to crop up with some regularity. The first is the area of department goals and objectives. The goals of colleges and universities change with societal needs and conditions, and department goals may have to be altered to remain consistent with the institution's larger goals. To avoid mere rhetoric, goals and objectives should be stated realistically within the institutional and societal framework.

A second area of change is the department curriculum. The curriculum should be consistent with the department's goals and responsive to the needs of students, the discipline or profession, the community, and the institution. While the curriculum necessarily reflects the capabilities of the faculty, it can become ossified if not monitored.

A third area of change is the department's research and service activities. Here, too, there is the question of whether the research activities of faculty members within the department are consistent with department goals. Another serious question concerns the relationship between the department's research and service activities and its curricular and instructional activities; some research and service activities might conceivably weaken the department's course offerings. Finally, departments can address the question of the quality and worth of the research carried out in the department. This question most commonly arises during considerations of promotion and tenure for faculty members, but it might be addressed more profitably in the context of a general department evaluation.

Hefferlin, in the article cited earlier, lists five techniques for implementing academic change: the administrator must determine the obstacles, provide reassurance, build on existing concerns, avoid rejection, and respect the past. Although Hefferlin is speaking of change at the institutional level, his techniques may be applied when implementing change within a department. If changes are contemplated, the chairperson should anticipate possible obstacles to implementing these changes. These obstacles may be internal or external. They may be due to apathy, indifference, or lack of information.

Change is sometimes threatening, and the threats can be real or imagined. The chairperson should think of ways to assuage fears and consider techniques of conciliation, cooptation, and confrontation in the attempt to implement changes. When discussing change, try to avoid distorting and misrepresenting ideas. The chairperson can avoid opposition by clarifying the ideas and activities being considered. The more information the faculty members receive, the more likely they are to feel reassured. Change that builds on the existing concerns of the department is more likely to gain acceptance than change that does not. Changes should address problems that the faculty sees as urgent. The task force approach to change, which allows interested faculty members to participate, is recommended as a way of channeling the concerns of faculty members.

One way to avoid rejection is to propose change for a specific experimental period. If such a proposal is rejected, an optional, parallel program can be suggested. Then, if the proposed change works well, the rest of the faculty is more likely to accept it. Optional, parallel programs work well in the area of curriculum.

Finally, change in academia may be garbed in tradition. Hefferlin cites President Lowell of Harvard, who, in 1938, said of the college president:

> If he desires to innovate he will be greatly helped by having the reputation of being conservative, because the radicals who want a change are little offended by the fact of change, while the conservatives will be likely to follow him because they look on him as sharing their temperament and point of view.[1]

This sage political advice can be applied to the governance of a department as well. Tradition should be respected while change is fostered.

In his article "Organizational Reform Is Not Enough," H. Bradley Sagen lists conditions that affect the adoption of academic innovation. His ideas, presented in terms of institutional changes, will be discussed here in terms of department changes. He favors incentives and institutional support for innovations. In fact, one common criticism voiced about department change is the lack of rewards for those who attempt to innovate. Sagen suggests that faculty members might be encouraged to develop new ideas, goals, and programs through such small incentives as secretarial assistance, student assistantships, and released time.

Proposed changes are also easier to implement if they do not conflict with the values held by the department faculty members. If proposed changes are compatible with the faculty members' values and beliefs, the changes should not meet with resistance. A chairperson interested in innovations should be aware of the faculty members' academic and personal values and should be able to show that proposed changes are compatible, or at least not too incompatible, with those values. Sagen also stresses the importance of "participative involvement" in bringing about change. Compatibility of values is a necessary part of participative involvement.

Another desirable prerequisite to change is the clarification of the present situation. To know where you are going requires not only a clear idea of how you are going to get there, but also a

---

1. J. B. Lon Hefferlin, "Hauling Academic Trunks," *Elements Involved in Academic Change.* (Washington, D.C.: Association of American Colleges, 1972), p. 10.

clear idea of where you are. Sagen also recommends identifying and using faculty leaders to facilitate change. Some faculty members are admired and respected by their colleagues for their intelligence, honesty, and integrity; their opinions and attitudes carry a good deal of weight with their peers. A chairperson who can mobilize department leaders to support desired changes may find the path to change smoother than the chairperson who ignores department leaders.

Dealing with Change and Resistance to Change

Clark Kerr, a former president of the University of California, once said that changing a university curriculum is like trying to move a cemetery. His statement aptly characterizes faculty resistance to change. Though colleges and universities are characterized by massive inertia, in the long run they too must yield to the pressure of changes. Because faculty members perceive change as threatening and manipulative, chairpersons tend to shy away from talking about it directly in order to avoid provoking anxiety and resistance. Faculty members feel less anxious, however, when discussing such subjects as self-renewal, organizational development, or faculty and staff development, all of which are actually efforts for planned change. For chairpersons to act as leaders or facilitators in these efforts, they should know and understand the process of change.

When faculty members resist change, what are they really resisting? Will a plan be automatically accepted if it is logical and educationally well conceived? Not necessarily. As we noted earlier, plans for change that rely exclusively on rationality are typically not successful. A faculty member's first reaction to a proposed change is to ask how it will affect him or her personally in terms of opportunity for professional development, promotion, salary increases, and work assignments. Faculty members will also be concerned about how the change will affect their future relationships with coworkers, students, administrators, colleagues, and so forth. To ensure the greatest likelihood of acceptance, therefore, a proposed plan for change should not only be logical and well conceived but should take into consideration the personal concerns of those involved. The chairperson should seek out those who feel that they will lose status if the change occurs. If their fears are unfounded, they should be given the necessary assurances. If indeed the change may cause them to lose status, the chairperson should think about what, if anything, could be done to make up for this loss or to improve their present status. When the chairperson shows proper concern and interest, resistance may be converted to support.

Proper and frequent communication with faculty members before, during, and after a change will help alleviate many of their personal concerns. Those who will be affected by a proposed change should be provided with as much information as possible about the situation. Lack of knowledge about what is going on causes insecurity, and insecurity increases resistance, regardless of the merits of the proposed change. Information that presents the rationale for suggested changes may be sufficiently persuasive to reduce resistance or gain support for a proposed plan. Changing a person's knowledge base is frequently a prerequisite for changing attitude and behavior.

Another impediment to change often results from the requirement that plans for proposed changes must be reviewed and approved by many persons and groups in the institution's governance hierarchy. Any faculty committee or administrator may veto an idea as it travels the hierarchy from department to dean's office to president's office. Whenever a new idea for change is presented to a faculty committee for the first time, the reaction is generally negative, and after the initial rejection, committee support for the idea is difficult to obtain. In some instances, it is better to discuss the idea individually with several members of the committee before making the presentation to the committee as a whole. If individual members are persuaded that the idea has merit, they will help obtain support from the rest of the committee. Proper and frequent communication with committee members and administrators during the development of the plan can reduce resistance.

Change involves considerable risk because it will not necessarily solve a problem. Not every new approach will prove effective, and when a change fails, the innovator may be criticized or even terminated. A wrong change could stir up conflict, upset sensitive balances and relations, and waste faculty members' energy. Therefore, before the chairperson decides to implement a plan for change, he or she could collect data that will help determine the probability of the plan succeeding without demoralizing the faculty. If the probability of success is low, the plan should not be implemented. Keep in mind also that the smaller the change, the less resistance it will generate. If a change is necessary, select one that will solve the problem in the simplest and least noticeable way. Do not amputate a leg to cure a toe infection. Remember also that if faculty members have not been involved in the planning, they will resist even the smallest change that might affect them.

What motivates faculty members to change? First, many are motivated by the desire for competence and the need to achieve. These persons are primarily interested in job mastery and professional growth and are constantly thinking of better ways of doing things. They are willing to participate in planning and implementing change for the sake of their own professional improvement and the department's improvement. Second, some faculty members are motivated to change only if they can anticipate a more tangible reward that they can share with their families. Third, some faculty members are motivated to change only when they consider the consequences of not changing—if, for example, they thought that unwillingness to change could cause them to lose privileges or face possible termination. A department with decreasing enrollments might be motivated to modify its recruitment policies, its curriculum, and its goals and activities if decreasing enrollment could lead to a reduced department budget and perhaps a reduced number of faculty positions. Faculty members' response to the need for change is generally based on a combination of all three factors, each of which may be weighted differently for different persons. But there are some faculty members who just won't change under any circumstances. The question of what to do with them is one of the challenges facing the department chairperson.

When considering the feasibility of implementing a plan for change, the chairperson should try to anticipate who will support the plan and who will resist it. The chairperson should make a list of potential supporters and the reasons for their support and another list of those who are expected to resist the plan and the reasons for their resistance. The supporting faculty members and their rationale can be thought of as "driving forces," the resisters and their rationale as "restraining forces."

Because the faculty members on each list will vary in the degree to which they support or resist the plan, the chairperson should rate the strength of each person's support or resistance on a scale of 1 to 5. When all the driving and restraining forces have been listed and the strength of each force has been rated, totals of the driving forces and the restraining forces can be calculated and then compared.

In his book *Field Theory in Social Science*, Kurt Lewin, a well-known social psychologist, has developed what is called the force field analysis theory, which says that change takes place when an imbalance occurs between the sum of the driving forces and the sum of the restraining forces. The greater the imbalance, the more acceptable the change will be. When the two sets of forces are balanced, the status quo continues. To bring about change, the driving forces must become strong enough to overcome the restraining forces, or the restraining forces must be sufficiently reduced or weakened to be overcome by the existing driving forces.

Applying Lewin's theory to the chairperson's role, we see that the chairperson should determine what kind of and how much influence is needed to attain the optimum pressure of driving forces necessary to bring about the desired change. He or she must then calculate whether there is enough support—or enough influence to obtain support—for the change. At this point the chairperson can decide whether the efforts for change are likely to be successful. If the decision is made to go ahead with the plan, a decision must also be made about the strategy to be used.

Strategies for bringing about change include the participative model and the power model. The participative, or involvement, model is used most often in organizations. In this model, new knowledge is made available to the group with the hope that the group will accept the data and develop a commitment to the desired change. The group is involved in reviewing the data and helping select or develop new methods for choosing the desired goal. In the power model, the chairperson imposes the plan for change on the faculty members in the hope that when they see how well it works, they will support it. In a university setting, the participative model is the most appropriate most of the time. The power model, however, can be more efficient and effective when the faculty's acceptance is not crucial to the implementation of the plan.

In evaluating the need for the change, the department chairperson must learn how to ask the right questions. He or she should talk to faculty members, the dean, other chairpersons, students, and recent alumni. The questions should include these: What is good about the department? What is not so good? What might happen in the future if the status quo remains unchanged? What would faculty members like to see happen in the future?

These questions will elicit mounds of useful information. Moreover, the process will generally please those who are asked to comment and will thereby earn the chairperson a measure of positive support. These interviews will result in a tentative list of proposed changes that should be considered.

In selecting and implementing plans for change, then, the following points should be kept in mind.

- Select changes that are most timely and appropriate for the department's current situation.
- Select plans for change that have a reasonable chance of success—e.g., sufficient faculty support, sufficient resources, and so forth.
- Select plans that require the least drastic change to solve a problem.
- Develop plans for responding to the personal needs of those who will be affected by the changes.
- Develop strategies for communicating appropriately with those who will be affected by the change as well as those who must approve it.
- Develop strategies for obtaining faculty members' commitment to supporting and participating in the implementation of the plan.
- Be sensitive to values held by members of the department.

In bringing about needed change, the department chairperson should have the ability to perform the following functions:

- provide guidance to the faculty in developing and updating department goals and objectives
- assess local, regional, and national needs for education services provided by the department
- develop action plans for the needed changes
- implement action plans for the needed changes

Examples of specific skills helpful to department chairpersons in dealing with change include these:

- ability to design and implement strategy for bringing about needed curriculum and program change
- ability to develop long-range plans and strategies—for example, strategies for timely appointment, promotion, tenure, and retirement of faculty members—that will enable a department to remain responsive to new and changing needs
- ability to identify and develop programs to meet the professional development needs of faculty members in times of retrenchment

Intervention Plans

For our purposes, an *intervention* is defined as a person's action or series of actions that causes a change in the behavior of another person or group. Literally, it is an interruption in the direction in which a person or group is moving. A department chairperson can devise an intervention plan that will move a department in the desired direction and at the same time improve faculty motivation and morale. A well-planned intervention may further the goals of collegiality and shared governance. In its simplest form, such a plan would consist of a statement of the intervention and its expected outcome. Evidence for these expectations should be specified so that a follow-up can determine whether the intervention was effective.

Some interventions seem especially appropriate to the university setting, with its horizontal structure and its traditional framework of collegiality. Nine particularly appropriate kinds of interventions are described below, with examples of how such interventions might be useful.

The first kind of intervention calls attention to a contradiction in action or attitudes. Recently a chemistry department had the opportunity to fill a vacant position at the associate professor level. In establishing the criteria for the application, the faculty members stipulated at least five years' teaching experience, significant publications in major journals, national visibility, demonstrated service in the profession, and the ability to direct graduate students. Some months later an assistant professor in the department with four years of teaching experience, two publications, a good service record to the university, and a pleasant personality applied for a promotion to the rank of associate professor. Since he was well liked and seemed to show promise as a researcher, the department members were anxious for him to be promoted. The chairperson called their attention to the discrepancy between their criteria for someone coming from outside the institution and their criteria for someone within the institution. After some discussion, they decided to ask the faculty member to wait another year and work toward coming closer to department standards. In this case, the department chairperson's intervention modified the way in which the department developed and used its human resources.

The second kind of intervention relies on the use of research findings or conceptual understandings to help faculty members broaden their perspective on a particular problem. A communications department chairperson was faced with the problem of having too many sections of an extremely popular speech course and too few instructors. The faculty's desire to maintain the twenty-to-one student-faculty ratio in the classroom was opposed by the dean, who said that he simply could not find the additional faculty positions to support so low a student-faculty ratio in a lower-division course. The chairperson looked into the research on students evaluating their peers' performance, which showed that students' evaluation of their fellow students was reliable and permitted a larger class size by reducing the amount of time the instructor spent on grading. She shared the information with the faculty members, who were convinced by the evidence. The appeal to research findings was persuasive and allowed the department chairperson both to double her class size and to maintain the faculty members' morale.

The third kind of intervention reexamines the existing methods for solving problems within the department. A new economics department chairperson wished to involve junior faculty members in the department's decision-making process. When he met resistance from the existing oligarchy, he used the occasion of a university self-study to appoint a committee composed of junior and senior faculty members to review the department's decision-making process. The committee concentrated on the methods used to make decisions and, with the input from the junior faculty members, recommended a revision of the department's decision-making processes. The committee workload was distributed more evenly and the senior faculty members' time used to better advantage.

The fourth kind of intervention focuses on lowering situational conflict within the group by improving group relationships. The faculty members of an English department were unable to modify their selection of requirements for their undergraduate general education courses. The modernist faction felt that the traditionalists were being stubborn in their devotion to the past, while the traditionalist faction felt that many of the modernists' innovations were too avant garde and that faculty members who espoused curricular revisions were merely trying to promote their own ends. Tensions had increased when the department chairperson organized a weekend retreat for the faculty members at the university convention center some twenty-five miles from campus. During the retreat, as the faculty members walked together on the beaches or sat in front of the fire, many of the superficial, emotional elements of the conflict were reduced. On the last day of the retreat, the faculty members were able to resolve the problem to everyone's satisfaction.

The fifth kind of intervention allows for the adoption of two or more options rather than a single forced choice. This approach is particularly appealing to science departments and other departments that are quantitatively oriented. Although the procedures for comparing courses of action are not scientifically exact, they do add an element of logic to the decision-making process. A graduate psychology department wished to modify its comprehensive examination procedures by substituting a research project assignment for the written examination. The faculty members disagreed about the apropriateness of this course of action, so the department chairperson allowed one group of doctoral students to select either the examination or the project for one academic year. After the year's experience with both options, the faculty decided to adopt the research project as an option for students.

The sixth kind of intervention identifies significant alternatives and examines the consequences that might follow the adoption of each alternative. The chairperson of a history department found that she was unable to provide adequate office space for a growing number of faculty members and graduate students. A morale problem developed. The dean told the chairperson that she could have all the office space she wanted in a vacant house on the edge of campus. The chairperson met with the faculty members to explore the advantages of being housed in spacious quarters but away from the center of campus life and the advantages of being housed in cramped quarters but close to the center of campus life. After much discussion, they decided in favor of more cramped quarters closer to classrooms and other students. The intervention resulted in increased understanding, thus reducing the morale problem.

The seventh kind of intervention objectively applies a historical perspective to the present situation. A geology department chairperson wished to encourage faculty members to solicit research proposals from outside agencies. To this end he conducted a review of outside funding received by the department over the preceding ten years and compared it with research activities and funding both of other science departments within the university and of other geology departments within the university system. The evidence indicated that the department was missing out on some research opportunities. Faculty members began to write proposals and to receive outside funding.

The eighth kind of intervention identifies the source of the problem as something related to an institutional policy or constraint. A humanities department chairperson was challenged by a group of her faculty members for her failure to secure enough travel money for them to attend the national convention. The department chairperson met with the group and reviewed the board of regents' budgetary procedures, the university's restrictions on travel, and appropriations of travel funds throughout the university. She was able to demonstrate that while the absolute amount of travel money was ridiculously low, the department had received more than its fair share, given the institutional constraints. She also indicated that those departments that had more travel money usually obtained it from outside sources. By showing the faculty members the structure of the system, she was able to spur their requests for funds from outside agencies.

The final kind of intervention relies on one of the strongest arguments of all—tradition. Faculty members, it has been said, never like to do anything for the first time; appeals to tradition can, therefore, be particularly persuasive. An education administration department chairperson wished to encourage the faculty members to be more active in ordering books for the library. Ordering books was consuming a great deal of his time, but he knew from experience that a general request for more book orders would generate little response. He began his strategy by assigning students in his own classes to read books that he considered basic to areas in his field but that were unavailable in the library. When students reported that the library did not possess the books that were assigned, the chairperson relayed those reports to a meeting of the faculty. At the meeting, the chairperson spoke of the great libraries at the universities at which many of the faculty members had earned their doctorates. He stated that funds were available to the department for the purchase of books in their respective fields; thus a library could be built that would at least equal those they had used as students. With the expertise of the faculty mobilized, a first-class collection representing the highest tradition of university scholarship could be amassed. As a result of the discussion, the book-ordering function was taken over by a faculty committee.

The nine intervention techniques that seem especially appropriate for use in universities may be summarized as follows.

1. Call attention to a contradiction in action or in attitudes.
2. Rely on the use of research findings or conceptual understandings.
3. Reexamine the existing methods for solving problems.
4. Focus attention on lowering intergroup conflict by improving group relationships.
5. Test the adoption of two or more options, as opposed to a single forced choice.

6. Identify significant alternatives and examine the consequences of adopting each alternative.
7. Apply a historical perspective to the present situation.
8. Identify the source of the problem as related to an institutional policy or constraint.
9. Argue from tradition.

In this chapter we have discussed the need for chairpersons to obtain information from faculty members when contemplating department changes. Faculty members who have not had the opportunity to become involved in the decision-making process sometimes resist, actively or passively, the implementation of the resulting decision, regardless of its potential benefit to the department. Too much involvement, however, can be just as detrimental as too little. We have described various ways of determining the extent to which faculty members should be involved, how to involve them, and how to help them overcome some of their feelings of resistance to a proposed change. Some attitudes of resistance, if unchecked, can develop into difficult conflict situations. Dealing with potential and active conflict is described in some detail in chapter 9.

Questions

1. What are some fairly important types of decisions that you as chairperson could make for your department without involving the faculty members in the decision-making process and that they would accept without serious complaint?
2. What are some fairly unimportant types of decisions that you could make without involving the faculty members in the decision-making process and that they would not accept?
3. What types of department decisions would your faculty members prefer that you make without bothering them?
4. *a)* Do you currently have a specific problem in your department, the solution to which requires a change that will be resisted by some faculty members?
   b) Thinking only about this specific problem, can you identify in your mind those faculty members who would support your idea and those who might oppose it?
   c) What interventions would seem to have the most positive effects on faculty members in your department?
   d) What procedures and strategies would you use to win over those faculty members who might create opposition?

82   *Chairing the Academic Department*

References

Argyris, Chris. "Interpersonal Barriers to Decision-Making." *Harvard Business Review*, February 1966, pp. 84–97.

Argyris, Chris, and Schon, Donald A. *Theory in Practice: Increasing Professional Effectiveness*. San Francisco: Jossey-Bass, 1974.

Bergquist, William H., and Philips, Steven R. "Components of an Effective Faculty Development Program." *Journal of Higher Education*, March 1975, pp. 177–211.

Birnbaum, Robert. "Using the Calendar for Faculty Development." *Educational Record*, Fall 1975, pp. 226–30.

Brown, David G., and Hanger, William S. "Pragmatics of Faculty Self-Development." *Educational Record*, Summer 1975, pp. 201–6.

Buhl, Lance C., and Greenfield, Adele. "Contracting for Professional Development in Academe." *Educational Record*, Spring 1975, pp. 111–21.

Burns, Tom, and Stalker, G. M. *Management of Innovation*. New York: Methuen, 1961.

Cartwright, Dorwin. "Achieving Change in People: Some Applications of Group Dynamics Theory." *Human Relations*, November 1951, pp. 381–92.

Cartwright, Dorwin, and Zander, Alvin, eds. *Group Dynamics: Research and Theory*. 3rd ed. New York: Harper and Row, 1968.

Chamberlain, Philip C. "Resistance to Change in Curriculum Planning." In *The Academic Department or Division Chairman: A Complex Role*, edited by James Brann and Thomas A. Emmet, pp. 250–62. Detroit: Balamp, 1972.

Coch, Lester, and French, John R. P., Jr. "Overcoming Resistance to Change." *Human Relations*, August 1948, pp. 512–32.

Florida Board of Regents. *Comprehensive Development Plan of the State University System of Florida*. Tallahassee: Board of Regents, 1970.

Etzioni, Amitai. "Human Beings Are Not Very Easy to Change, After All." *Saturday Review*, 3 June 1972, pp. 45–47.

Group for Human Development in Higher Education. *Faculty Development in a Time of Retrenchment*. New Rochelle, N.Y.: Change Magazine Press, 1974.

Guest, Robert H.; Hersey, Paul; and Blanchard, Kenneth H. *Organizational Change through Effective Leadership*. Englewood Cliffs, N.J.: Prentice-Hall, 1977.

Hammons, James O., and Wallace, Terry H. Smith. "Sixteen Ways to Kill a College Faculty Development Program." *Educational Technology*, December 1976, pp. 16–20.

Hefferlin, J. B. Lon. *Dynamics of Academic Reform*. San Francisco: Jossey-Bass, 1969.

———. "Hauling Academic Trunks." In *Elements Involved in Academic Change*, edited by Charles U. Walker, pp. 1–10. Washington, D.C.: Association of American Colleges, 1972.

Ladd, Dwight R. *Change in Educational Policy: Self-Studies in Selected Colleges and Universities,* with commentary by Katharine McBride. New York: McGraw-Hill, 1970.

Lawrence, Paul R. "How to Deal with Resistance to Change." *Harvard Business Review,* May–June 1954, pp. 49–57.

Lewin, Kurt. *Field Theory in Social Science,* edited by Dorwin Cartwright. Westport. Conn.: Greenwood, 1975.

Lionberger, Herbert F. *Adoption of New Ideas and Practices.* Ames, Ia.: Iowa State University Press, 1960.

Lippitt, Ronald, et al. *Dynamics of Planned Change: A Comparative Study of Principles and Techniques.* New York: Harcourt Brace, 1958.

McGannon, Barry James, S. J. "Guide to Academic Planning—St. Louis University." In *The Academic Department or Division Chairman: A Complex Role,* edited by James Brann and Thomas A. Emmet, pp. 269–96. Detroit: Balamp, 1972.

Marrow, Alfred J.; Bowers, David G.; and Seashore, Stanley E., eds. *Strategies of Organizational Change.* New York: Harper and Row, 1967.

Milgram, Stanley. "Group Pressure and Action against a Person." *Journal of Abnormal and Social Psychology,* August 1964, pp. 137–43.

Miller, Richard I. *Evaluating Faculty Performance.* San Francisco: Jossey-Bass, 1972.

National Training Laboratories. *Explorations in Human Relations Training.* Washington, D.C.: National Education Association, 1969.

Richardson, Richard C., Jr. "Staff Development: A Conceptual Framework." *Journal of Higher Education,* May 1975, pp. 303–11.

Ronken, Harriet O., and Lawrence, Paul R. *Administering Changes: A Case Study of Human Relations in a Factory.* Boston: Harvard University Press, 1952.

Sagen, H. Bradley. "Organizational Reform Is Not Enough." In *Elements Involved in Academic Change,* edited by Charles U. Walker, pp. 20–29. Washington, D.C.: Association of American Colleges, 1972.

Steele, Claude M., and Green, Stephen G. "Affirmative Action and Academic Hiring: A Case Study of a Value Conflict," *Journal of Higher Education,* July 1976, pp. 413–35.

Tannenbaum, Robert, and Schmidt, Warren H. "How to Choose a Leadership Pattern." *Harvard Educational Review,* March-April 1957, pp. 95–101.

Von Haden, Herbert I., and King, Jean Marie. *Educational Innovator's Guide.* Worthington, Oh: Charles A. Jones, 1974.

Walberg, Herbert J., ed. *Evaluating Educational Performance: A Sourcebook of Methods, Instruments, and Examples.* Berkeley: McCutchan, 1974.

Wergin, Jon F.; Mason, Elizabeth J.; and Munson, Paul J. "Practices of Faculty Development: An Experience-Derived Model: Virginia Commonwealth University." *Journal of Higher Education,* May 1976, pp. 289–308.

5

Faculty Development:
Encouraging Professional Growth

||||||| |||||||||||||||||||||||||||||||||||| |||||||||||||||||||||||||||||||||||||| ||||||||||||||||||||||||| ||||||||||||||||||||||||||

The case can be made that the department chairperson's most important function is to foster the growth and development of faculty and staff members within the department. Experts in staff and personnel development contend that an organization's effectiveness depends heavily on an ongoing, self-renewing program of human resources development. In the same way, an academic department's effectiveness depends largely on *faculty development*, a term coined to denote self-renewing activities for faculty members. In this regard, one vital question emerges: To what extent should the department chairperson help faculty members acquire the requisite knowledge, skills, and attitudes for maintaining their effectiveness, improving their approach to fulfilling responsibilities, and making satisfactory adjustments to the changes in their environments?

Although the need for staff or personal development has been recognized in the past, such development has been mainly a "background" activity. Sometimes it was relegated to the chairperson, for whom it was probably a minor concern. Occasionally, sabbaticals were granted to those who could afford to survive on a reduced income for a limited time. More recently, centers for the improvement of instruction have been established to help faculty members improve the quality of their instruction. By and large, however, faculty development has been allowed to happen naturally through ongoing professional activity, such as attending or participating in conferences or consulting with old friends and colleagues.

In times of expanding resources and faculties, the need for a deliberate faculty development effort was perhaps not as acute or obvious as it is now. New ideas were imported with the ever-flowing stream of new faculty members. With the influx of new and energetic talents, it was easy to cover up or overlook maturing but nonproductive faculty members. But circumstances have changed. Colleges and universities are now faced with steady-state or declining budgets, a population of maturing faculty members who hold tenure and have little chance of obtaining more rewarding positions at other institutions, and the mixed opportunities of unionization. In addition, enrollment is declining, and a growing number of nontraditional students demand that their rights and expectations be upheld.

How then should institutions of higher education respond to these powerful forces that demand change? Before addressing this question, colleges and universities must first identify the nature of such forces and formulate a reasonable guess as to how these forces may affect university systems, institutions, departments, and ultimately the faculty, which actually delivers the services. Then the question may be raised: What is the department chairperson's responsibility in enhancing faculty members' continuing development to meet emerging institutional needs, their own needs, and the needs of students?

A Case for a Deliberate Development Effort

The following trends that have begun to emerge may well compel college faculty members, as individuals and as department members, to reexamine their professional careers:

- a decline in the growth of higher education due to the decline in the 18–22-year-old population
- a decline in the level of public support, resulting in an economic crunch for universities and for students
- an emerging awareness of new skills and understandings that will be required for effective functioning in a changing society
- the decreased mobility of faculty members and administrators
- a high percentage of tenured faculty members, most of whom are in their forties and fifties
- a buyer's market for students with regard to educational opportunities
- an increasing number of students who are not awed by a teacher's authority and who are willing to bring legal action if they don't get what they pay for
- an increased demand for accountability by parents, members of governing boards, legislators, and the general public

Four trends from this list deserve special consideration in light of their effect on faculty members; namely low mobility of faculty members and administrators; decline in the growth of higher education; decline in public support for higher education; and the demand for new knowledge, skills, and attitudes in a changing society.

Low Mobility of Faculty Members and Administrators. After several years of unprecedented growth, higher education enrollments are now leveling off and quite possibly even declining. This trend, coupled with an overabundance of Ph.D.'s, has resulted in fewer faculty vacancies and, therefore, in less mobility for existing faculty members. Unless enrollment increases significantly, there will be little need for "new hires" before 1990. Without regular faculty turnover, the responsibility for updating curricula will increasingly rest with existing staff members. As a result, a deliberate faculty development effort may be required to assist faculty members in refreshing and upgrading their command of their disciplines.

Decline in the Growth of Higher Education. How can colleges and universities be sure that enrollment growth will not increase again soon? They can be quite sure within specified time periods, as long as they include present census data as a point of reference. For example, the number of children born in 1970 can help institutions determine the number of eighteen-year-olds in the year 1988. But how many of these eighteen-year-olds will attend college? According to U.S. Office of Education enrollment projections, total enrollment in higher education will peak about 1980, begin to decrease, and then bottom out about 1988. Although this projection takes into account the increasing number of high school graduates pursuing postsecondary education, this increase cannot compensate for the plunge in the number of college-age youth through the 1980s. The increasingly severe national economic picture, coupled with the absence of a military draft for the next ten years, would reduce even further the number of college-age youth who actually attend college during this period.

Given existing demographic data and trends, it is clear that fewer and fewer youth and young adults will attend colleges and universities in the years ahead. What is not so clear is whether older adult learners, many of whom need or want to continue their education at the college or university level, will fill the gap left by the younger students. Many urban universities and community colleges have discovered that they are now enrolling more adult part-time learners than recent high school graduates.

In addition, this "new clientele" for higher education is composed of different kinds of learners, with wide ranges of abilities, interests, and life experiences. They may have more experience than the instructor and be as knowledgeable in some subjects. They often challenge time-tested and traditional ways of perceiving how knowledge is organized and may not want credit or degrees for their efforts. Adult learners may also desire learning that is relevant to current issues and problems, since most are not in training for a position or job. Finally, they may wish to be involved in educational decision-making processes, such as needs assessment, goal setting, selection of content and method, and evaluation.

The major question facing higher education today may well be, To what extent can faculty members learn to relate effectively to the learning needs, styles, and personal attributes of adult students, a potential clientele larger than the total number of persons now enrolled in the education system, from kindergarten through graduate school? To address such changes, a faculty development effort may include activities that familiarize faculty members with research about learning characteristics of adults.

Decline in Public Support for Higher Education. Unfortunately, public confidence in higher education is declining at the same time that financial support is eroding. If universities and colleges could count on a constant level of financial support in the face of declining enrollment, this situation would be tolerable. The public, however, is telling higher education to do more with less. This adaptation will be difficult because of the relative affluence of the past decade. With the curtailment of institutional funds to support many valued activities, faculty members may be required to develop skills in obtaining funds from external sources to support these activities. For example, one strategy would be to initiate a deliberate effort to help faculty members acquire skills in grantsmanship to support their research interests.

Demand for New Knowledge, Skills, and Attitudes. Perhaps the most compelling reason for planned renewal efforts can be derived from analyses and forecasts made by futurists, such as Alvin Toffler, Herman Kahn, and Daniel Bell. For example, Toffler forecasts negative psychological and sociological consequences brought about by accelerating social change and details these negative consequences under the now familiar concept of "future shock." Toffler is highly critical of current education and refers to it as "a hopeless anachronism" because of its orientation toward the past rather than the future. He argues that education appropriate for an industrial age is no longer adequate for the postindustrial age. As he puts it, "For education the lesson is clear: its prime objective must be to increase the individual's 'copeability'—the speed and economy with which he can adapt to continual change. And the faster the rate of change, the more attention must be devoted to discerning the pattern of future events."[1] In Toffler's view, a curriculum is required that effectively helps students learn how to learn, how to relate to others, and how to clarify their values so that they can effectively choose among competing alternatives.

Approaching the problem from another perspective, the futurists Kahn and Bruce-Briggs envision a traumatic future for the human race. In *Things to Come: Thinking about the Seventies and Eighties*, they point out the irony that technology—the means of production that has raised our standard of living so dramatically—may also be responsible for a series of environmental and economic disasters. They predict a world-wide crisis around 1985 brought on by thoughtless use of technology. Perhaps Toffler is correct in advocating values clarification and the opportunity to choose among competing alternatives as appropriate curricular goals. Values based on consumption and growth may have to be changed to values based on conservation and more humanistic concerns if these predicted disasters are to be averted.

Daniel Bell, in his book *The Coming of Post-Industrial Society*, describes several changes that create strain as society moves from an industrial to a postindustrial age. The sources of strain include the inclusion of disadvantaged groups into society; the growth of global economic interdependence and the creation of international societies; the increasing substitution of political decision making for market decision making; the creation of fully urbanized societies and the erosion of an agricultural population; and the introduction of a multitude of technological products. Acording to Bell, the "elite" approach to higher education must change to accommodate the ever-increasing number of students from lower- and working-class backgrounds. Bell sees the university as becoming society's primary institution for the dissemination of required survival skills. Many of these skills can be deduced from his analysis: the ability to codify, store, and retrieve theoretical knowledge for the purpose of solving human problems; ability to coordinate human behavior in complex systems; ability to engage in participatory decision making; ability to play;

1. Alvin Toffler, *Future Shock* (New York: Random House, 1970), p. 357.

ability to regulate individual and group behavior; and ability to resolve conflict. Bell posits that decision-making processes will be political in nature in the postindustrial society. As a result, tension and conflict will probably increase, and conflict resolution will become a necessary skill.

Analyses by these futurists provide much food for thought. Observation of recent trends and events lends credibility to many of their forecasts. We need only examine the advent of legislative mandates for minimum contact hours, collective bargaining by public employees, land use legislation, affirmative action programs, energy control legislation, and pollution control legislation to find evidence of the new kinds of decision-making processes and interest groups described by Bell. Clearly, each of these trends has critical significance for the role of faculty members in higher education.

In response to such dramatic changes in society, renewal activities for faculty members may include an introduction to the concepts of global interdependence, to techniques in values clarification, and to principles of attitude development and change. Nevertheless, perhaps the most compelling rationale for a deliberate faculty development effort is the severe curtailment and ineffectiveness, due to these trends, of the informal and spontaneous forces that have fostered faculty growth, development, and change in the past. Faculty members must now accept greater responsibility for conducting and managing their own change and renewal processes. Without these processes, stagnation and irrelevance in both teaching and research may well increase.

State of the Art

Given a case for a deliberate faculty development effort, what are some of the ways in which such efforts have been conducted? One salutary effect of the student unrest of the mid- and late 1960s was that it drew attention to the quality of college teaching. Not surprisingly, the American Council on Education chose as the theme for its 1966 Annual Meeting the topic of improving college teaching. Papers and commentaries on "teaching the teachers" were presented there; proceedings of the conference were published the following year. Interestingly enough, Calvin Lee, who edited the papers (*Improving College Teaching: Aids and Impediments*) noted that only two paragraphs were devoted to the teaching of older teachers, but at least the matter was raised.

Several relevant monographs on the topic have appeared since then, however. *Career Development of the Effective College Teacher*, by Kenneth E. Eble, appeared in 1971 through the sponsorship of the American Association of Colleges and the American Association of University Professors. Jossey-Bass, in its New Directions for Higher Education series, featured a collection of essays by Mervin Freedman entitled *Facilitating Faculty Development*. Perhaps the most cogent and provocative statements regarding the teaching of older teachers can be found in the book *Faculty Development in a Time of Retrenchment*, by the Group for Human Development in Higher Education. The work that resulted in this latter monograph was supported at various times by the Carnegie Corporation, Lilly Endowment, and the Hazen Foundation. As a matter of fact, the Lilly Endowment has committed funds to several liberal arts schools for the purpose of establishing faculty development programs. The question no longer seems to be whether or not but when and how.

When we examine the existing literature on faculty development, we find that nearly all of it focuses on only one of the faculty members' roles—teaching. Yet in most institutions faculty members serve as researchers, curriculum developers, information analysts, disseminators of knowledge through the mass media, theory builders, providers of service, problem solvers, consultants, advisors, and counselors. Some also serve as administrators, managers, and members of government committees. Thus, faculty roles and responsibilities span far more than the teaching function itself. The term *faculty development*, as used in this chapter, therefore, refers to establishing activities and procedures that assist faculty members in acquiring knowledge, skills, and attitudes that enable them to become more effective in performing all functions related to professional academic life.

What, then, are some activities that could aid a department faculty development effort? The following list includes only a few of the many possible activities, some of which may already be available at some institutions. Two criteria govern the selection of the activities listed here: faculty members can engage in such activities without great cost to the university and without the assistance of elaborate service facilities or massive bureaucratic effort; and little effort beyond individual initiative is required in order to participate. The list was adapted from a list compiled by David G. Brown and William S. Hanger.[2]

2. David G. Brown and William S. Hanger, "Pragmatics of Faculty Self-Development," *Educational Record* (Summer 1975): 202-6.

SUGGESTED SELF-DEVELOPMENT ACTIVITIES FOR FACULTY MEMBERS

A. New experiences
   1. Exchanges and sabbaticals
      a) Exchanges within your college or university
      b) Exchanges between colleges and universities regionally, nationally, and internationally
      c) Short visits to neighboring colleges or universities
      d) Exchanges with government, industry, or foundations
      e) Joint appointments
      f) Assignments in other universities or institutes
      g) New, unusual, or unfamiliar committee assignments
   2. Special assignments in administrative posts
      a) Work in dean's office
      b) Work in contracts and grants office
      c) Prepare a grant proposal for a faculty development project sponsored by your institution
B. Development of expertise
   1. Research practices
      a) Submit articles, monographs, books, book reviews, or poetry for publication
      b) Attend research colloquia within and outside the department
      c) Team with a colleague from outside the department to write a grant proposal or article
      d) Join a research center or institute
      e) Participate in local, regional, or national conferences
      f) Participate in consortia activities)
      g) Read literature in your field
   2. Developments in peripheral areas
      a) Audit courses given in your field or a related field
      b) Enroll in a new degree program
      c) Take a continuing education course
      d) Enroll in an undergraduate short course
      e) Attend a dissertation defense in another discipline
      f) Read literature about higher education (e.g., *Chronicle of Higher Education, Journal of Higher Education, Educational Record, Change, Higher Education and National Affairs,* and so forth)
C. Instructional development
   1. New techniques and materials
      a) Organize or participate in instructional improvement seminars or luncheons
      b) Visit classes conducted by colleagues
      c) Sponsor a session at a professional conference or convention on teaching techniques within your discipline
      d) Develop and use audio-visual aids
      e) Experiment with one of the new teaching technologies—computer-assisted instruction (CAI), individually guided instruction (IGI), instructional television (ITV), simulation and gaming
      f) Talk with book salesmen or equipment dealers

        g) Write and distribute to students clear objectives for the courses you teach

        h) Vary teaching techniques—for example, if you teach primarily by lecturing, introduce some discussion techniques

        i) Try the case-study method

  2. New skills and knowledge about the teaching and learning processes

        a) Take a psychology course or education course in language development or cognitive development

        b) Seek out colleagues familiar with objective test design, criterion-referenced assessment, evaluation strategies, performance testing

        c) Make an item analysis of your tests

  3. Curriculum development

        a) Develop a new specialty area

        b) Attempt to assess and evaluate the effectiveness of a series of courses or a program

        c) Learn about competency-based education

  4. New teaching experiences

        a) Prepare to teach a new course in your discipline or in a related discipline

        b) Teach a continuing education course

        c) Teach an in-service workshop for practicing professionals

        d) Take over a colleague's class in another discipline when he or she is away

        e) Teach an intensive short course

        f) Teach a high school class or a graduate seminar for a few days

        g) Team teach with a colleague or student

  5. Evaluation

        a) Have students evaluate your teaching effectiveness

        b) Form a student feedback committee to advise you on teaching effectiveness

        c) Invite a teaching specialist to sit in on your classes and offer constructive criticism

        d) Xerox your lecture notes and have peers react to them

        e) Videotape your lectures and have colleagues critique them

        f) Develop a peer evaluation system with your colleagues

D. Service

  1. Advisement

        a) Solicit current information about employment possibilities for students majoring in your discipline

        b) Study counseling techniques and human development theories

        c) Advise a campus student group (fraternity or sorority, political group, campus newspaper, service clubs, and so forth)

        d) Keep up with rules and regulations regarding curriculum options outside your discipline

        e) Help with registration advisement or drop-add advisement

        f) Learn to recognize abnormal behavior patterns persons use when coping with stress or anxiety

g) Find out about community mental health services and how to make referrals

h) Learn about campus services available to students

2. Interaction with students

    a) Entertain students in your home

    b) Live in a residence hall for two days

    c) Host a foreign student

    d) Attend an intercollegiate athletic event

    e) Lead a group of students to Europe, Mexico, Asia

    f) Participate on a faculty intramural team

3. Community involvement

    a) Run for local office

    b) Serve on local or state government committees and councils

    c) Do volunteer work with a hospital board or local charity

    d) Consult

    e) Participate in academic fairs, workshops, or other activities with elementary and secondary teachers or counselors

4. Work for the college or university

    a) Assist the admissions office in recruiting students

    b) Prepare attractive materials or publications for recruiting students to your field

    c) Call on prospective donors of gifts and bequests asking for time, money, equipment, artifacts

    d) Serve on an admissions committee

E. Personal development

1. Personal knowledge

    a) Enroll in a skill development course such as typing, book-keeping, auto repairs

    b) Enroll in a continuing education course

    c) Enroll in a leisure education course

    d) Join a group to watch a public television course

    e) Participate in an "outward bound" program

    f) Try to attend a dozen special lectures on campus next year

    g) Analyze how you spend your free time

    h) Attend a personal growth group (assertiveness training, stress management, interpersonal communication, and so forth)

    i) Join a book club

2. Cultural experiences

    a) Attend an artist series on campus

    b) Travel to a foreign country

    c) Learn a new foreign language or sign language

3. Career development

    a) Schedule brown-bag sessions to discuss life and careers of important or interesting persons

    b) Organize a panel on nonacademic career opportunities related to your discipline

    c) Develop a contract with your department chairperson that allows you to pursue a special area of interest in the year ahead

      d) Work at another profession or develop new sources of in-
         come that complement but do not detract from academic
         responsibilities
  4. Physical development
      a) Jog with a group of colleagues
      b) Form a faculty intramural team
      c) Learn a new sport

The Question of the Chairperson's Role

In all likelihood, when aspiring faculty members assumed their roles as chairpersons, no clause was included in their contracts or job descriptions that alluded to responsibilities regarding faculty development. The question naturally follows, How much responsibility should a chairperson have in ensuring that faculty members continue to upgrade their knowledge and skills as researchers and instructors? Below are three short scenarios describing possible role models for the ways in which chairpersons might respond to this issue.

The Caretaker

Chairperson Smith, fifty-five years old, has been a department chairperson for four years. The faculty members in his department are all tenured; half are associate professors, and the other half are full professors. Most are between the ages of thirty-five and fifty-five, and they are generally satisfied with their lot professionally. Smith has noticed lately, however, that many of them are beginning to invest more of their effort in nonprofessional activities—such as camping, jogging, and community affairs—and that department productivity in research and student credit hours is beginning to fall off.

Smith recognizes the need for faculty development in general but feels that each person should assume complete responsibility for finding activities that foster his or her own growth and development. He does, however, have a good reputation for help-‑‑‑ing faculty members who come to him for advice, and he encourages them to pursue their own initiatives, particularly in research. Merit pay is awarded primarily on the single criterion of research productivity. Smith sees his role as chairperson mainly as that of a caretaker who manages routine administrative duties. He plans to resume eventually the role of full-time faculty member.

The Broker

Chairperson Jones, fifty years old, has been department chairperson for three years. Approximately 20 percent of the department faculty members are untenured. Ten percent are assistant professors; 30 percent are associate professors; and 60 percent are full professors. Their ages range from thirty to sixty; forty-five is the median age. Jones has stated that the primary criterion for determining merit pay should be effective teaching, but the department's tenure and promotion committee clearly rewards those who demonstrate productivity in research. The department enrollment has held steady over the past several years and probably will continue to do so since the department's admissions standards are now somewhat selective. Should applications decline, the department would simply decrease admissions standards to compensate. The faculty morale is good, but none of the faculty members are exerting unusual efforts—such as serving on editorial boards or establishing clearly focused research programs—to distinguish themselves nationally.

Jones's view of her role regarding faculty development is that of facilitator and broker. She is familiar with services available to faculty members within the institution and in the community. During the annual evaluation conferences, she reviews with the faculty members their career objectives, suggests resources to help them, and often makes referrals to the contracts and grants office, the instructional design center, and, for personal and career problems, the campus or community counseling centers. But she definitely sees her role as helping faculty members realize their personal and professional goals by encouraging them to seek help from specialized services outside the department. To this end, she maintains a complete file of brochures pertaining to faculty development services and opportunities for growth, such as sabbaticals and exchange programs. Jones has stated publicly that she does not seek a higher administrative office, but she has indicated to close associates that if she were nominated for the position of dean, she would accept the nomination.

The Developer

Chairperson Adams, forty-five years old, has been chairperson for three years. The department faculty members are all tenured; 65 percent are associate professors, and 35 percent are full professors. The median age is forty. The faculty members are highly competitive and ambitious. Adams, who entertains the goal of some day assuming greater administrative responsibility as a dean, seeks to help his department gain a strong regional and perhaps even a national reputation. The department's goals are to increase the number and quality of students enrolled in the program, to have each faculty member in the department establish a focused research program, and to have each member demonstrate service to the profession and the community in ways that will enhance the first two goals.

As a result, Adams has established and organized a rather sophisticated faculty development effort. He has established a committee on research that coordinates and encourages grant-writing efforts and publication. A seminar on grantsmanship is held once a year, and a colloquium in which faculty members report their research efforts is held once a month. A curriculum committee is also active; it coordinates matters concerning the content of the curriculum and encourages new delivery mechanisms as well. To expand enrollments, the curriculum committee plans an outreach effort to offer, through the continuing education office, special interest courses to the community. Through this effort the department hopes to enroll many students in full-credit courses or degree programs. The chairperson realizes that the faculty members have had little experience in conducting programs like that planned by the curriculum committee and feels that a series of seminars is necessary to help them acquire the requisite skills for the new program.

Thus Adams views his role regarding faculty development as that of developer. He actively helps faculty members acquire skills and knowledge to implement department goals. The faculty members realize that by contributing toward department goals, they, in turn, will be more able to attain individual professional goals. Adams has also established a reward system that recognizes achievement in these areas and requires that faculty members demonstrate how they have helped the department achieve its goals.

Whether a department chairperson acts as a caretaker, broker, or developer or wishes to assume some other role depends on several factors, such as his or her career goals, self-image, or leadership skills. These factors then interact with the collective will of the department faculty. Does the department want to be led by a caretaker, broker, or developer? A department's capability to survive and grow in an era of declining resources may well depend on the chairperson's ability to lead within the constraints of the faculty's expectations and aspirations.

If the idea of a faculty development program seems attractive, the chairperson and each department faculty member should ponder the following questions: What important trends will af-

PROGRAM COMPONENTS			
Curriculum	Faculty Members	Students	Research
More adult learners 1. Ways of crediting prior experience will be developed. 2. More evening classes will be required. 3. More in-service training will be required. 4. Practical application will be emphasized.	1. Faculty members may be required to teach in evenings or on weekends. 2. Faculty members must become knowledgeable about how adults learn. 3. Faculty members may be threatened.	1. New services may be required (e.g., babysitting). 2. There may be less collegiality among students.	1. Research moneys will be available to address problems of adult learners.
Energy shortage 1. Delivery systems must rely on low-cost dissemination. 2. Ways of learning through media at home or at work will be explored.	1. Faculty members may be required to go to students rather than vice versa. 2. Instruction may take place through media and correspondence.	1. Skills in independent learning may be crucial. 2. Transportation costs to schools may be prohibitive for commuter students.	1. There will be less mobility to travel to conventions. 2. There will be more emphasis on journals to keep informed. 3. Funds will be available to explore ways of disseminating information through low-cost media.
More working women 1. Ways of coping with sex bias will be included in curriculum. 2. Ways of removing stereotyping will be included in curriculum materials.	1. Faculty members may be required to adjust teaching methods to working mothers or single parents. 2. Faculty members' values regarding the career woman, dual-career families, and single-parent families may be tested.	1. More men may pursue elementary education as a career. 2. More women may pursue math and science as careers.	1. Studies in processes of stereotyping will be encouraged. 2. Studies in the educational development of children from dual-career families will be encouraged.

TRENDS

Fig. 5.1. Sample of matrix analysis: trends affecting an education department, 1980–85.

fect the department in the next five to ten years? What should be the department's response to these trends? Where does each faculty member want to be, with respect to his or her own life and career, five or ten years from now? Tentative answers to these questions can provide the foundation on which to build a faculty development program and a serious commitment to professional development.

Planning a Development Program

Once the faculty has decided to explore the possibility of establishing a deliberate faculty development effort, a first step in planning is to analyze how local, regional, and national trends might affect the department. One planning technique that is helpful in analyzing how trends may affect a department is the matrix method. One dimension of the matrix lists important trends, while the other identifies components of a program, such as curriculum, faculty members, students, and research (see figure 5.1). Intercepts in the matrix show how the trends will affect particular program components. Using a five-year planning horizon might be helpful—i.e., project how the trend will affect the program component five years from now. Information organized in this way can provide a basis for establishing priority goals and activities in the area of faculty development. Figure 5.1 presents hypothetical data on how certain local and national trends may affect a department in a school of education.

Anyone using the matrix technique must be able to identify those trends that would exert the strongest influence. Otherwise, one may plan to scratch where no itch develops. Assuming, though, that the predictions resulting from this analysis are correct—or at least defensible—gaps between the existing state of affairs and the desired state of affairs become readily apparent.

Initiating a Development Program: Six Caveats

After analyzing important trends and ways in which it could effectively respond, the department should consider strategies for change. Certain caveats should be kept in mind when initiating faculty development activities.

1. *Aim for cooperation.* For faculty development to become an ongoing process, it must be a cooperative effort involving the faculty members, department chairpersons, and other administrators. Lack of support at any of the three levels could result in wasted effort.

2. *Think big, but start small.* A well-planned activity for a small

group of interested faculty members is more likely to be success-ful than a large-scale, general effort, which may suit no one. A low-profile, low-key approach keeps expectations at realistic lev-els and provides a better basis to begin working with faculty members. A hard-sell approach tends to alienate or intimidate many faculty members and thereby creates difficulties in work-ing with them later. A small group of satisfied and motivated vol-unteers will soon set an example for their colleagues.

3. *Involve faculty members in planning development activities.* This approach will help ensure content validity for the partici-pants and enhance their commitment to follow through. The cli-ché "Begin where the people are" is as pertinent when working with the faculty as with any other group of adult learners. The goals to be achieved should be set by the faculty members them-selves, not by other persons in the academic hierarchy. Given adequate performance counseling, faculty members should as-sume the ultimate authority for determining the direction and nature of change.

4. *Be eclectic in approach.* When planning a faculty develop-ment program, the department may be tempted to concentrate on a single new technique. No single technique is suitable for ev-eryone, however, and a variety of possible techniques would en-able faculty members to choose some that suit their own style and needs.

5. *Start where the chances of success are high.* First impres-sions are crucial, and a few small but highly successful efforts will soon pave the way for more ambitious projects and activi-ties.

6. *Institutionalize faculty development efforts.* A meaningful program of faculty development must address itself to the ques-tion of long-term efforts and how these efforts can be formalized to ensure longevity, adaptability, and relevance.

Strategies for Initiating a Development Program

If the chairperson has decided to begin a faculty development program and has determined his or her level of responsibility for administering it, he or she should analyze some of the conditions that would foster or inhibit the implementation of a program. Two approaches, described below, may be appropriate for initi-ating a faculty development program.

1. *Faculty development as a means to individual development.* This strategy begins with an activity in which a reasonable num-ber of faculty members have agreed to participate. Determining

the topic could be accomplished through the use of a questionnaire administered by a department faculty development committee. After collating the data, the committee would set priorities and consult with the chairperson for endorsement of its
plans. The advantage of this strategy is that the faculty members
assume the responsibility for determining areas in which they
would like to improve.

2. *Faculty development as a means to department development.*
Another strategy is to make faculty development a means to help
the department achieve its goals. The department determines its
goals by analyzing perceived trends that will affect its future. In
addressing these trends and the changes required to meet them,
the department should consider whether the faculty is currently
qualified to meet the new demands. A faculty development program then is anchored to department goals agreed upon by the
faculty. This approach addresses the matter of motivation—i.e.,
why faculty members should participate in an organized faculty
development effort. The faculty members can then collectively
monitor their progress in attaining department goals. Obviously,
when faculty members perceive a faculty development effort as
a means for enhancing both their individual goals and a department's goals, an optimum state of affairs exists.

Conditions That May Inhibit Faculty Development

Faculty development programs have met resistance for various reasons. The chairperson should be aware of common problems that impede the implementation of a program.

- The faculty members' personal goals may not be congruent
  with the goals of the department or the college. In this case,
  faculty members may fail to identify with any effort to alter the status quo.
- Faculty members often perceive development activities as
  unnecessary infringements on their already crowded
  schedules. They need to be convinced of the value of deliberate efforts toward professional growth.
- Even when faculty members become aware of the need for
  such involvement, they often have little idea of where to go
  or whom to ask for assistance.
- Some chairpersons see as a barrier the lack of funds to buy
  books or materials, to pay for travel, or to hire consultants.
  Some programs require little or no funding, however, and
  the chairperson should encourage development efforts
  even when moneys are not available.

- Physical isolation from colleagues deprives some faculty members of opportunities for stimulation and learning.
- In some departments a spirit of apathy exists, and faculty members are indifferent to the idea of continuing their professional growth. Other departments may have faculty members who feel that they have already achieved perfection and therefore see no need for organized development activities.

Many of the conditions that inhibit development efforts may be overcome by proper leadership on the part of the chairperson.

Assessing Readiness for Involvement

Before embarking on a faculty development effort, a chairperson may wish to obtain an indication from the faculty members regarding their interests. Identifying interest areas could be accomplished through a questionnaire listing areas of development and relevant activities. The following list includes some possible activities that department chairpersons can adapt for use with their faculty members.[3]

AREAS OF DEVELOPMENT AND POSSIBLE ACTIVITIES FOR FACULTY MEMBERS

A. Professional development
   1. Acquiring visiting professorships
   2. Locating and applying for sabbaticals
   3. Getting published
   4. Preparing grant proposals
   5. Establishing your own research program
   6. Exploring professional exchanges with business, industry, and government
   7. Setting up joint appointment possibilities
   8. Conducting an effective committee meeting
   9. Exploring techniques for department curriculum planning
B. Instructional development
   1. Developing course objectives
   2. Preparing and using media in the classroom
   3. Preparing and delivering a lecture
   4. Stimulating class discussions
   5. Preparing classroom tests
   6. Using computers for testing students
   7. Using atypical classroom procedures
      a) Keller Plan (using student tutors to teach subsections of large lecture courses)
      b) Personalized systems of instruction

3. This list is part of the Professional Seminars and Workshops Questionnaire, prepared by the Institute for Departmental Leadership, Florida State University, with the cooperation of the Instructional Systems Institute.

        c) Competency-based education
        d) Self-instructional systems
    8. Evaluating students' writing skills
  C. Personal development
    1. Managing time efficiently
    2. Improving relationships with colleagues
    3. Improving relationships with department chairpersons
    4. Learning about faculty career patterns
    5. Using assertiveness techniques with students and peers
    6. Training in stress management
    7. Dealing with job frustrations
    8. Overcoming boredom
    9. Developing effective communication skills
    10. Exploring local recreational opportunities
    11. Improving your physical health
    12. Managing the dual-career family
    13. Countering sexism in higher education
    14. Exploring tax-deductible professional activities
  D. Service
    1. Becoming a consultant for government, private industry, or other consumers
    2. Exploring consultation techniques
    3. Getting appointed to state, regional, and national professional committees
    4. Teaching special interest courses
    5. Evaluating your service contribution to the university
    6. Finding opportunities for public speaking
    7. Learning to speak effectively
    8. Planning and conducting workshops and conferences
    9. Advising students about courses and careers
    10. Recognizing, coping with, and referring troubled or disruptive students
    11. Exploring career possibilities for students in your discipline
    12. Participating on department committees
    13. Securing public support for your program

Staff, or professional, development activities existed long before the term *faculty development* was coined. Nevertheless, before a chairperson expends a great deal of energy in organizing a deliberate faculty development effort, he or she should determine whether faculty members perceive a need for it. Not surprisingly, most faculty members consider themselves "above average" teachers, and some openly claim to be among the best. With such perceptions of perfection, it is no wonder that faculty members are sometimes unresponsive to efforts to induce them to improve their teaching skills. Faculty members must perceive a need to change before they will commit themselves to participating in a faculty development effort, whether in teaching or some other professional area. Without a cogent rationale, however, such efforts will probably not elicit much faculty response.

This chapter has highlighted three critical factors that chairpersons should consider before embarking on a deliberate faculty development effort: (1) the significant local, regional, and national trends that may require of the faculty members new skills for serving their students; (2) the chairperson's own perceptions of his or her role in the area of faculty development; and (3) the extent to which individual faculty members' goals can be met by meeting the department's goals. Unless faculty members themselves can be convinced of the need to be involved in some form of faculty development and are willing to participate in a program, however, the probability of success for these types of activities is not great.

Questions and Exercises

1. In view of the changes that may well affect higher education in general, select three trends or changes that are likely to have the most effect on your department during the next five years..

2. For each trend you cited above, how would your department's curriculum, faculty, students, and research be affected? Construct a matrix similar to the one shown in figure 5.1 (page 97).

3. *a)* After surveying the list of suggested activities that could be included in a faculty development effort (pages 91–94), list three activities that would be appropriate for helping faculty members in your department acquire knowledge and skills to cope more effectively with each of the three trends you listed in question 1.

   b) Having read the three scenarios in the text describing ways in which a chairperson could approach faculty development, formulate an approach that would have the best chance of success in your department.

References

Bailey, Stephen K. "People Planning in Postsecondary Education: Human Resource Development in a World of Decremental Budgets." In *More for Less: Academic Planning with Faculty without New Dollars*, edited by James N. Nesmith, pp. 3–11. New York: Society for College and University Planning and Educational Testing Service, College and University Programs, 1975.

Bell, Daniel. *The Coming of Post-Industrial Society: A Venture in Social Forecasting.* New York: Basic Books, 1973.

Bennis, Warren G. *Organization Development: Its Nature, Origins, and*

Prospects, edited by Edgar Schien et al. Reading, Mass.: Addison-Wesley, 1969.

Bergquist, William H.; Philips, Steven R.; and Quehl, Gary H. *A Handbook for Faculty Development*. Washington, D.C.: Council for the Advancement of Small Colleges, 1975.

Boyer, Ronald K., and Crockett, Campbell, eds. "Organizational Development in Higher Education." *Journal of Higher Education*, May 1973 (special issue), pp. 339–51.

Brown, David G., and Hanger, William S. "Pragmatics of Faculty Self-Development." *Educational Record*, Summer 1975, pp. 201–6.

Chickering, Arthur W. *Education and Identity*. San Francisco: Jossey-Bass, 1969.

Crow, Mary Lynn; Milton, Ohmer; Moomaw, W. Edmund; and O'Connell, William R., Jr., eds. *Faculty Development Centers in Southern Universities*. Atlanta: Southern Regional Education Board, 1976.

Eble, Kenneth E. *Career Development of the Effective College Teacher*. Washington, D.C.: Association of American Colleges and the American Association of University Professors, 1971.

————. *Professors as Teachers*. San Francisco: Jossey-Bass, 1972.

Feldman, Kenneth A., and Newcomb, Theodore M. *The Impact of College on Students*. 2 vols. San Francisco: Jossey-Bass, 1969.

Freedman, Mervin. *Facilitating Faculty Development*. San Francisco: Jossey-Bass, 1973.

Gaff, Jerry G. *Toward Faculty Renewal: Advances in Faculty, Instructional, and Organizational Development*. San Francisco: Jossey-Bass, 1975.

Gagne, Robert M., and Briggs, Leslie J. *Principles of Instructional Design*. 2nd ed. New York: Holt, Rhinehart, & Winston, 1979.

Group for Human Development in Higher Education. *Faculty Development in a Time of Retrenchment*. New Rochelle, N.Y.: Change Magazine Press, 1974.

Kahn, Herman, and Bruce-Briggs, B. *Things to Come: Thinking about the Seventies and Eighties*. New York: Macmillan, 1972.

Lee, Calvin B. T., ed. *Improving College Teaching: Aids and Impediments*. Washington, D.C.: American Council on Education, 1966.

Mager, Robert F. *Preparing Instructional Objectives*. 2nd ed. Palo Alto, Calif.: Fearon-Pitman, 1975.

Morris, Celia. "A Call for Faculty Reform." *Change*, Winter 1973–1974, pp. 13–15.

Noonan, John F. "Curricular Change: A Strategy for Improving Teaching." In *The Expanded Campus: Current Issues in Higher Education 1972*, edited by Dyckman W. Vermilye. San Francisco: Jossey-Bass, 1972.

O'Connell, William R., Jr., and Meeth, L. Richard. *Evaluating Teaching Improvement Programs*. New Rochelle, N.Y.: Change Magazine Press, 1978.

Seldin, Peter J. "Fostering Faculty Talent." *Change,* September 1976, pp. 10–13.

Stone, James C., et al. *Toward Excellence in Teaching, Too.* Berkeley: University of California Press, 1974.

Toffler, Alvin. *Future Shock.* New York: Random House, 1970.

Wilson, Robert C.; Gaff, Jerry G.; Dienst, Evelyn R.; Wood, Lynn; and Bavry, James L. *College Professors and Their Impact on Students.* New York: John Wiley & Sons, 1975.

6

Faculty Evaluation

||||||||||||||||||||||||||||||||||||||||||||||||||||||||||||||||||||||||||||||||||||||||||||||||||||||||||||||||||||||||||||||||

Evaluation of faculty performance is one of the chairperson's most difficult and important responsibilities. Probably no other activity has more potential for strengthening or weakening the department over a period of years. Handled properly, evaluation can be a valuable communications device; it can improve faculty morale and result in a strong, effective department. Handled improperly, evaluation can destroy morale, decrease the chances for the department's success in meeting objectives, and place the chairperson on the receiving end of a long succession of grievances. Most colleges and universities have or should have official documents that provide specific information about the evaluation process, such as how often evaluations will be conducted, who will do the evaluating, in what form the evaluations will be submitted, who may use them, how they will be used, and what may be placed in the faculty member's personnel file.

A necessary condition for effective evaluation is clear, specific criteria. In addition, there must be a reasonable, definitive assignment of activities and an ongoing system of performance counseling. If faculty members' assignments are sufficiently clear and if discussion between chairperson and faculty members regarding performance becomes a regular activity, evaluation will no longer be seen as a dreaded annual exercise. In effect, the process could become no more than a report of a faculty member's performance—a report that would hold no surprises for either the faculty member or the chairperson.

This chapter will focus on four questions: Why is evaluation necessary? What should be evaluated? Who should do the evaluating and what should be the process? and How can performance be evaluated?

Why Is Evaluation Necessary?

Every department chairperson who has held the position for at least a year has been faced with the need to evaluate staff and faculty members. Evaluation is required by the dean, the collective bargaining contract (if the institution has one), the vice president, the president, the board of trustees, and even the faculty. One basic purpose of evaluation has always been to provide faculty members with some measure of how well they are performing in their professional role so that they can improve their performance. Sooner or later, however, all evaluation activity must serve as a basis for decision making in matters of promotion, tenure, salary increases, and other benefits. In times of limited resources and static or declining university growth, competition becomes intense and decisions are sometimes challenged. State legislators, parents, and citizens are requiring more accountability with regard to the quality of teaching, benefits from research, and time away from campus for service.

Faculty members themselves are no longer satisfied with an arbitrary and paternalistic evaluation by a department chairperson. They insist on a more formal evaluation based on specific criteria, and this desire seems to increase as the discretionary funds available for merit raises decrease. Faculty members also want the option to appeal in the event that they disagree with the evaluation. Leaders in education, therefore, need to find ways to perform evaluations that are reliable and acceptable to students, to the faculty, to faculty unions, to university administrators, and to state legislators and other groups responsible for providing financial support.

What Should Be Evaluated?

The central academic functions of most colleges and universities are teaching, research, and service. The activities performed by faculty members will fall under one or more of these categories; thus, a department committee or the department as a whole will have little trouble developing a list of activities that should be evaluated. Questions about the minimal level of performance quality and the kinds of evidence that will be accepted for the evaluation, however, are considerably more difficult.

One point that has emerged in the last several years, especially at those institutions that have faculty unions, is the importance of evaluating only what has been formally assigned. Penalizing faculty members for failing to complete unassigned duties or for failing to accomplish more than what has been assigned has created legal problems in some instances when faculty members were not subsequently promoted or awarded tenure. It behooves chairpersons, therefore, to anticipate what activities within each major category will be evaluated and to include them in the formal assignments.

Performance Areas to Be Evaluated

Performance areas to be evaluated are generally listed in various official documents, such as the university constitution, the state system personnel policy manual, or a union contract. The list may vary in detail from one university to another, from one department to another within the same university, or from one faculty member to another. Most lists, however, will include the following performance areas, compiled from a variety of official documents. Note the mixture of activities, outcomes, and the quantitative and qualitative characteristics included.

Teaching. Teaching involves the presentation of knowledge, information, and ideas by methods that include lecturing, discussion, assignment and recitation, demonstration, laboratory exercise, practical experience, direct consultation with students, and so forth. In an evaluation, the use and effectiveness of each method should be considered. The evaluation of teaching effectiveness should also be related to the written objectives of each course, which should have been given to each class at the beginning of the term. Evaluation of teaching should include consideration of:

- correlation of imparted knowledge and skills to course objectives
- stimulation of the students' critical thinking and creative ability in light of the course objectives
- the faculty member's adherence to accepted standards of professional behavior in meeting his or her responsibilities to students

In an informal sample taken in 1979, chairpersons in two major state universities in Florida listed the following as their preferred sources of evidence for evaluating teaching: (1) systematic rating by students; (2) chairperson's evaluation; (3) colleagues' opinions; (4) committee evaluation; (5) content of course syllabi and examinations; (6) informal rating by students; (7) colleagues' ratings based on classroom visits; (8) long-term follow-up of students' performance; (9) faculty member's interest in teaching improvement activities (workshops and so forth); (10) faculty member's self-evaluation or report; (11) students' examination

performance; (12) popularity of elective courses (e.g., enrollment); and (13) opinions of alumni.[1]

Research and Other Creative Activities. Contribution to and discovery of new knowledge, new educational techniques, and
other forms of creative activity should be considered for evaluation. Evidence of research and other creative activity should include, but not be limited to, published books; articles and papers
in professional journals; paintings and sculpture; works for performance (musical compositions, dances, plays, and so forth);
papers presented at meetings of professional societies; and current research and creative activity that has not yet resulted in
publication, display, or performance. Evaluation of research and
other creative activities should include consideration of:

* quality and quantity of productivity of both short-term and
  long-term research and other creative programs and contributions
* recognition by the academic or professional community of
  work accomplished (for judgments pertaining to the decision to award tenure, evaluation should be sought from
  qualified scholars in pertinent disciplines both within and
  outside the university)

Service. Service should include, but not be limited to, involvement in department, college, and university committees, councils, and senates; service in appropriate professional organizations; involvement in organizing and expediting meetings,
symposia, conferences, and workshops; participation in radio
and television; and service on local, state, and national governmental boards, commissions, and other agencies. Only those activities that are related to a person's field of expertise or to the
university's mission should be evaluated. Evaluation of service
should include consideration of:

* contribution to the orderly and effective functioning of the
  academic administrative unit (program, department, school,
  college) and the whole institution
* contribution to the university community
* contribution to local, state, regional, and national communities, including scholarly and professional associations

Other University Duties. Reasonable duties other than those
usually classified as teaching, research or other creative activity,
or service are occasionally assigned to faculty members. The
performance of these duties—which might include academic ad-

1. Informal survey conducted by Allan Tucker, unpublished.

ministration, academic advising, career counseling, or the supervision of interns—should also be evaluated. A dean or director may be the best person to conduct the evaluation of these activities, so the chairperson should consult them about correct procedures.

Evaluation Based on Assignments

If evaluations are to be based on assignments, then the assignments must specify what constitutes successful and acceptable completion. Such specification requires an understanding of the difference between activities and outcomes, for both may be evaluated. Typically, faculty members are paid for participating in an acceptable set of professional activities, such as conducting classes, preparing syllabi and other materials for classes, advising and counseling students, serving on department and institutional governing committees, reviewing manuscripts, collecting and analyzing data, conducting research, and so on. Simply assigning activities without some idea of what is expected or what constitutes satisfactory completion of the assignment, however, makes it difficult to differentiate the performance of faculty members, especially when they are given similar activity assignments—the same number of courses to teach, the same percentage of time to conduct research, and so forth.

Outcomes are the results of activities. Whereas activities emphasize process, outcomes focus on achievements and end products. Examples of simple outcome assignments made by department chairpersons include preparing and duplicating for students a research bibliography on subject X for course Y; completing the first draft of the third chapter of a book manuscript on topic Z; and reviewing the professional literature on subject R for inclusion in a consulting paper for government agency A. All these outcomes are clearly observable.

Examples of complex outcome assignments would be completing manuscript M and finding a publisher for it; submitting a completed proposal for funding and having it accepted in principle; and completing a consulting project by a specific deadline date and arranging for publication of the final report. These outcome assignments are "complex" because they include more than one condition that must be met. Two other complex outcome assignments, drawn from the literature of educational performance objectives, are teaching introductory course S so well that at least 75 percent of the students believed it was worthwhile and teaching course R so well that 85 percent attain a grade of *C* or higher on the final exam. Some controversy surrounds the idea that outcomes can be clearly specified, particularly when an arbitrary figure—such as 85 percent—appears in the statement. Such figures should be specified only after careful thought about what constitutes a satisfactory outcome; they should not be included merely to give an appearance of precision. Note that faculty members can meet these kinds of performance objectives by lowering standards.

Outcome assignments, if properly made, lend themselves more easily to an objective evaluation of performance quality than do activity assignments, which usually focus on quantity rather than quality of performance. Chairpersons who try to evaluate faculty performance on the basis of outcomes usually consult in advance with their faculty members to determine what each person plans to accomplish during the year and to stipulate the intended outcomes. The chairperson and the faculty member together develop the annual assignment, incorporating as far as possible the faculty member's plan. Some chairpersons and faculty members claim that faculty members generally resist a request to provide an advance list of the individual activities, projects, and outcomes that they plan for the coming year. They do not object, however, to submitting a detailed list of their accomplishments and their performance outcomes during the past year in order to prepare for an annual performance evaluation.

An interesting exercise for chairpersons would be to review some lists prepared by faculty members of their accomplishments of the past year, changing the tense of the verbs from past to future. By doing so, chairpersons can see what the anticipated outcome of assignments made at the beginning of the year might have been. Would these faculty members have been able to anticipate their accomplishments one year in advance? Would it have been helpful to them and to the department if they had been required to think in terms of intended accomplishments? Each person has his or her own opinion on these issues, and the arguments on both sides would provoke an interesting discussion.

Chairpersons who wish to specify desired outcomes in faculty members' annual assignments should obtain the following information about each person's activities. As far as teaching is concerned, the chairperson should know what level of effectiveness the faculty member plans to attain in helping students reach stated course objectives; what innovations are anticipated; how much effort will be expended in preparing for class; and what level of satisfaction will be expected from the students. If research or creative activity is part of the faculty member's assignment, the chairperson should know what progress can be expected by the end of the year and what kind of evidence (short of a published article or book) is acceptable to demonstrate that progress has been made; whether a grant proposal will be written by the end of the term; whether a rough draft of an article for publication will be completed; whether a special seminar or recital will be given; whether a specified amount of progress can be expected on a research project; and whether a library literature search will be completed by the end of the year. If a service assignment is made, the chairperson should know what outcome is expected; whether attendance at committee meetings is all that is expected; whether, if the assignment is on an ad hoc department committee, a report is due and who has responsibility for writing the report; whether contacts with potential students are part of a service assignment; and, if so, how many contacts are expected. These are the kinds of questions that department chairpersons should consider in making faculty assignments on which evaluations are based.

Obvious and specific procedures are necessary for interpreting whatever evidence is deemed appropriate for a faculty evaluation. For example, there must be procedures for reading and interpreting student ratings of teachers and some basis for assigning an overall quality rating, i.e., for stating whether the faculty member's teaching is "outstanding," "very good," "satisfactory," "weak," or "unsatisfactory." Similarly, standard procedures for interpreting all other evidence are also needed, so that a chairperson can demonstrate the extent to which the final evaluation is based on objectively assessed evidence.

Who Should Do the Evaluating and What Should Be the Process?

Evaluation of a faculty member's performance is usually derived from some or all of the following sources: the faculty member's chairperson or other administrator; the faculty member's self-evaluation; the faculty member's peers; professional colleagues at other universities (in matters of promotion and tenure); students; and other university officials.

The department chairperson is usually the person responsible for collecting evaluations about each faculty member from these sources. Even though a faculty committee may have assisted the chairperson in the evaluation, most universities hold the department chairperson responsible for the official evaluation. Each faculty member should be told who will perform the official evaluation, the nature of the process, the performance criteria to be used, and so on. Similarly, all persons involved in submitting evidence or making judgments should be informed of their particular roles. One point cannot be overemphasized: the chairperson's official evaluation rests on his or her informed judgment of all the appropriate evidence. The evaluation process gains substantial legitimacy in the eyes of the faculty members if they have been able to participate in the development of department goals and objectives.

Another way to involve faculty members in their own evaluation is to have each of them prepare a "brag sheet" describing his or her activities and accomplishments. Faculty members should be afforded the opportunity to describe in detail what they consider their important contributions to the department, the institution, the profession or discipline, and the community. Sometimes they cannot easily enumerate their outstanding accomplishments on a standardized form. Therefore, the self-evaluation could be written in narrative form, which would allow them the freedom to describe their achievements in their own words. Faculty members feel more confident that their actions are appreciated and valued if they have the opportunity to describe them adequately. On the other hand, the chairperson, when reading the brag sheets, should be able to distinguish between rhetoric and reality.

Students are often invited to participate in the institutional evaluation of faculty members. At some institutions they also conduct their own evaluation of teaching faculty members and publish the results for the benefit of fellow students. The results of these evaluations are quite interesting, to say the least.

How Should Performance Be Evaluated?

The questions of what should be evaluated and who should do the evaluating are relatively simple to answer compared with the question of how performance should be evaluated. The art of evaluating the performance of faculty members is not that well developed. Experts who are invited to make presentations on how to evaluate such performance will adequately explain why evaluation is important, what should be evaluated, who should do the evaluating, and what procedures should be followed to obtain maximum involvement of appropriate faculty members, students, and administrators in the evaluation process. Usually, however, these experts are unable to provide a magic formula that will make the evaluation process more simple or less painful.

The evaluation system that a department uses will depend on a variety of factors—the institution's requirements, the school or college's procedures, and so forth. The chairperson must remember, however, that basically four kinds of personnel decisions based on performance evaluation data must be made each academic year: (1) promotion decisions; (2) tenure decisions; (3) annual assessments; and (4) recommendations for merit pay. Two or more of these decisions may use the same evaluation data and thus may be scheduled simultaneously, but at most institutions these decisions are distinct in terms of legal requirements. Moreover, each personnel decision should be based on evaluation data that represent more than the subjective and arbitrary response of a chairperson or a committee of peers. Therefore, as these decisions become more complex, the chairperson should seek to implement or improve quantitative evaluations rather than avoid them.

Not every faculty member in a department is outstanding, but the difficult task for the chairperson is to differentiate among the members, most of whom perform their assigned duties at least satisfactorily. The department faculty members should help determine the specific criteria to be used for personnel decisions, whether these decisions are related to promotion, tenure, annual assessment, or merit recommendations. The chairperson must work with the faculty to delineate the particular evaluation criteria used in each part of the evaluation. The chairperson should also state how the criteria will be applied to the evidence in each person's evaluation folder.

In thinking about devising a system for evaluation, the chairperson and the faculty members together must confront several questions: First, what constitutes 100 percent of a full-time workload for a given term or year? Does a 100 percent assignment demand all a faculty member's professional time and effort, regardless of the number of hours worked? Or does it consist of a specified number of hours, say forty hours per week? Is a formal definition of what constitutes 100 percent of a full-time workload even necessary? Will a faculty member's teaching duties alone make up 100 percent of his or her assigned full-time workload, with research and service activities considered as "add-ons"? If so, will such additional activities be required or voluntary? Will the performance of these additional activities, even though they are not part of a formal assignment, be evaluated for promotion and tenure purposes? Will a subjective evaluation be made of each faculty member's overall worth to the department without separate evaluations of the performance in each activity and regardless of whether the activity was formally assigned?

After the chairperson and the faculty members have thought through these questions and arrived at answers that are acceptable to them as a department, they must consider further questions. If each faculty member is expected to engage in some teaching, research, and service activities, will this expectation be stated formally in an assignment contract? If activities in these three areas are formally or informally assigned, will each faculty member receive a separate performance rating for each area? Will a faculty member's overall performance evaluation be determined by simply averaging the three ratings? Or will the ratings also take into consideration the amount of time and effort expended in each area? Is good teaching just as important to the department as good research? If a faculty member receives an "outstanding" rating for research and a "poor" rating for teaching, will the "poor" rating for teaching pull down his or her overall evaluation?

Evaluation processes can vary greatly. They can range from simple to complex, from subjective to objective. Whatever type of evaluation process is chosen, department chairpersons and faculty members alike must realize that human judgment is involved. All these types of evaluation, no matter how complex, do not eliminate the need for judgment and common sense. A very complicated, highly quantified type of evaluation may seem to be the most objective, but, in the final analysis, it might be very unfair.

Taking this warning into consideration, we can outline a series of evaluation processes, beginning with a simple, subjective type. In this type of evaluation the chairperson bases his or her evaluation on the faculty member's performance of department activities without necessarily listing the activities and without prescribing what percentage of time or effort of full-time workload is to be spent on each activity. The chairperson reviews each faculty member's performance over the past year, including the self-evaluation report, and then asks the question, How valuable, in my opinion, is this faculty member to the department? This process is repeated for all the faculty members, and then they are ranked according to how much the chairperson values their contributions to the department. In the process of ranking, the chairperson assigns a number to each subjective evaluation and by so doing gives a quantitative measure to each faculty member's performance. This simple type of evaluation, as well as the types described later, may be done by the chairperson alone, with or without the help of consultants; by a department committee headed by the chairperson; by a department committee without the chairperson's participation; or by the entire department.

At this point, the matter of rating faculty members as "above average" should be mentioned. Every department chairperson must face the fact, difficult as it may be to acknowledge, that all the members of his or her department are not necessarily "above average." If the evaluations of all faculty members in a single department are averaged, the evaluation of some faculty members will be below that average. To evaluate faculty members as "above average" or "below average" does not make sense unless the group with which they are being compared can be clearly specified. Is the reference group another department in the same school or college, another department in the institution, or a similar department in another university? To give ratings higher than faculty members deserve simply because everyone else is doing so is not good policy.

Performance Ratings

Performance ratings can range from simple to complex. A chairperson might simply rate the faculty members as "O.K." or "not O.K.," "merit" or "no merit," or "acceptable" or "not acceptable." Faculty members can also be rated on a three-point scale, such as "high merit," "low merit," and "no merit." The difference between a rating of 73 percent and 75 percent, however, may be insignificant in determining whether the performance of one faculty member should be rated higher than another's.

An evaluation procedure based on a four-point scale is also suggested for use.[2] This approach is helpful because the scale is familiar to anyone who has graded academic performance. Simply translate the value terms "outstanding," "very good," "satisfactory," "weak," and "unsatisfactory" to the numbers 4.0, 3.0, 2.0, 1.0, and 0 (see figure 6.1 for performance rating key). For example, if the performance of a teaching activity is evaluated as "very good," the faculty member would receive a performance

2. Developed by Allan Tucker.

rating of 3.0. This scale will be used in subsequent discussions of more complex systems of evaluation, but it should be remembered that other schema can be used with equal effectiveness.

Level of Performance	Performance Rating
Outstanding	4
Very good	3
Satisfactory	2
Weak	1
Unsatisfactory	0

Fig. 6.1. Performance rating key

Before a number system is adopted to designate levels of performance as "outstanding," "very good," "satisfactory," and so forth, the chairperson and the department should have some idea of what those ratings imply. In terms of performance, what is the difference beween being "outstanding" and just "satisfactory"?

The simplest system sets the question of value in terms of the faculty member's overall contribution to the department without requiring a separate detailed scrutiny of each activity performed by the faculty member. The question of value at the next level of complexity takes into account the faculty member's contributions in each of the three major performance areas—teaching, research, and service. In this system, the faculty member's performance in each area is rated separately on a four-point scale, and his or her ratings are averaged. Figure 6.2 shows the performance ratings, by area and based on the four-point scale, of three faculty members.

Area of Performance	FACULTY MEMBERS		
	Jones	Smith	Brown
Teaching	4.0	2.0	2.0
Research	3.0	4.0	1.0
Service	3.0	3.0	3.0
Total of Ratings	10.0	9.0	6.0
Average Rating	3.33	3.0	2.0

Fig. 6.2. Rating of faculty members, by area of performance, using four-point scale

In our example, Jones comes out with an average rating of 3.33, which can be interpreted as somewhere between "very good" and "outstanding." Smith's average rating is "very good," and Brown's is "satisfactory." If this type of evaluation were being done by a committee rather than the chairperson, each committee member could give each department member a separate rating for each area of performance. These ratings could then be averaged to produce a committee rating for each performance area.

The system described above is used in departments that are not particularly concerned with the percentage of full-time workload that is assigned to any given activity. These same departments probably consider teaching, research, and service equally important in achieving department goals and do not rate outstanding researchers higher than outstanding teachers. Faculty members in some departments, however, are not satisfied with a laissez-faire system of assignment. They want evaluations to take into account the percentage of full-time workload that is assigned to each of the three major performance areas; in addition, they want the evaluations to count activities that fall under a fourth category called "other." The fourth category generally includes assignments such as administrative duties, career counseling, supervision of interns, and so forth. Such calculations are not difficult.

Subsequent discussion will make use of the following terminology:

- *Performance ratings* (PR)—These ratings are based on a four-point scale and are used to differentiate "outstanding," "very good," "satisfactory," "weak," and "unsatisfactory" performance (see figure 6.1).
- *Rating points* (RP)—Rating points are calculated for a given area or activity by multiplying the performance rating for that activity by the percentage of full-time workload assigned to that activity. For example, if 60 percent of a faculty member's full-time workload is assigned to teaching and if her rating for that assignment is "outstanding," she would receive 240 rating points (4×60).
- *Rating point average* (RPA)—The rating point average is calculated by totaling the rating points obtained for the areas of performance being evaluated and dividing that total by the sum of the percentages of the full-time workload assigned to the several areas or activities being rated.

For example, Faculty Member A is rated 4.0 for his

teaching assignment, which constitutes 60 percent of his full-time workload. He therefore would receive 240 rating points (4 × 60) for the area of teaching. He is rated 3.0 for his research assignment, which constitutes 30 percent of his full-time workload. For the area of research, therefore, he would receive 90 rating points (3 × 30). His assigned percentage of full-time workload for service was 5 percent; his assigned percentage of full-time workload for "other," which consisted of supervising interns, was also 5 percent. For each of the latter two areas he was rated 3.0 and thus received 15 rating points (3 × 5) for each. The total number of rating points for the four areas—teaching, research, service, and "other"—therefore was 360 (240 + 90 + 15 + 15). The sum of assigned percentages of full-time workload for the four areas was 100 percent (60 + 30 + 5 + 5). The rating point average (RPA) for this faculty member was 3.6 (360 ÷ 100). (The calculations used to derive the RPA also appear in figure 6.3.) Since "full time" constitutes 100 percent of a faculty member's workload, the sum of the percentages assigned to the several areas cannot exceed 100 percent, and since 4.0 is the highest performance rating that can be given to any area, a rating point average can never be greater than 4.0.

Following are examples of assignments and ratings given to two other faculty members in the same department, Faculty Member B and Faculty Member C. Forty percent of Faculty

Area of Performance	I Performance Rating	II Assigned % of Full-Time Workload	Rating Points (RP) (I × II)
Teaching	4.0	60	240
Research	3.0	30	90
Service	3.0	5	15
Other	3.0	5	15
Total	13.0	100	360

$$\text{Rating Point Average (RPA)} = \frac{\text{Total of Rating Points}}{\text{Total of Assigned Percentages}} = \frac{360}{100} = 3.6$$

Fig. 6.3. Rating of Faculty Member A's performance, by area of performance and by percentage of full-time workload assigned to each area

Member B's full-time workload was assigned to teaching, for which she was rated 2.0; 40 percent was assigned to research, for which she was rated 4.0; 10 percent was assigned to service, for which she was rated 3.0; and 10 percent was assigned to "other" (in this case, administrative duties), for which she was rated 2.0. Sixty-five percent of Faculty Member C's full-time workload was assigned to teaching, for which he was rated 1.0; 20 percent was assigned to research, for which he was rated 1.0; 10 percent was assigned to service, for which he was rated 4.0; and 5 percent was assigned to "other" (in this case, career counseling), for which he was rated 3.0. Figures 6.3, 6.4, and 6.5 show how the rating point averages (RPAs) can be calculated for each faculty member.

Had Faculty Member A's ratings been averaged without regard for the percentage of full-time workload assigned to each area, he would have received a rating of 3.25 (13÷4). Taking the percentage of full-time workload assigned to each area into account, his rating point average is 3.60. Faculty Member B, who would have received an average rating of 2.75 (11÷4), receives a rating point average of 2.90 when consideration is given to the percentage of full-time workload assigned to each area. Faculty Member C, who would have received an average rating of 2.25 (9÷4), now receives a rating point average of 1.40 when percentage of full-time workload assigned to each area is considered.

Keeping in mind that human judgment is a factor to be reckoned with in the assessment of faculty members' performance,

Area of Performance	I Performance Rating	II Assigned % of Full-Time Workload	Rating Points (RP) (I × II)
Teaching	2.0	40	80
Research	4.0	40	160
Service	3.0	10	30
Other	2.0	10	20
Total	11.0	100	290

$$\text{Rating Point Average (RPA)} = \frac{\text{Total of Rating Points}}{\text{Total of Assigned Percentages}} = \frac{290}{100} = 2.9$$

Fig. 6.4. Rating of Faculty Member B's performance, by area of performance and by percentage of full-time workload assigned to each area the chairperson must address the question of the quantity of work completed in the amount of time assigned to the effort. For example, if a faculty member receives an "outstanding" rating for assigned research that constitutes 10 percent of a full-time workload, should that person receive an "outstanding" rating for the same effort and end product if research constitutes 30 percent of a full-time workload?

So far we have discussed two types of evaluation: (1) a simple type based only on performance rating without regard for percentage of full-time workload assigned to each area and (2) a more complex type that takes into account separate performance ratings for each area and the percentage of full-time workload assigned to each of the areas rated. We have not yet considered the question of priority of performance areas.

Some departments prize research more highly than other performance areas and wish to reward good research more highly than good teaching or good service. On the other hand, some departments with enormous undergraduate teaching loads are primarily concerned with encouraging and rewarding their outstanding teachers. Such departments not only evaluate faculty members in terms of their assigned duties, as already illustrated, but also assign priority factors to the various areas according to the priority given to each. If a department wishes to encourage its members to do more research, for example, it could reward its more productive members by assigning larger percentages of their full-time workload to research, or it could assign a higher priority factor to the research portion of the assignment.

Area of Performance	I Performance Rating	II Assigned % of Full-Time Workload	Rating Points (RP) (I × II)
Teaching	1.0	65	65
Research	1.0	20	20
Service	4.0	10	40
Other	3.0	5	15
Total	9.0	100	140

$$\text{Rating Point Average (RPA)} = \frac{\text{Total of Rating Points}}{\text{Total of Assigned Percentages}} = \frac{140}{100} = 1.4$$

Fig. 6.5. Rating of Faculty Member C's performance, by area of performance and by percentage of full-time workload assigned to each area

Figures 6.3, 6.4, and 6.5 describe a department that assigns a priority factor of 1 to each performance area; in this way the department indicates that it believes all areas to be of equal importance and that "outstanding" performance should be rewarded equally, regardless of area. A department that wishes to give more priority to research than to other assigned areas can do so in several ways within the four-point system. A chairperson, after consulting with department members, could arbitrarily decide that research is 1.5 times as important as any other area and accordingly multiply each faculty member's assigned percentage of full-time workload devoted to research by a priority factor of 1.5.

Consider Faculty Member B, who in figure 6.3 was assigned 40 percent of her full-time workload to research and received a rating of 4.0 for research. If Faculty Member B's assigned percentage of full-time workload for research is multiplied by a priority factor of 1.5, her adjusted assigned percentage of full-time workload for research becomes 60 percent (40 percent × 1.5). Figure 6.6 shows these calculations. When Faculty Member B's percentage of full-time workload assigned to research (40) is multiplied by the area priority factor for research (1.5), her rating point average rises from 2.90 to 3.08.

If a priority factor is applied to the percentage of full-time workload assigned to a given performance area for one faculty member, then the same priority factor has to be applied to that

Area of Performance	I Performance Rating	II Assigned % of Full-Time Workload	III Area Priority Factor	IV Adjusted Assigned % of Full-Time Workload (II × III)	V Adjusted Rating Points (I × IV)
Teaching	2.0	40	1.0	40	80
Research	4.0	40	1.5	60	240
Service	3.0	10	1.0	10	30
Other	2.0	10	1.0	10	20
Total	11.0	100	N/A	120	370

$$\text{Adjusted Rating Point Average (RPA)} = \frac{\text{Total Adjusted Rating Points}}{\text{Total Adjusted Assigned \%s}} = \frac{370}{120} = 3.08$$

Fig. 6.6. Rating of Faculty Member B's performance, by area of performance and by percentage of full-time workload assigned to each area, taking into account the area priority factor performance area for all faculty members. The adjustment described in figure 6.6 would result in a lower rating point average for Faculty Members A and C. Faculty Member A's would drop from 3.60 to 3.50, and Faculty Member C's would drop from 1.40 to 1.35. These differences might affect the distribution of merit money. Note that the higher the priority factor in any activity, the greater will be the change in the rating point averages.

A chairperson who does not want to assign a priority factor that could be considered arbitrary might conduct a survey of the faculty members, asking each to indicate on a ten-point scale the value that should be given to each assigned area. For example, on a form similar to figure 6.7, each faculty member would circle the number that, in his or her opinion, reflects the priority of the performance area to the department's mission.

Teaching	1	2	3	4	5	6	7	(8)	9	10
Research	1	2	3	4	5	6	7	8	9	(10)
Service	1	2	3	4	(5)	6	7	8	9	10
Other'	1	2	3	4	(5)	6	7	8	9	10

Fig. 6.7. Faculty rating of the priority of performance areas to the department's mission

Area of Performance	I Performance Rating	II Assigned % of Full-Time Workload	III Area Priority Factor	IV Adjusted Assigned % of Full-Time Workload (II × III)	V Adjusted Rating Points (I × IV)
Teaching	2.0	40	8.0	320	640
Research	4.0	40	10.0	400	1600
Service	3.0	10	5.0	50	150
Other	2.0	10	5.0	50	100
Total	11.0	100	N/A	820	2490

$$\text{Adjusted Rating Point Average (RPA)} = \frac{\text{Total Adjusted Rating Points}}{\text{Total Adjusted Assigned \%s}} = \frac{2490}{820} = 3.09$$

Fig. 6.8. Rating of Faculty Member B's performance, by area of performance and by percentage of full-time workload assigned to each area, taking into account the area priority factor

The average of the faculty members' responses for each performance area would be the priority factor for that area. In figure 6.7, therefore, the department has given a priority factor of 8 to teaching, 10 to research, 5 to service, and 5 to "other." In figure 6.8, Faculty Member B's assigned percentages of full-time workload have been adjusted by multiplying the assigned percentages by the department priority factor for each area.

By the same method of calculation, Faculty Member A's rating point average would become 3.58 and Faculty Member C's 1.25. Note that the effect of applying priority factors, while not great, has increased the rating point average (RPA) of the department's best researcher, Faculty Member B, from 2.90 to 3.10, thus raising her evaluation on the four-point scale from "satisfactory" to "very good." This adjustment, however, has not greatly reduced the other faculty members' rating point averages.

In the calculations thus far, performance ratings have been used for the major categories of teaching, research, service, and "other." Each of these major categories may be broken down into several components. For example, the area of teaching can be divided into these components: amount of teaching; fulfillment of educational objectives; use of innovative techniques; and student evaluations. Each component could then be rated individually on the four-point scale, and from these individual ratings a composite rating for the area of teaching could be calculated. The areas of research and service can also be broken down into component activities and rated accordingly.

Some departments have developed a point system to help in the evaluations. They have a comprehensive list of all activities in each area, and a specific number of points is awarded for the completion of each activity. For example, some departments award a certain number of points for publications in refereed journals and fewer points for those in nonrefereed journals. In some fields there exists a well-known and generally accepted hierarchy of journals, and publications in the most prestigious journals are awarded more points than publications in less prestigious journals. A small number of points might be given for submitted publications and a larger number of points for accepted publications. A certain number of points may be given for papers presented at national meetings and a smaller number for papers presented at regional or local meetings of professional societies. The number of points given for the publication of a book might differ according to the publisher's prestige.

In the area of service, questions about allocation of points may be complex and difficult. Consideration might be given to the number and importance of committees on which the faculty member serves. A department might award more points for chairing a committee than for serving on it and might vary the number of points for service on national, regional, and state committees. The number of points earned by each faculty member for each activity is then totaled. The department must then determine how to translate these totals into performance ratings. This system is mentioned as a matter of information but is not necessarily advocated for use.

Following is an example of a point system for evaluation developed by a small, primarily research-oriented department. The system specifies the number of points to be awarded for each activity included in the areas of teaching, research, and service.[3]

SAMPLE OF POINT SYSTEM FOR FACULTY EVALUATION

A. Teaching
 1. Teaching load
    a) Graduate courses—each 0.50 points × number of credit hours
    b) Undergraduate courses—each 0.30 points × number of credit hours
    c) Directed individual study, supervised research, or supervised teaching—each 0.10 points
 2. Students' evaluation of faculty member; evaluation of peer or supervisor may also be conducted according to this form
    a) 90th percentile ranking—20 points
    b) 75th–89th percentile ranking—16 points
    c) 60th–74th percentile ranking—12 points
    d) 50th–59th percentile ranking—8 points
 3. Supervisory committees or positions
    a) Director of doctoral committee—5 points for each Ph.D. granted during faculty member's evaluation period; 3 points for each ongoing doctoral committee
    b) Member of doctoral committee—2 points
    c) Director of master's committee—3 points for each master's degree granted during faculty member's evaluation period; 2 points for each continuing student
    d) Member of master's committee—1 point
    e) Graduate student advisor—1 point for every three students
    f) Laboratory director—10 points
B. Research and scholarly activity
 1. Publications
    a) Writing
       1) Article for refereed national journal—5 points

3. Point system used by a small, primarily research department at Florida State University until 1978.

    2) Article for nonrefereed national journal—3 points
    3) Article for state journal—2 points
    4) Book with major publishing company—15 points
    5) Revised book—7 points
    6) Section of book with major publisher—5 points
    7) Book with local publisher—5 points
    8) Section of book with local publisher—2 points
   b) Editorial activities
    1) Editor of book—7 points
    2) Editor of national professional journal—15 points
    3) Editor of state professional journal—10 points
    4) Associate editor or reviewer for national journal—10 points
    5) Associate editor or reviewer for state journal—5 points
    6) Manuscript reviewer for major publisher—2 points each manuscript
    7) Reviewer for federal agency—5 points
  2. Research projects
   a) Author of R&D project funded by outside agency—15 points
   b) Author of R&D project funded by university—10 points
   c) Author of R&D project submitted to outside agency but not funded—15 points
   d) Author of R&D project submitted to university but not funded—3 points
  3. Papers and speeches
   a) Presented at national or international meeting, by invitation—10 points
   b) Submitted to national or international meeting—5 points
   c) Presented to regional or state meeting, by invitation—5 points
   d) Submitted to regional or state meeting—3 points
   e) Presented at another institution, by invitation—5 points
   f) Presented at local meeting—1 point
 C. Service
  1. Committee activities
   a) Chairperson of university committee—10 points
   b) Member of university committee—5 points
   c) Chairperson of school or college committee—5 points
   d) Member of school or college committee—3 points
   e) Chairperson of area or program committee—3 points
   f) Member of area or program committee—1 point
   g) Member of faculty senate—7 points
   h) Chairperson of search committee—5 points
   i) Member of search committee—3 points
  2. Professional activities
   a) Chairperson of national committee—5 points
   b) Member of national committee—3 points
   c) Chairperson of regional or state committee—3 points
   d) Member of regional or state committee—1 point
   e) Officer at regional or national level—10 points
   f) Officer at state level—7 points

  g) Leader for in-service training—3 points
  h) Organizer for workshop—5 points
  i) Member of professional association—1 point
  j) Attendance at professional meeting—1 point each
 3. Consulting (each visit—2 points)

This point system was used until the department was merged with several others that were less research oriented. The resulting larger department felt that this system was too rigid and too specific and abandoned it.

This system is highly quantitative in that it assigns a number of points for each activity. It is also qualitative, however, in that it allocates more points to good teaching performance than to average teaching performance, more points for papers published in prestigious journals than for papers published in lesser journals, and more points for membership on important committees than for membership on less important committees.

Another system of point allocation used by some departments rates faculty members' teaching performance on a ten-point scale, with "outstanding" performance receiving a full ten points and "poor" performance receiving no points at all. The average score for faculty members in the department is fixed beforehand at five points. Thus a department with ten members will have a total of fifty points to be divided among all the faculty members for teaching performance. This system is sometimes called the "constant sum" method. If a rater gives three faculty members ten points each for teaching performance, there would be only twenty points left to be divided among the other seven members. The same method is used for evaluating research and service.

This rating system, by limiting the total number of points that can be allocated, keeps a department from giving high ratings to all its members. In practice, if a small committee does the rating, the result will be sharp differentiations between faculty members, with some receiving high scores and others receiving low scores. When a large number of persons does the rating, the result will be a regression towards the mean, and the system loses much of its discriminating force.

The Evaluation Folder

The rules and regulations governing faculty members usually require that an official evaluation folder be established for each member. The folder is to be accessible only to the faculty member and to administrators who must make evaluative decisions. It may contain any information that will be used in the evaluation process, including summaries of performance counseling actions as well as annual formal evaluations prepared by the department chairperson.

In this age of due process, a faculty member may challenge any item placed in the evaluation folder and, by mutual agreement, the item may be removed from the folder. Also note that anonymous material, except systematic student evaluations and committee summaries, may not be placed in the folder. Some state laws may give even greater protection to personnel files.

Linking Merit Increases to Rating Point Averages

The following example will focus only on the allocation of moneys for merit increases. Assume that cost-of-living increases and other types of salary adjustments, if any, have already been made. The four-point system can link merit increases with performance evaluations in several ways. In this example, merit is divided into several levels—"high merit," "medium merit," "low merit," and "no merit." The department has seven members. They have been evaluated using the four-point system, and their rating point averages are as follows: Faculty Member A—3.8; Faculty Member B—3.4; Faculty Member C—3.2; Faculty Member D—2.8; Faculty Member E—2.6; Faculty Member F—2.5; and Faculty Member G—1.9.

The first question the department must address is, Where should the lines be drawn to differentiate the levels of merit? In this example, the lines will be drawn as follows: "high merit"— 3.5–4.0 RPA; "medium merit"—3.0–3.4 RPA; "low merit"—2.5– 2.9 RPA; and "no merit"—0–2.4 RPA. This merit level key is shown in figure 6.9.

	RPA
High merit	3.5 – 4.0
Medium merit	3.0 – 3.4
Low merit	2.5 – 2.9
No merit	0 – 2.4

Fig. 6.9. Merit level key

Three units of money are allocated for "high merit," two units for "medium merit," and one unit for "low merit." The number of faculty members in each merit category and the number of merit units are illustrated in figure 6.10.

Assume that $3,900 has been made available to the department for merit increases. The total number of merit units in the example is 10, and each unit is therefore worth $390 ($3900÷10). The amount of merit raise that each faculty member in the department will receive is shown in figure 6.11. If the department had decided to draw the lines differently, the money would have been allocated differently. The fewer the merit units, the greater would be the dollar value per unit. The fewer the faculty members earning merit raises, the greater would be the amount of money per faculty member deemed meritorious. In some departments, less than 50 percent of the faculty receive merit money. Determining policy in the allocation of merit money is a vexing matter and the subject of some controversy.

At institutions that have faculty salary schedules, merit moneys are often allocated not in dollars, but in units. The central administration takes upon itself the responsibility of determining the dollar value of each unit and specifying the number of units each department will receive. At such institutions, the chair-

	Rating Point Average	Number of Faculty Members		Merit Units Per Faculty Member		Total Merit Units
High merit	3.5 – 4.0	1	×	3	=	3
Medium merit	3.0 – 3.4	2	×	2	=	4
Low merit	2.5 – 2.9	3	×	1	=	3
No merit	0 – 2.4	1	×	0	=	0
				Total	=	10

Fig. 6.10. Calculation of number of merit units available for distribution

Faculty Member	Number of Merit Units		Value of Merit Unit		Merit Raise
Faculty Member A	3	×	$390	=	$1170
Faculty Member B	2	×	$390	=	$ 780
Faculty Member C	2	×	$390	=	$ 780
Faculty Member D	1	×	$390	=	$ 390
Faculty Member E	1	×	$390	=	$ 390
Faculty Member F	1	×	$390	=	$ 390
Faculty Member G	0	×	$390	=	$ 0

Fig. 6.11. Calculation of merit raises

person has the responsibility for determining only the number of units to be awarded to each faculty member. The process used could be the same as described above.

The art of evaluating the quality of faculty members' performance is and has been a perplexing problem ever since there have been faculty members. Quantity of performance can be measured in many ways, but quality of performance is, in most instances, measured in terms of the opinions, values, and perceptions held by students, peers, alumni, and other persons who have actually observed or been the beneficiaries of the performance. Scientifically derived numbers to describe quality are difficult to compute. Quality of performance is best described with words and phrases, but words and phrases cannot be added, multiplied, or averaged. To overcome this difficulty, numbers are often assigned to various words and phrases that describe quality of performance. Numbers can be processed mathematically for the purpose of yielding a final number that supposedly represents a faculty member's overall evaluation. This final number can then be transposed into words or phrases that describe the quality of the overall performance. The number, regardless of how sophisticated the mathematical process that yielded it, still represents a collection of human judgments. Attempting to quantify the quality of faculty performance, nevertheless, does force the evaluator to examine more carefully all facets of the faculty member's professional life.

If a chairperson subjectively feels that Faculty Member X is the most valuable member in the department and if an evaluation procedure based on statistical analysis shows that Faculty Member Y far surpasses Faculty Member X in performance, the chairperson is faced with the problem of reconciling these opposing evaluations. He or she can do so by modifying the statistical evaluation procedure or by reconsidering his or her personal evaluation of both faculty members. Perhaps the statistical procedure needs to be refined, or perhaps the chairperson's personal evaluations of these two faculty members are no longer relevant. The exercise of quantifying performance should not be avoided just because it has not yet been perfected. Used properly, this tool can help chairpersons evaluate faculty members.

Questions and Exercises

1. Do you conduct your own evaluations of faculty members, do you use a committee, or do you do both?

2. Is your faculty reasonably satisfied with the procedure used in your department for faculty evaluations?
3. Are you satisfied with the procedure?
4. Has your faculty as a department developed criteria, policies, or procedures for faculty evaluations? Are these currently being implemented?
5. Identify the faculty member whom you consider the most valuable to your department. Also identify the faculty member whom you would consider the least valuable. Using the four-point scale and the format described in this chapter, calculate the rating point average (RPA) of each of the two faculty members. Assume that all activities—teaching, research, service, and so forth—are of equal importance to the department's mission and that for each faculty member you have either formally assigned percentages of full-time workload to each activity or you know the percentage of effort devoted to each activity.

References

Allen, Paul M.; Barnes, William D.; Reece, Jerald L.; and Robertson, E. Wayne. *Teacher Self-Appraisal: A Way of Looking over Your Own Shoulder.* Worthington, Oh.: Charles A. Jones, 1970.

Argyris, Chris, and Schon, Donald A. *Theory in Practice: Increasing Professional Effectiveness.* San Francisco: Jossey-Bass, 1974.

Astin, Alexander W., and Lee, Calvin B. T. "Current Practices in the Evaluation and Training of College Teachers." *Educational Record,* Summer 1966, pp. 361–75.

Cadenhead, Kenneth, and Newell, Laura. "Personalizing Teacher Education." *Educational Technology,* March 1973, p. 51.

Cook, Marvin J., and Neville, Richard F. "The Faculty as Teachers: A Perspective on Evaluation." ERIC Clearinghouse on Higher Education, Report no. 13. Washington, D.C.: George Washington University, 1971.

Eble, Kenneth E. *Professors as Teachers.* San Francisco: Jossey-Bass, 1972.

"Evaluating Administrative/Supervisory Performance." *Educational Research Service,* circular no. 6. Washington, D.C.: Educational Research Service, 1972.

Gaff, Jerry G.; Wilson, Robert C.; et al. *The Teaching Environment: A Study of Optimum Working Conditions for Effective College Teaching.* Berkeley: Center for Research and Development in Higher Education, 1970.

Gray, Charles E. "The Teaching Model and Evaluation of Teaching Performance." *Journal of Higher Education,* November 1969, pp. 636–42.

Hildebrand, Milton. "How to Recommend Promotion for a Mediocre

Teacher without Actually Lying." *Journal of Higher Education,* January 1972, pp. 44–62.

Hildebrand, Milton, and Wilson, Robert C. *Effective University Teaching and Its Evaluation.* Berkeley: Center for Research and Development in Higher Education, 1970.

Hind, Robert R. "Evaluation and Authority in a University Faculty." Ph.D. dissertation, Stanford University, 1968.

Hind, Robert R.; Dornbusch, Sanford M.; and Scott, W. Richard. "A Theory of Evaluation Applied to a University Faculty." *Sociology of Education,* Winter 1974, pp. 114–28.

Lindman, Eric L. "The Means and Ends of Accountability." *Proceedings of the Conference on Educational Accountability.* Conference sponsored by the Educational Testing Service, Chicago, Illinois, June 1971.

Mager, Robert F. *Preparing Instructional Objectives.* 2nd ed. Belmont, Calif.: Fearon-Pitman, 1975.

Miller, Richard I. *Evaluating Faculty Performance.* San Francisco: Jossey-Bass, 1972.

National Center for Higher Education Management Systems. *Faculty Activity Analysis: Interpretation and Uses of Data.* TR 84. Boulder, Colo.: NCHEMS, 1974.

———. *Faculty Activity Analysis: Overview and Major Issues.* TR 24. Boulder, Colo.: NCHEMS, 1971.

———. *Faculty Activity Analysis: Procedures Manual.* TR 44. Boulder, Colo.: NCHEMS, 1973.

National Science Foundation. *Systems for Measuring and Reporting the Resources and Activities of Colleges and Universities.* NSF 67-15. Washington, D.C.: National Science Foundation, June 1967.

Scott, Robert A. *Lords, Squires, and Yeomen: Collegiate Middle Managers and Their Organizations.* AAHE-ERIC/Higher Education Research Report no. 7. Washington, D.C.: American Association for Higher Education, 1978.

Scott, W. Richard; Dornbusch, Sanford M.; Busching, Bruce C.; and Laing, James D. "Organizational Evaluation and Authority." *Administrative Science Quarterly,* June 1967, pp. 93–117.

Smith, Albert B. *Faculty Development and Evaluation in Higher Education.* ERIC/Higher Education Research Report no. 8. Washington, D.C.: American Association for Higher Education, 1976.

Smith, Richard, and Fiedler, Fred E. "The Measurement of Scholarly Work: A Critical Review of the Literature." *Educational Record,* Summer 1971, pp. 225–32.

Van Haden, Herbert I., and King, Jean Marie. *Educational Innovator's Guide.* Worthington, Oh.: Charles A. Jones, 1974

Walberg, Herbert J., ed. *Evaluating Educational Performance: A Sourcebook of Methods, Instruments, and Examples.* Berkeley: McCutchan, 1974.

7

Performance Counseling and Dealing with Unsatisfactory Performance

The Importance and Purpose of Performance Counseling

Performance counseling offers the chairperson a valuable communications tool that, properly used, can significantly enhance relations with faculty members and improve the department's chances for attaining its goals. *Performance counseling* is here defined as a regular although not necessarily formal contact between the chairperson and individual faculty members for the purpose of discussing successes and failures in completing assignments and duties. It is a two-way communications device that affords chairpersons and faculty members an opportunity to express their concerns and needs. Failure to provide this opportunity can become a grievance issue in the case of faculty members whose performance has been labeled deficient at evaluation time. At many institutions, performance counseling is required by state law, institutional policy, or collective bargaining agreement.

Some department chairpersons shirk the responsibility of providing performance counseling because they view this activity as nonprofessional or even degrading. They regard faculty members as professional peers and feel that infringing on or criticizing a fellow faculty member's professional activities is unjustifiable. This attitude is particularly prevalent in institutions in which department chairpersons serve on a rotating basis; it also exists in departments in which the chairperson's academic rank happens to be lower than that of his or her peers. Both chairpersons and faculty members will find performance counseling more acceptable, however, when they see that it can pave the way for more palatable decisions about promotion, tenure, and salary increases.

Chairpersons are also reluctant to provide performance counseling because it demands a complete understanding of department goals and objectives, the ability to make specific assignments for faculty members, and experience in assessing what constitutes acceptable performance standards. Meeting these requirements is no small matter and requires a great deal of thought and maturity. Further, the skills involved cannot easily be taught, because they require an intuitive judgment that not all chairpersons possess equally.

Perhaps the most important advice that can be given to performance counselors is, Avoid distorting the record. Chairpersons often tend to look for strong points that can offset weak points or to gloss over problems, especially those considered minor. Another distortion results when justifiable criticisms are turned into compliments. For example, a faculty member who gives unreasonably difficult examinations and fails an excessive number of students may be described by the chairperson as a teacher who "demands a high standard of excellence from students"! Such distortions merely avoid the issues and undermine the counseling approach, if not the entire evaluation procedure.

Dealing with Unsatisfactory Performance

One of a chairperson's most difficult and unpleasant duties is to inform faculty members that their performance has been unsatisfactory. Nevertheless, unsatisfactory performance must be dealt with, since bad situations often deteriorate even more if left unattended. Because chairpersons are colleagues of the faculty members whose performance is deemed inadequate, the problem of how to confront those colleagues is often perplexing. Some basic principles, practices, and techniques can be useful when attempting to remedy certain situations.

Unsatisfactory performance is handled most effectively if it is identified early. Early detection of an unhealthy situation allows time for diagnosis and remediation. How, then, does a chairperson recognize a developing problem that requires attention? First, the faculty member's performance must be compared with predetermined standards of satisfactory performance (see chapter 5). In this discussion we will assume that the department has developed criteria that are used to determine whether or not a faculty member's performance is acceptable in the areas of teaching, research, service, and other assigned duties.

Some unsatisfactory behaviors, such as unethical or illegal conduct, must simply be stopped to prevent irreparable harm. Other problems that occur because of rule or policy infractions generally are easily handled *provided* the chairperson adopts a strong managerial position. Institutional policy statements, faculty constitutions, or collective bargaining agreements may give the chairperson significant authority in such matters. For example, most institutions require that faculty members who accept outside employment report such employment before beginning the work. Such activity may well affect performance, especially if the faculty member is off campus one or more days per week. A faculty member's failure to follow this rule should be dealt with directly and firmly if the violation appears to be intentional.

Another example of unacceptable behavior is a faculty member's failure to hold office hours as required by university regulations or to meet scheduled classes. Repeated behavior of this type simply cannot be tolerated. The chairperson's job is *not* to be a policeman but to correct actions that are not in the best interests of students and the department. The effective chairperson may initially make light of the problem, but direct action, through informal as well as formal means, is appropriate if the situation does not improve.

Unsatisfactory performance, like most behavior, usually has a discernible cause or cluster of causes. The chairperson must learn to search for possible causes before attempting to discuss with the faculty members the behavior in question. Most instances of unsatisfactory performance are usually linked to personal matters, environmental matters related to employment, or both.

Personal matters that may cause unsatisfactory performance include the following:

1. *Lack of competence.* Incompetence takes various forms. A faculty member may perform poorly in teaching a certain course because he or she was trained in another area and does not possess the requisite knowledge to teach the assigned course. Other persons may lack pedagogic skills or may be unable to organize course content, to manage field experiences, and so on.

2. *Lack of mental or physical ability to carry out assigned duties.* Certain faculty members not only demonstrate incompetence but also seem unable to acquire necessary skills, no matter how hard they try. For example, a biology professor whose training was in taxonomy lacked the detailed knowledge of biochemistry and physiology necessary for teaching courses in modern biology. Furthermore, he seemed to lack the mental ability to master the new material. Another example is an education professor who lacked the physical stamina required to travel extensively while

supervising interns. A few faculty members perform poorly because they are simply too lazy to devote the necessary effort to their tasks.

3. *Lack of understanding of what is expected.* Some faculty members do not have a clear idea of what their duties are, or their view of their responsibilities conflicts with the views of the chairperson and the department. For example, a faculty member who felt that teaching was her main responsibility received a poor evaluation because of her lack of research activity. She did not understand that all members of her department were expected to conduct research. Another faculty member thought that teaching off-campus courses fulfilled his service responsibilities and refused to serve on committees. As a result, his overall evaluation in the area of service was unsatisfactory.

4. *Lack of proper attitude or appropriate temperament.* Some faculty members do not have the appropriate temperament or attitude to carry out certain assignments. For example, some extremely competent scholars seem temperamentally incapable of teaching undergraduate general education courses. Although very successful with graduate courses in their specific fields, they lack patience and understanding with students whose major interests may lie elsewhere. Other faculty members are resentful of duties that they consider demeaning. Such duties may include undergraduate counseling, off-campus teaching, service on certain committees, attendance at official functions, and so forth. These negative attitudes often lead to poor performance.

Environmental matters that may contribute to poor performance include the following:

1. *Social pressures and lack of acceptance by colleagues.* A faculty member's apathy and poor performance may be linked to lack of acceptance by colleagues. There are many reasons why some faculty members are not socially accepted. Some are perceived as having abrasive personalities. Others may be thought of as unwelcome intruders thrust upon the department as a result of reorganization. Still others may be rejected because of differences in age, sex, or lifestyle. Some persons collapse under the pressure of trying to emulate successful colleagues.

2. *Lack of incentives.* Some faculty members are not motivated to perform well because of insufficient incentives. These incentives may include adequate financial rewards, public recognition for achievements, and perquisites such as travel expenses for professional meetings or even parking space.

3. *Lack of appropriate facilities and pleasing environment.* A

faculty member's performance may suffer because of inadequate physical facilities and resources such as laboratory equipment, office space, libraries, and classroom environments. Dissatisfaction with the social and physical climate of the community at large may also affect the quality of his or her performance.

4. *Lack of adequate leadership.* In some instances a faculty member's poor performance may be directly related to counterproductive interaction with the department chairperson. The faculty member may receive insufficient encouragement, praise, direction, or supervision. As a result, he or she may perceive a lack of concern on the chairperson's part. Other chairpersons may supervise too closely, thereby causing undue anxiety and tension.

In attempting to deal with a faculty member whose performance is considered unsatisfactory, the chairperson should first learn as much as possible about the personal and environmental matters that may be affecting the faculty member's behavior. Some of these circumstances may be known to the chairperson from personal observation, some from observations of other faculty members. In most instances it is advisable for the chairperson to meet with the faculty member in question to discuss the matter. The chairperson should prepare for the encounter by giving thought to the following suggestions.

First, it is difficult to tell someone that his or her performance has been unsatisfactory without provoking a defensive reaction. Defensiveness is natural, and even the chairperson may become defensive when confronting a faculty member whose performance is unsatisfactory. But defensiveness is counterproductive and should be minimized whenever possible. If the discussion regarding the faculty member's performance is seen as a counseling session rather than as an interview for formal evaluation, any potential defensiveness may be diffused. The discussion should be just that—a discussion, not a lecture. The chairperson should try to involve the faculty member, rather than reprimand him or her. As mentioned earlier, the chairperson should start a dialogue with a faculty member at the first hint of difficulty and continue the dialogue at regular intervals. In this way, discussion of instances of poor performance will arise within a context of openness and will not provoke an immediate negative reaction. The chairperson should avoid lumping all a faculty member's shortcomings into one bundle and dumping it on the unsuspecting person without warning.

The chairperson may perceive unsatisfactory faculty performance as a personal insult or as a poor reflection of his or her leadership abilities. He or she may also feel guilty about a faculty member's shortcomings. These reactions should not be allowed to become anger or hostility toward the faculty member. The chairperson should be as self-controlled and as calm as possible, since emotional responses may get out of hand. Yet the chairperson needs to recognize his or her feelings and anxieties and not try to repress them completely. At times, however, poor performance may be caused by the chairperson's behavior. In such cases, the chairperson should admit to this possibility and not try to project an image of omniscience and infallibility.

The faculty member should be made to feel that the chairperson is genuinely interested in bringing about positive changes and is willing to spend as much time and effort as is necessary to do so. The faculty member should also be made to feel that his or her poor performance need not be shouldered alone, that it is a problem for the whole department and can be solved cooperatively for the good of the department. What must be determined, therefore, is how best to solve the problem, not who should be blamed. Problem solving requires the chairperson's empathetic understanding of the faculty member and the ability to see the other person's point of view. To relieve the faculty member's anxiety, the chairperson must point out that others have had similar problems that have been successfully resolved.

When the chairperson has achieved the proper frame of mind for performance counseling, he or she should again review the personal and environmental matters discussed earlier to see if anything can be done to change the situation. The faculty member should be encouraged to participate in the dialogue and make suggestions for change. If the dialogue goes well, some of these suggestions may correspond to those the chairperson has thought of. At the same time, the chairperson should be flexible enough to change his or her mind when new insights emerge as the result of dialogue. Some measures within the realm of the department's authority or control include providing opportunities for retraining faculty members who lack certain competencies; providing opportunities for reassignment for those who lack the ability to gain competence or whose health requires less demanding tasks; providing more preparation time for those who are overloaded or overworked; and changing or upgrading facilities for a better research atmosphere. Faculty members who are experiencing a personal crisis may benefit from a new assignment, for the change may give them a renewed sense of importance and productivity.

Sometimes unsatisfactory performance cannot be remedied. Although an attempt should be made to resolve the problem, the chairperson must be able to recognize and accept the fact that some faculty members' performance cannot be improved.

Initiating and Conducting a Dialogue about Unsatisfactory Performance

The importance of dialogue in solving problems of poor performance has been emphasized. Following are some concrete suggestions to the chairperson about how to initiate and conduct a discussion with a faculty member.

- Do not send a memorandum to the faculty member listing his or her areas of unsatisfactory performance and asking that an appointment be made with you to discuss them. It is better to make a personal contact, during which you can invite the faculty member to meet with you to talk about his or her progress towards reaching performance expectations. A private and uninterrupted meeting should be arranged for this purpose.
- Try to allay the faculty member's anxiety by being calm and cool. Let the faculty member know that his or her personal worth is respected and that his or her abilities are appreciated, but that specific changes in performance are necessary.
- Be open-minded, tolerant, and cooperative, and encourage the faculty member to express his or her point of view. Be considerate. Listen attentively to what is being said without interrupting, and keep sufficient control over the discussion so that it does not develop into a shouting match or an abusive argument.
- Be as empathetic as possible and give credit where credit is due, but try to focus on those areas that need improvement and on the possible solutions to the problem. Feelings of friendship should not be allowed to stand in the way of challenging unsatisfactory performance.
- When pinpointing poor performance, be specific and descriptive, rather than ascribe a blanket negative value to the performance. Be ready to offer concrete suggestions about what needs to be done, especially when the faculty member seems unable to develop his or her own plan. At the same time, keep the plan flexible.

The meeting should result in the development of a course of action that is agreed upon by both chairperson and faculty member and that includes specific objectives and a schedule for achieving them. The chairperson should arrange additional meetings, if necessary, and keep a written record of the dialogue and its conclusions. The faculty member deserves to have a copy of the record of the meeting. A note of caution: The chairperson should not try to give psychological counseling to the faculty member or even suggest that it is needed. Experience has shown that giving this kind of advice, even when it is solicited, sometimes results in legal action against the chairperson or the university or both.

Encouraging Good Performance

A department recently hired a temporary faculty member to teach two classes. During the term, she spent an inordinate amount of time on the assigned courses and developed some innovative activities that were adopted for continued use in the class. An evaluative questionnaire completed by the students rated both the classes and her teaching "excellent." At the end of the term, the chairperson's only comment to her was, "You may be interested to know that I didn't receive any negative comments on your work this term." Needless to say, the faculty member did not feel that her efforts were sufficiently appreciated!

In facing the day-to-day problems of running a department, the chairperson can easily overlook the importance of encouraging acceptable performance. Most faculty and staff members feel encouraged when their chairperson makes the effort to identify good performance and offers a sincere comment on the work. Chairpersons must find time to compliment special efforts by faculty members. Obvious performance—such as unusually high student ratings, a published paper, a successful grant proposal, or an outstanding presentation to a group of local businessmen— is easy to identify and deserves favorable comment. The recognition of less obvious accomplishments—such as completing an assignment ahead of schedule, spending extra time with a group of students, or being available to help with an unexpected problem— can be an even greater boost for a faculty member's morale.

The chairperson should also take every opportunity to encourage actions by faculty members that will lead to successful promotions and tenure decisions and to ensure that good performance is properly documented. The chairperson's task is *not* to build the case for the faculty member but to have as much supporting evidence as possible when making a case for promotion or tenure.

Maintaining a Record of Performance Counseling

The chairperson's responsibility for maintaining a record of performance counseling, including comments on successful and outstanding accomplishments as well as problem areas, is increasingly important. This record need not be extensive or detailed, and it should not be kept secret from the faculty member involved. It can be as valuable to the faculty member as it is to the chairperson, since the faculty member soon gains a clearer picture of the performance standards expected by the chairperson. The performance counseling record is a valuable document when decisions about promotion, tenure, and salary adjustments are made. When promotion, tenure, or salary adjustments must be denied, the chairperson must be able to document that a reasonable effort has been made to assist the faculty member to improve poor performance. Summaries of performance counseling actions should go in the faculty member's evaluation folder.

The department chairperson, then, should establish a regular pattern of performance counseling with department faculty members. This effort may be formal or informal, but the real purpose of the counseling is to establish a close working relationship with faculty members and to encourage actions that the chairperson feels will benefit both the faculty member and the department. Counseling must be based on clear, definite assignments and on reasonable standards of performance in each major academic area—teaching, research, and service. The chairperson must document performance counseling activities as accurately and as quantitatively as possible without overreacting with either positive or negative comments.

The improvement in faculty members' performance as a result of performance counseling can play a significant role in promotion, tenure, and salary adjustment decisions. Performance counseling may also prove to be important to the chairperson as a way of establishing and maintaining meaningful communication with faculty members.

Questions and Exercises

1. Identify one or two faculty members in your department or in another department who have performed unsatisfactorily in

teaching, research, service, or some other area that is important to the department.
2. For each faculty member so identified, ask yourself the following questions:
   a) In what way was the performance in each case unsatisfactory? Against what criteria was each performance compared?
   b) Are you familiar with any personal and environmental factors that may have contributed to the poor performance of
   the faculty members concerned?
   c) To your knowledge, did the faculty members in question
   receive any kind of performance counseling? What kind, if
   any?
   d) Assuming that you have decided to provide these faculty
   members with performance counseling, how would you go
   about it? Prepare a mental script that you would use with
   each faculty member. Under what circumstances would
   you meet with each of them? Anticipate their response.
   What kind of assistance would you offer them? How
   would you motivate them?

An Unsuccess Story

This case is based on an actual incident that occurred after a
chairperson attended a department leadership seminar sponsored by the Institute for Departmental Leadership, Florida State
University.

When Harry Casper, a social science department chairperson,
returned home from a workshop on collegial administration for
the 1980s, he decided to test his new knowledge. The first problem he wanted to approach was the issue of inequitable workloads among the faculty members. This problem was uppermost
in his mind because it was time to work out the class schedule
for the next term. After several days of effort he developed an
assignment plan using several ideas that were discussed at the
workshop. He designed a basic system of points for various activities and a form for recording the planned assignments. To
make sure the plan was understandable and that the point
weights reflected the priorities agreed upon by the faculty members, he sought out some of his colleagues to get their reactions
and made a few important changes based on their suggestions.
While creating and obtaining acceptance of the plan, Casper
contemplated ways of making assignments that would be equita-

ble and at the same time allow for faculty development that could be recognized and rewarded. As he reviewed the latest student evaluations of faculty members' performance and considered those persons who were most strongly criticized, his thoughts turned especially to one faculty member, Anne Stone.

Stone, an associate professor, was the first woman social scientist recruited by the department search committee. She had been an outstanding undergraduate social science major, graduating cum laude from this very institution. She completed her doctorate at Indiana University six years ago and had continually done good research. She published regularly and had a book manuscript in process. Her otherwise good record was marred by continuous complaints about her teaching. Students reported that she was uninteresting, disorganized, unfriendly, and rarely available to those seeking advice. In fact, of the department's nineteen full-time faculty members, she always had the lowest rating for teaching.

Stone's record seemed to be getting worse, and Casper wanted to make some special assignments that would enable her to improve her performance. He began work on an assignment that would provide released time for consultation with some instructional design professionals in the university; he also would propose that she teach a few small sections of the introductory courses, as well as a reduced graduate teaching load. In all, he spent almost two weeks working out the details for her faculty development program and for each term of the next academic year's assignment. He felt a genuine sense of accomplishment, tinged with altruism, and felt that Stone would be pleased with his plan for improving her teaching and advising capabilities.

A meeting with Stone was scheduled for the Wednesday morning preceding Thanksgiving holidays. She came into his office, seeming a bit fidgety; her manner was friendly, but she showed some anxiety. Casper explained the new assignment system first, then elaborated on the special assignments that could be worked out for her growth and development as a faculty member. As he began to unfold the details of the plan, her face changed from a look of mild curiosity to one of growing anger. Her first response was to ask why Casper did not like her teaching, and he answered that his plan was based on complaints about her teaching. She responded forcefully that she was one of the best teachers in the department and that he was judging her on the basis of incomplete, unreliable, and bad evidence. Casper tried to reason with her, offering to change the plan in any way that she thought would help improve her teaching. At the end of the third exchange about the plan, Stone jumped from her chair and without another word walked out and slammed the door. Casper made some minor changes in her assignment and then prepared for the consultation with the next faculty member.

Just before the term ended at Christmas, Casper received a call from the president that surprised, saddened, and angered him. Stone had filed an official faculty grievance against him. She claimed that he was harassing her and embarrassing her by requiring that she seek help in improving her teaching from professionals who were not faculty members when she already was an accomplished and experienced teacher. An informal conference with the president's faculty grievance representative could not resolve the issues, so they were to be heard formally by a university grievance committee at the end of January.

1. Assuming that the chairperson was well-intentioned in his attempt to help Stone improve her performance, why were his efforts rebuffed?
2. What could or should the chairperson have done to have aroused a less negative response from Stone?
3. Was Casper wrong in trying to design an annual assignment for Stone that included a program to help her improve her teaching?
4. Should Casper have involved other faculty members of the department in designing an improvement program for Stone? If so, how should they have been involved?
5. How would you have handled the situation?

References

Bolton, Robert H. *People Skills: How to Assert Yourself, Listen to Others, and Resolve Conflicts.* Englewood Cliffs, N.J.: Prentice-Hall, 1979.

Brammer, Lawrence M. *The Helping Relationship.* 2nd ed. Englewood Cliffs, N.J.: Prentice-Hall, 1979.

Egan, Gerard, and Cowan, Michael A. *People in Systems: An Integrative Approach to Human Development.* Monterey, Calif.: Brooks-Cole, 1979.

Fournies, Ferdinand F. *Coaching for Improved Work Performance.* New York: Van Nostrand Reinhold, 1978.

Hasenfeld, Yeheskel, and English, Richard A. *Human Service Organizations: A Book of Readings.* Ann Arbor, Mich.: The University of Michigan Press, 1974.

Leavitt, Harold J., and Pondy, Louis R., eds. *Readings in Managerial Psychology.* 2nd ed. Chicago: University of Chicago Press, 1974.

Shertzer, Bruce E., and Stone, Shelley C. *Fundamentals of Counseling.* 3rd ed. Boston: Houghton Mifflin, 1980.

Steinmetz, Lawrence L. *Managing the Marginal and Unsatisfactory Performer.* Reading, Mass.: Addison-Wesley, 1969.

8

Faculty Grievances and Unions

IIIIIIIIIIIIIIIIIIIIIIIIIIIIIIIIIIIIIIIIIIIIIIIIIIIIIIIIIIIIIIIIIIIIIIIIIIIIIIIIIIIIIIIIIIIIIIIIIIIIIIIIIIIIIIIIIIII

In the days of rapid expansion of colleges and universities, little attention was given to resolving problems relating to the conditions and procedures of employment of faculty members. Because the academic market was strong, faculty members who were dissatisfied with their jobs could escape their problems by changing institutions. Moreover, many faculty members were of patrician background, and their upbringing taught them to disdain strident, overt conflict. Colleagues "were done in quietly": they simply disappeared in June, to emerge at another school the following September.

By the end of the 1960s, much had changed. Students had frightened university administrators into making various reforms, and issues of war and peace had become campus concerns. Faculty members from the working class, ethnic backgrounds, and, to a lesser degree, minority cultures had joined the profession. Legislators voted to punish university communities for real or imagined transgressions, and most traditional disciplines faced declining markets. For many faculty members the idea of organizing themselves and their professions no longer seemed outlandish.

At one time, faculty members who were denied tenure or whose contracts were not renewed might have respectably transferred to other institutions. With few employment opportunities available, they now were increasingly willing to challenge negative evaluations by administrators and colleagues. They tried to retain their jobs through existing, though sometimes impotent, procedures, and their cases frequently reached federal or state appellate courts.

Some institutions changed their procedures, although most did not. A few institutions, especially those supported primarily by private sources, developed formal procedures that were included in their constitutions and faculty handbooks. Others, particularly those state universities supervised or coordinated by state boards of higher education, developed procedures that became part of state law. At some institutions where procedures were actually included in the law, faculty members still felt that they had no strong advocates to ensure that the procedures were applied impartially. When they were not satisfied with the implementation of the procedures and mechanisms designed for appealing individual nonrenewals, *de facto* tenure quotas, or layoffs, faculty members often designated unions to represent them in negotiating with the administration and in filing grievances. This cooperation frequently resulted in the development of official faculty union contracts that contained conditions and procedures of employment. Contracts at some state universities—for example, the state universities in Florida—contain the same conditions and procedures as those stipulated in the state law concerning university personnel policies.

In several states the difference between the legislation and the contracts is that the contracts are monitored by union officials who act as faculty advocates. In states with legislation but no negotiated contract, the conditions are monitored by the administration, a situation that many faculty members perceive as the fox guarding the henhouse. The spirit of the legislation appears to be remarkably similar to the spirit of the negotiated contracts. Perhaps if a mechanism were developed that carried out the legislative intent fairly, faculty members might not feel such a strong need to unionize.

Faculty personnel problems occur whether a union exists or not. In fact, although the power and influence of faculty unions are increasing dramatically in some areas of the country, the personnel problems facing faculty members have remained the same. These problems have led to formal grievances or informal complaints, depending on the procedures at any given institution.

Regardless of whether a faculty union exists, a department chairperson may confront many kinds of grievances. The following list contains examples of typical problems that have led to grievances:

- conflict with colleagues, administrators, students, or community over teaching methods, course content, research design, or subject matter
- complaints about rank or pay; claims that inequities were due to discrimination against race, sex, religion, or handicap

- dissatisfaction with status or classification; claims that existing status or classification did not reflect training, experience, or responsibilities
- disagreement over assignment; claims that assignment was made late, represented an undesired overload, constituted disciplinary action, or was made arbitrarily and capriciously
- problems concerning evaluation; claims that evaluations were biased, that supervisors failed to notify employees of the results of their observations, that the evaluation procedures and instruments used were in violation of the contract, that the evaluation file was stacked with negative information, or that evaluation was based on materials not contained in the evaluation file
- problems concerning nonrenewal of contract; claims that employees were not notified of nonrenewal within contractual time limits, that reasons for nonrenewal were not provided on request, or that reasons provided were in violation of the contract, the law, or university rules or constitution
- problems concerning layoff; claims of failure to follow contractual guidelines for layoff or failure to pursue actively recall and placement procedures
- problems with peer review; claims of failure to conduct peer reviews so that administrative decisions would be based on consistent criteria and procedures established by the contract, the law, or university rules
- problems concerning promotion and tenure; claims that decisions were not based on established criteria, were arbitrary and capricious, or contradicted supportive materials in the evaluation folder; claims of unwillingness to overturn an erroneous review on its merits; claims of total disregard for a favorable peer review
- problems concerning reprimand or censure; objections to negative letters placed in personnel file; objections to suspension or termination
- problems concerning access to records, documents, or information; disagreements over administrative use of "relevance" or "privilege" arguments to refuse access
- problems concerning efforts to solve problems; claims that administrators failed to observe time lines, to conduct impartial meetings, or to make good faith efforts to reach a

settlement or to issue decisions based on the merits of the grievance

The issues of greatest conflict between faculty members represented by a faculty union and the board of regents in one state university system have been identified in a recent dissertation. The study found that during the period from 1 January 1977 to 1 January 1978, 114 conflicts reached the second step of the formal grievance procedure—i.e, review by the chancellor of the board of regents or his or her representatives. These conflicts arose from complaints about salary inequities (24 cases); tenure and promotion decisions (24 cases); assignment of responsibilities (12 cases); nonrenewal (11 cases); evaluation (11 cases); salary schedule not established by board of regents (5 cases); sabbaticals (5 cases); academic freedom (2 cases); holidays (2 cases); failure to hold informal conferences (2 cases); and other issues (16 cases, each different).[1]

Most of the inequity grievances grew out of a sex discrimination clause of the contract. Once the initial inequities were rectified, this cause of grievances became of secondary importance in subsequent years. Tenure, promotion, assignments, nonrenewals, and evaulations still remained major grievance areas. Since these 114 cases reached an advanced step in the grievance process, certain matters of faculty relations clearly deserve close scrutiny. With these conflicts in mind, the chairperson may be able to anticipate personnel problems. In many cases, when the reason for a problem is understood, the potential difficulty can be resolved to everyone's benefit before it becomes critical.

Sometimes personnel problems result in formal grievances. A *grievance*, as the term will be used here, is a claim that a contract negotiated under collective bargaining has been violated or that university or college rules, state statute, federal law, or constitutional rights have been violated. When a faculty union perceives that its members have a problem, it may "find" an article of the contract that it will claim is being violated. Such a claim does not necessarily mean that a violation has occurred but that the union can be expected to interpret the contract liberally when the interests of its clientele are involved. If a faculty member's unhappiness stems from something other than a violation of the contract or of any of the above laws, rules, or rights, he or she may

1. Chris Parnell Plyler, "The Grievance Appeals Process in the State University System of Florida: A Case Study." Unpublished doctoral dissertation, Florida State University, 1978, p. 53.

simply choose to write a letter of complaint to some upper-level administrator in the college or university.

An unusually large number of complaints or grievances within a department, whether based on alleged violations of a faculty contract or not, is often symptomatic of deep-seated conflict. A wise chairperson will try to create a department environment that minimizes grievances and maximizes openness and trust. In discussing how to minimize grievances, we have assumed that a better understanding of grievance procedures will lead department chairpersons to adhere to the spirit and letter of the faculty contract (if one exists) or of current university rules and regulations governing faculty personnel. Unfortunately, some department chairpersons are not cognizant of these rules and regulations or choose to ignore them. As faculty members expend greater efforts defending their rights, it is increasingly important for chairpersons to understand the faculty contract or other operative personnel rules and regulations, as well as alternatives for dealing with personnel problems.

A chairperson can minimize grievances, contractual or other, by assigning responsibilities in a clear and forthright manner; providing a process for faculty members to dispute and change an arbitrary or capricious assignment; regularly evaluating employees on the basis of their assignments, rather than on personality or social considerations; instructing committees engaged in peer evaluation also to evaluate a faculty member on the basis of that person's assigned responsibilities; and counseling faculty members who have performed poorly. A good personnel policy is one that is fair, provides means of improvement, and minimizes complaints and grievances.

When a faculty member files a grievance, considers doing so, or simply has a complaint or problem, the chairperson should be willing to discuss the problem with the potential grievant and his or her representative. A chairperson should not be offended if a department member feels the need for a representative when dealing with a serious career matter. Unions usually advise faculty members to have a colleague witness such discussions with supervisors. Moreover, to the chairperson, the faculty member may be a colleague, but to the faculty member with a problem, the chairperson may simply be the "boss." Even a professional may need the moral support of a colleague or grievance specialist.

Faculty members with grievances are under enormous pressure. They do not want to offend friends or administrators, but they do want a just resolution of their problem. A simple description of the grievance process does not begin to reveal the strain that a grievance creates, even among innocent bystanders in a department or college.

Resolving personnel problems is easier when the complaints are still informal. Clearly, doing whatever possible to eliminate potential causes of grievances and attempting to solve them informally is in the best interests of all persons in the university community. Possibilities of settlement may arise at informal meetings early in the grievance process and should be seriously pursued. An experienced party might be recruited to suggest solutions. Early resolution keeps the complaint within the chairperson's control; avoids time-consuming hearings, depositions, or court appearances; spares upper-level administrators the need to deal with the department's headache; and prevents the intradepartment bloodletting that often results when factions form behind protagonists.

The Grievance Procedure

If the problem is not resolved, it may become a formal grievance. When a contract exists, only matters covered by the contract may constitute the subject of a grievance. The contract encourages administrators and employees to communicate openly and to make every attempt to resolve problems before a grievance is filed. Once a grievance is filed, however, the contract stipulates three steps to be followed in the attempt to settle the grievance. The grievance procedure for the State University System of Florida will serve as our model for the three-step grievance procedure.

The first step consists of the grievant and his or her representative presenting evidence supporting the grievance to the university president or his or her representative. At this time, the "acts or omissions" leading to the grievance and the university officials involved are identified, and a solution is proposed. The president or his or her representative must give a written decision within a defined time. If the grievance is not satisfactorily resolved within the institution, the process moves to the second step, which consists of a prompt review by the chancellor of the university system or his or her representatives, who must give a decision with supporting reasons within a defined time. If no satisfactory resolution results, the third step is taken at the discretion of the union. This step consists of a process of arbitration conducted by a neutral arbitrator chosen from a preselected panel. The arbitrator's decision is binding on the board of regents, the union, and the grievant, though the arbitrator's decision may be appealed to a court of law if he or she appears to have acted outside his or her jurisdiction.

The three-step approach gives the impression that grievances are primarily resolved at one of the three official levels. Many grievances, however, never reach the first step but are worked out informally between the local union steward or chapter grievance specialist and the department chairperson or, occasionally, a dean. In addition, many grievances are worked out along the way as "settlements" that are satisfactory to both sides. Still others end in ad hoc committees, acceptable to both the administration and the faculty union, which successfully resolve the problems. The distasteful prospect of arbitration encourages both sides to strive for an acceptable settlement. The grievance procedure with the possibility of a review by a neutral party introduces an element of accountability into contract administration.

The situation is considerably different when a union contract does not exist. At universities that provide due process, usually one or several peer committees exist to deal with complaints. The committees may be appointed by administrators, chosen by senates, or elected at large. Such committees hear charges, examine evidence, and keep records. The committee members are colleagues of the grievant and rarely, if ever, have authority to change personnel decisions on their own. Their charge is to make a recommendation to a high-level management representative, who may or may not choose to follow the recommendation.

Several states have legislation modeled on the federal Administrative Procedures Act, and a considerable number of academic rules and procedures for state universities are usually included in these state statutes. Florida law, for example, provides for standard university governing policies, such as criteria for tenure and promotion, acceptable reasons for nonrenewal, and even the relationship of teaching to research and publication in the promotion criteria. The state's Administrative Procedures Act provides a mechanism for faculty members to deal with violations of those procedures.

The shortcomings of the Administrative Procedures Act in Florida, however, are typical of those throughout the country. Under this act, a party has the right to have a grievance placed before a neutral hearing officer, who is chosen on the basis of his or her expertise in the matter in question. In the absence of a collective bargaining contract, the hearing officer's ruling on whether a faculty member's rights have been violated is only a recommendation to the university. If the university does not choose to implement the recommendation, the aggrieved faculty member can litigate, but in so doing faces considerable financial costs. Moreover, in Florida the courts have rarely upheld the hearing examiner when he or she ruled against management. The unions, of course, point out that the standard grievance procedures in collective bargaining contracts culminate in neutral arbitration, which the courts almost universally support. For this reason neither management nor labor enters into litigation over arbitration decisions, except in the rare instance in which the arbitrator exceeds his or her authority.

The chances of a grievant winning his or her argument seem to be much greater on those campuses where faculty members have union contracts. Nevertheless, the chairperson may face even greater involvement in a noncontractual case because so many separate hearings may need to be conducted for a single case. The strain on the department, the loss of faculty members' time, and diversion of department administrative effort can be significant. For example, one standard noncontractual tenure grievance case was in intrauniversity system hearings for two years and in litigation for another three years. Faculty members and especially chairpersons are frequently required to take part in hearings and litigation. Although the department will not have to incur legal costs for such cases, the university will. In addition, upper-level administrators will have to take part in this unpleasant diversion. University administrators may view chairpersons who are involved in a great many grievances as problems in themselves. Chairpersons should not acquiesce to unreasonable claims made by some department members but should understand the rules under which they function and minimize grievances through sound personnel practices.

A grievant or the union will occasionally blame the chairperson for the problem leading to the grievance. The grievant will sometimes demand that the chairperson be disciplined or receive psychiatric counseling. Grievants often vent their hostility in this way, and the chairperson should not succumb to emotional reactions. Such reactions not only may make resolution more difficult and final adjustment to the situation unlikely, but they also may weaken the argument for the chairperson's position. The goal of both sides is to reach an equitable settlement, but the chairperson will have to live with whatever settlement is attained. Department members may have difficulty accepting an uncomfortable situation, but the chairperson must acquiesce gracefully for the sake of the department and its development. In such instances, it helps for the chairperson to have a thick skin.

A Case Study of a Grievance Filed under a Union Contract

The following case study is based on a grievance that took place in the State University System of Florida. The procedures that were followed are outlined in a contract for 1978–1981 negotiated between the United Faculty of Florida and the Florida Board of Regents. The Florida contract is not presented as a model for other states to follow, nor is this study to be viewed as advocating or opposing the cause of faculty unions. It is presented in order to inform department chairpersons of the dynamics of a grievance process. Other states with similar contracts usually have similar, though not necessarily identical, processes. This case study should also be of interest to chairpersons in institutions that do not have union contracts, because it deals with a grievance about tenure and closely resembles cases that have occurred in the absence of a contract.

The facts of the case presented here have been slightly modified in order to protect the privacy of the persons involved. The actual case involved several steps, but it has been restructured as only a one-step case. The names of the persons have been changed, minor facts altered, and some events deleted, but the case is based on an actual incident.

A Brief Background of the Case

John O'Hara, a member of the department of educational foundations for six years, filed a grievance after being denied tenure. During his fifth year he had been promoted to associate professor, and the promotion was unanimously approved by his department's tenure and promotion committee. When he applied for tenure the next year, the same committee rejected him unanimously. When O'Hara formally asked why he had failed to receive tenure, the university president's representative responded that the department would state only that it had rejected O'Hara because a majority of the committee had voted against him.

O'Hara filed a grievance citing several documents: a letter from the department chairperson, C. B. Rhodes, a collective bargaining unit member [at certain institutions in the State University System of Florida some chairpersons are designated as members of the collective bargaining unit and some are designated as part of management]; a letter from Jason Smith, the chairperson of the tenure and promotion committee; and a letter from James Deles, the leading scholar among the full professors serving on the committee. The initial series of letters supported O'Hara's promotion; a subsequent series supported his tenure approval. These letters were uniformly positive, praising O'Hara's qualities as both a teacher and a scholar. Deles, for example, described him as "the strongest scholar in the department." O'Hara also included letters from the same persons that were written following the department's rejection of his request for tenure. These three letters, all written in a remarkably similar style, considerably modified the earlier praise and indicated unspecified doubts about the candidate.

The file contained several other letters. Among them were two unsolicited communications to O'Hara from nationally known scholars praising his latest book and a related article of his that had appeared in the leading journal in the field. The file also included a copy of the chairperson's annual evaluation of faculty members, which rated as "excellent" O'Hara's teaching and research for each year that he had served at the university. Student evaluations of O'Hara's teaching were also quite positive. His publications list was formidable.

In the area of service, however, O'Hara had received only a "satisfactory" rating for his first three years with the department; for the last three years, he was not evaluated for service. Included in the grievance file was a statement by O'Hara pointing out that he did not understand why he had received only a "satisfactory" rating for meeting his service obligations. O'Hara noted that he had served on as many committees as anyone else in the department, had several doctoral students working under him, and had obtained more money in grants in the last four years than the three most successful grants recipients in the department had obtained in their combined academic careers. O'Hara also coached a pee-wee league softball team, an activity he felt constituted community service of a sort. He stated, however, that he was not sure what "community service" meant for someone in the field of philosophy of education. O'Hara noted that when he asked Rhodes what he should do to improve his service rating, Rhodes assured him—verbally—that O'Hara need not worry about the matter. Subsequently, he was not assigned a service obligation for the last three years.

An Informal Attempt to Deal with the Problem

A union grievance representative brought the O'Hara matter

to the attention of the dean of the college of education, Carmine Calabrezi. The dean chose not to have the assistant to the president for labor relations present, indicating that on principle he would not overturn a unanimous vote of a department. In addition, Dean Calabrezi emphasized that he had utmost confidence in the department chairperson, Rhodes. Dean Calabrezi would not speak of the substance of the grievance. If Rhodes indicated to him that a serious error had taken place, Calabrezi assured the representative that he would be happy to reconsider the tenure recommendation.

The union representative then met informally with Rhodes, who also refused to discuss the substance of the case. Rhodes began by noting that the union had filed this grievance only after the dean had rejected O'Hara's tenure. Rhodes emphasized, "I'm in the collective bargaining unit, not an administrator who has to justify his decisions." After his meeting with Rhodes, the union grievance representative gave a report of "no progress" to O'Hara.

Grievance Meeting

O'Hara's grievance meeting was held on 3 April 1979. Grievance meetings at this stage in the process take on different forms at different institutions. At some universities, the president's representative meets first with the representatives of one party and then with the representatives of the other. At O'Hara's grievance meeting, the union's representative and the president's representative remained for the entire meeting.

At the meeting, O'Hara and his union representative discussed the grievance matter with the president's representative. O'Hara based his argument on documents from his personnel file and on relevant sections of the collective bargaining contract, board of regents rules, and state law. The president called on O'Hara's department chairperson, Rhodes, to testify against O'Hara's charges. The union representative asked Rhodes many questions, but Rhodes refused to cite any specific reasons for the denial of O'Hara's request for tenure other than the fact that a peer committee had unanimously made that recommendation. He also refused to answer any substantive questions regarding the case, citing the secrecy of the tenure process. In addition, he claimed that, as a collective bargaining unit member, he had no official responsibility in the matter.

The representatives of the union and the president both countered that merely citing the unanimous vote against O'Hara's tenure application was an inadequate response by the chairperson. The president's representative added that although Rhodes was a unit member, a chairperson serves in a management role when deciding about promotion and tenure matters and should be responsible enough to aid the grievant in his right to due process. The representative added that any chairperson who does not accept supervisory responsibilities should meet with the dean to redefine the chairperson's role or else resign the position. He also pointed out that if the chairperson were not able to provide the evidence on which the rejection of O'Hara's request was based, the department would have to grant O'Hara tenure. "If, Mr. Rhodes, you persist in hiding behind the argument that you are in the unit, you will be stuck with a man you claim you do not want in your department," the president's representative said.

Other members of the tenure and promotion committee appeared at the meeting or were contacted directly by the president's representative. All but one member of the committee presented the same arguments as Rhodes and refused to give any substantive reason for opposing O'Hara's request for tenure.

The one exception, Jason Smith, chairperson of the department's tenure committee, stated that he did not feel strongly about O'Hara's request for tenure one way or the other. He considered O'Hara an "overly aggressive man who cared only about research and his own career" and stated that O'Hara had little loyalty to the department. The union representative asked Smith if any criteria such as "department loyalty" or "lack of aggressiveness" were included in the qualifications for tenure drawn up by the university or the board of regents. Smith said that he was not familiar with the specifics of tenure criteria found in official documents. His vote had been based on his intuition, on information he had received from students and colleagues, on his personal impression of the grievant, and on a careful examination of O'Hara's promotion file. He also noted that because of O'Hara's overconcern with research, he had a weak service record. Smith stated, however, that he intended to vote for O'Hara's tenure next year. [In this institution, candidates could be considered for tenure during the seventh year even though they have been formally notified of nonrenewal.] Smith felt that another year of seasoning would provide O'Hara with some much needed humility.

Before examining the president's decision about O'Hara's grievance, let us review certain relevant excerpts from the contract between the Florida Board of Regents and the faculty union, as well as excerpts from the Florida Administrative Code, the Board of Regents Manual.[2] Chairpersons should have some familiarity with the language of contracts, statutes, and rules that define the rights and responsibilities of faculty members and administrators. Note that the language of each is similar.

EXCERPTS FROM THE FLORIDA ADMINISTRATIVE CODE,
FLORIDA BOARD OF REGENTS MANUAL, 1979

> Each faculty member, tenured and non-tenured, shall be evaluated at least once annually on the basis of his or her individual total performance in fulfilling responsibilities to the university. The basic purpose of the evaluation is faculty improvement in the functions of teaching, research, service, and any other duties that may be assigned, with the resulting enhancement of learning, cultural advancement, and the production of new knowledge. This evaluation shall precede and be considered in recommendations and final decisions on tenure, promotions, and salary for tenured and non-tenured faculty members and on retention or non-renewal for non-tenured faculty members. [6C-5.05(1)(a)]

> When first employed, each faculty member shall be apprised of what is expected of him or her, generally, in terms of teaching, research and other creative activities, and service, and specifically if there are specific requirements and/or other duties involved. If and when these expectations change during the period of service of a faculty member, that faculty member shall be apprised of the change. [6C-5.05(1)(b)]

> Tenure is that condition attained by the faculty member through highly competent teaching and research, or other scholarly activities, service, and contributions to the university and to society .... [6C-5.06 (1)(a)]

> Each nomination for tenure shall be acted upon with careful consideration being given to the qualifications of the faculty member, including evaluations by colleagues and the immediate superior .... [6C-5.06(2)]

> Tenure recommendations shall be based on the institution's evaluation procedures. ... [6C-5.06(4)(a)]

> [The areas of performance to be evaluated are:]
>   (a) Teaching ....
>   (b) Research and Other Creative Activities—Contribution to the discovery of new Knowledge, development of new educational tech-

---

2. The BOR has contended that such BOR rules, state law, and state and federal constitutions do not, as such, constitute the subjects of a grievance. The union has continually cited BOR rules and state law in grievances. The issue has not yet been decided either in arbitration or litigation. Whether the BOR or the union eventually prevails in this issue, the chairperson should understand the material involved. Also nonunit grievants will likely utilize these citations.

niques, and other forms of creative activity shall be considered and evaluated. Evidence of research and other creative activity shall include, but not be limited to: published books; articles and papers in professional journals; . . . and current research and creative activity that has not yet resulted in publication, display, or performance. The evaluation shall include consideration of:

1. Productivity, including quality and quantity of what has been done during the year, and of the faculty member's long-term research and other creative programs and contributions, and;

2. Recognition by the academic or professional community of what is done.

(c) Service—Service shall include, but not be limited to, service on departmental, college, and university committees, councils, and senates; service in appropriate professional organizations; involvements in the organization and expedition of meetings, symposia, conferences, workshops; participation in radio and television on local, state, and national governmental boards, agencies and commissions. Only those activities which are related to a person's field of expertise or to the mission of the university shall be evaluated. [6C-5.05]

In evaluating the competency of a faculty member, primary assessment shall be in terms of his performance of the assigned duties and responsibilities, and such evaluation shall be given adequate consideration for the purpose of salary adjustments, promotions, re-employment, and tenure. . . . Flexible criteria for rewarding faculty members, consistent with the institution's educational goals and objectives, shall be established, which criteria shall include quality teaching as a major factor in determining salary adjustments, promotions, re-employment, or tenure. [Florida Statute 241.731, a portion of what is known as the Omnibus Education Act of 1973]

[Although not a part of the statute proper, the Title of the bill conveys the legislative intent] that no denial of promotions, salary adjustments, re-employment or tenure be solely for failure to do research, publish, or perform other scholarly activities. . . . [Laws of Florida, Chapter 73–338]

ARTICLES FROM THE FLORIDA BOARD OF REGENTS–UNITED FACULTY OF FLORIDA AGREEMENT, 1978–81

Article 8
APPOINTMENT
8.4 When first employed, each employee shall be apprised of what is expected, generally, in terms of teaching, research and other creative activities, and service, and specifically if there are specific requirements and/or other duties involved. If and when these expectations change during the period of service of the employee, that employee shall be apprised of the change.

Article 9
ASSIGNMENT OF RESPONSIBILITIES
9.1 The professional obligation is comprised of both scheduled

and non-scheduled activities. The parties recognize that it is a part of the professional responsibility of employees to carry out their duties in an appropriate manner and place. For example, while instructional activities, office hours and other duties and responsibilities may be required to be performed at a specific time and place, other non-scheduled activities are more appropriately performed in a manner and place determined by the employee.

9.2 Employees shall be apprised in writing, at the beginning of their employment and at the beginning of each year of employment thereafter, of the duties and responsibilities in teaching, research and other creative activities, service, and of any other specific duties and responsibilities assigned for that year.

9.3 Except for an assignment made at the beginning of an employee's employment, the person responsible for making an assignment shall contact the employee prior to making the final written assignment. Such contact shall also take place prior to changes which become necessary in an assignment, and such changes shall be specified in writing. The employee shall be granted, upon request, a conference with the person responsible for making the assignment to express concerns regarding:

    (a) the employee's qualifications and preferences; and

    (b) the character of the assignment, including the number of hours of instruction, the preparation required, whether the employee has taught the course in the past, the number of students and time required by course, whether travel to another location is required, the number of preparations required, the employee's assignments in other quarters, and the availability and adequacy of materials and equipment, secretarial services, student assistants, and other support services needed to perform the assignments.

An employee may request which three of four quarters the employee wishes to work and this request shall be honored where appropriate. Available assignments to a fourth quarter shall be offered equitably and as appropriate to qualified employees in sufficient time to allow voluntary acceptance or rejection.

9.4 . . . No employee's assignment should be arbitrarily and capriciously imposed. If an employee believes that the assignment has been so imposed, the employee should, prior to the effective date of the assignment, take the matter up with the individual who has the responsibility for making the assignment. If that discussion does not resolve the dispute, the employee may discuss the matter with the dean or other appropriate administrator. If no satisfactory resolution is accomplished after consultation with the dean or appropriate administrator, UFF may, prior to the effective dates of the assignment, refer the matter to a neutral umpire acceptable to both parties or, failing agreement, to a member of the Arbitration Panel in accordance with the procedures in Article 20.11. The umpire shall determine whether or not the employee's assignment has been arbitrarily and capriciously imposed. Upon a finding that the assignment has been so imposed, the President or designee shall take appropriate corrective action. . . .

Article 10
ANNUAL EMPLOYEE PERFORMANCE EVALUATION

10.1 Employees' performance shall be evaluated at least once annually and they shall be advised of the quarter during which such annual evaluation will be made. Personnel decisions shall take such annual evaluations into account, provided that personnel decisions need not be based solely on written employee performance evaluations.

10.2 The employee, if assigned teaching duties, shall be notified at least two weeks in advance of the date, time and place of any direct classroom observation or visitation made in connection with the employee's annual evaluation.

10.3 The evaluation shall be in writing and shall be discussed with the employee prior to being placed in the employee's evaluation file. The evaluation shall be signed by the person performing the evaluation, and by the person being evaluated, who may attach a concise comment to the evaluation. A copy of the evaluation shall be made available to the employee.

10.4 Those persons responsible for supervising and evaluating an employee shall endeavor to assist the employee in correcting any performance deficiencies reflected in the employee's annual evaluation.

10.5 The annual performance evaluation shall be based upon assigned duties, and shall take into account the nature of the assignments, in terms, where applicable, of:

(a) Teaching effectiveness, including effectiveness in presenting knowledge, information, and ideas by means or methods such as lecture, discussion, assignment and recitation, demonstration, laboratory exercise, practical experience, and direct consultation with students. The evaluation shall include consideration of effectiveness in imparting knowledge and skills, and effectiveness in stimulating students' critical thinking and/or creative abilities, and adherence to accepted standards of professional behavior in meeting responsibilities to students.

(b) Contribution to the discovery of new knowledge, development of new educational techniques, and other forms of creative activity. Evidence of research and other creative activity shall include, but not be limited to: published books; articles and papers in professional journals; musical compositions, paintings, sculpture; works of performing art; papers presented at meetings of professional societies; and current research and creative activity that has not yet resulted in publication, display, or performance. The evaluation shall include consideration of the employee's productivity, including the quality and quantity of what has been done during the year, and of the employee's long-term research and other creative programs and contributions; and recognition by the academic or professional community of what is done.

(c) Service on departmental, college, and university committees, councils, and senates; service in appropriate professional organizations; participation in meetings, symposia, conferences, workshops; participation in radio and television; and service on local, state and national governmental boards, agencies and commissions. Evaluation of service shall include consideration of contribution to:

   (1) the orderly and effective functioning of the employee's academic unit (program, department, school, college) and/or the total university;
   (2) the university community; and
   (3) the local, state, regional and national communities, and scholarly and professional associations.

   (d) Other assigned university duties, such as advising, counseling, and supervision of interns, or as described in a Position Description, if any, of the position held by the employee.

   (e) Such other responsibilities as may be appropriate to the assignment.

Article 11
PERSONNEL EVALUATION FILE

11.1 There shall be one file in which all written materials used in the evaluation process are maintained. When evaluations and personnel decisions are made, the only documents which may be used are those contained in that file. Employees shall be notified upon request of the location of the personnel evaluation file and the identity of the custodian.

11.2 An employee may examine the evaluation file upon reasonable advance notice, during the regular business hours of the office in which the file is kept, and under such conditions as are necessary to insure its integrity and safekeeping. Upon request and the payment of a reasonable fee for photocopying, an employee may obtain copies of any materials in the evaluation file and may attach a concise statement in response to any item therein. A person designated by the employee may examine that employee's evaluation file with the written authorization of the employee concerned and subject to the same limitations on access that are applicable to the employee.

11.4 In the event a grievance proceeds to arbitration, the Board, UFF, the arbitrator, and the grievant shall have the right to use copies of materials from the grievant's evaluation file relevant thereto in the arbitration proceedings.

11.5 No anonymous material shall be placed in an evaluation file, except for student evaluations which are part of a regular evaluation procedure of classroom instruction.

11.6 Evaluative materials or summaries thereof prepared by peer committees as part of a regular evaluation system may be placed in an evaluation file when signed by a representative of the committee.

11.7 Materials shown to be contrary to fact shall be removed from the file. This section shall not authorize the removal of materials from the evaluation file when there is a dispute concerning a matter of judgment or opinion rather than fact. Materials may also be removed pursuant to the resolution of a grievance.

11.8 Except as noted above, only university and Board officials responsible for the supervision or evaluation of employees shall have access to such files except upon order of a court of competent jurisdiction.

Article 15
TENURE PROCEDURE

15.1 A tenured employee may be terminated only for cause in accordance with the provisions of Article 16, Termination and Other Actions, or laid off only in accordance with the provisions of Article 13, Layoff and Recall.

15.3 Except for employees who, by virtue of prior service credited at time of appointment, are eligible for consideration earlier, an employee shall normally be considered for tenure during the fifth year of continuous service in a tenure-earning position or, at the option of the employee and with the concurrence of the appropriate administrative officials, during the sixth such year in a tenure-earning position. Part-time service of an employee employed at least three academic quarters out of four in any 12 month period shall be accumulated. For example, one year (at least three quarters) of half-time service shall be considered one-half year of service for purposes of tenure eligibility. By the end of six full years of service within the State University System, an employee eligible for tenure shall either be awarded tenure or given notice that further employment will not be offered. The notice shall be accompanied by a statement of reasons by the President or representative why tenure was not granted.

15.4 The decision of the Board to award or deny tenure shall be made by September 15 and the employee shall be notified in writing by the President within five days of the decision of the Board. An employee being considered for tenure prior to the sixth year may withdraw from consideration on or before April 15 without prejudice.

15.5 The performance of an employee during the entire term of employment at the institution shall be considered in determining whether to grant tenure.

Grievance Finding

A grievance report was drawn up by a member of the president's committee, which acted in lieu of a single representative. After reading the report, the president sent a letter to O'Hara indicating that he would recommend to the Board of Regents that O'Hara be granted tenure. The president cited the following reasons for his decision.

1. The documentary evidence indicated that without any doubt John O'Hara had fulfilled two of the three standard criteria for tenure, those of teaching and research, in an exceptional manner. These criteria, it should be noted, had been cited to all chairpersons by the dean of faculties in a memorandum dated 8 October 1976. [The established criteria for promotion and tenure are cited in Florida Statutes 241.731, the Florida Administrative Code Section 6C-5.06, and the BOR/UFF Collective Bargaining Agreement, Articles 10 and 15.]

2. Neither the members of the tenure and promotions committee nor the department chairperson could or would adequately explain their negative votes. They could not explain how O'Hara failed to meet the existing criteria for tenure. Only one member of the tenure committee even discussed the substance of the grievance, and that member's only relevant argument was that O'Hara's service record had been weak. O'Hara had been rated "satisfactory" in the area of service for three years and had not been given a service assignment during the next three years. If he had not performed the service responsibilities well, this weakness should have been noted on the evaluation forms. In addition, the chairperson should have counseled O'Hara about the matter and given him an opportunity to improve in that area.

3. Senior faculty members in the department had repeatedly rated O'Hara's performance in both research and teaching as "excellent," ratings that were recorded on the evaluation forms used for considering his requests for promotion and tenure. O'Hara had letters in his file from program leaders indicating strong support for his candidacy. In addition, he had received two "high merit" raises. [Criteria for such salary adjustments are the same as for promotion and tenure under Florida Statute 241.731.] The tenure committee could not adequately explain the inconsistency of O'Hara's continued high ratings and the negative tenure vote. If the committee had not changed the criteria on which its earlier judgments had been based, then this judgment was clearly inconsistent, arbitrary, and capricious. If the criteria had in fact changed, O'Hara had not been informed of the changes. Failure to inform him of such changes is in violation of Florida Administrative Code 6C-5.05 (1)(6) and Article 8.4 of the BOR/UFF agreement.

4. Before the vote on the tenure application, the department chairperson had at no time informed O'Hara of any inadequacies in his performance of his teaching, research, or service responsibilities. Following the tenure vote, the tenure committee and the department chairperson evaded O'Hara's request to cite specific inadequacies on his part so that he could work to overcome these immediately. By not informing O'Hara of his inadequacies, if in fact they existed at all, the department and the chairperson clearly violated both Florida Administrative Code/BOR Rule 6C-5.05 (1)(a), which states that those being considered for tenure shall be evaluated in order to improve "the functions of teaching, research, service," and Article 10.4 of the BOR/UFF Collective Bargaining Agreement, which states that "persons responsible for supervising and evaluating an employee shall endeavor to assist the employee in correcting any performance deficiencies. . . ." To refuse to reveal the inadequacies of the candidate clearly contradicts the purpose of the evaluation, namely faculty improvement.

Rhodes, the department chairperson, had the specific responsibility of ensuring that the department tenure committee not act in an arbitrary and capricious manner. Clearly, Smith, who chaired the tenure committee, had little knowledge of the official criteria. In addition, Rhodes, who had the responsibility of ensuring that O'Hara knew of his performance inadequacies in time to correct them before the tenure vote, had been totally unresponsive and continued to insist that a peer committee vote should not be overruled on any grounds. This argument was rejected since it would deny O'Hara his due process in any grievance or appeal process following a peer committee vote. In addition, Rhodes argued that the BOR/UFF Agreement provisions were new and that therefore it was unnecessary to follow them this year. When it was pointed out to him that these provisions had recapitulated long-standing Board of Regents rules, university rules, and state law, he claimed that these rules had not been traditionally followed. In all, Rhodes's approach to the tenure process and the appeal procedure seemed to be at best cavalier. O'Hara should not be penalized because of his chairperson's poor judgment and inadequate leadership.

5. Rhodes's position that as a chairperson in the bargaining unit he had no responsibility in the matter was rejected. This argument is not unique. Some members of the state university system collective bargaining unit who supervise and evaluate other members have filed grievances stating that they should no longer have the obligation to evaluate members of their own bargaining unit. The viewpoint is invalid since the collective bargaining contract was never intended to change the assignment of any unit members. The collective bargaining agreement also gives the administration the right to make assignments and to determine the types of duties and responsibilities. Faculty members in the unit have, of course, traditionally taken on management roles such as the evaluation of peers for tenure and promotion purposes. Chairpersons should continue in a similar manner.

The president concluded that the administration of the department of educational foundations violated both the letter and the spirit of the BOR/UFF Collective Bargaining Agreement, Florida Statute (241.731), Board of Regents rules, and reasonable standards of academic administrative judgment. He would add O'Hara's name to the recommended tenure list and officially forward it to the Board of Regents.

After the case was completed and the decision rendered, other facts that revealed the source of O'Hara's actual problems with his colleagues came to light. O'Hara's tenure was opposed primarily because his peers resented his large grants and because he made little effort to include any of them in his bounty. In fact, he did invite several members from another department within the university to join him in his work. Although O'Hara had rejected collaboration with his department colleagues, he had nevertheless fulfilled all the requirements for tenure. Incidentally, O'Hara had never been specifically told of the department's resentment, and neither the union's representative nor the president's representative had even surmised the crux of the problem.

Other Case Studies

Following are brief descriptions of other grievances filed under a variety of conditions. Some of them have been resolved; others have not. These abbreviated case studies are examples of the kinds of grievances chairpersons might face, regardless of whether a union contract exists.

Grievance Heard before a Faculty Senate Committee

The following grievance was processed through university procedures at an institution that had no collective bargaining contract.

Three associate professors in the classics department argued that the dean had rejected their promotion requests even though each of them had fulfilled all the department's requirements for promotion. In a subsequent memo, the dean noted that the classics department promotion committee did not recommend any of the three applicants for promotion and that the chairperson supported the committee's recommendation. In response to the grievants' requests for the reasons for not being promoted, the dean replied that the information he had received from the department chairperson indicated that none had adequate publishing records.

In the formal grievance the candidates for promotion pointed out, with substantial supporting evidence, that the publishing records of previously promoted candidates were rarely stronger than their own records and often appeared somewhat weaker. In addition, they noted that the only senior woman in the department was promoted, even though she had a publishing record considerably weaker than any of theirs. They claimed that she was promoted because of affirmative action pressure. The grievants also pointed out that the classics department consisted mostly of full professors; that the department's promotion and tenure committee was made up entirely of full professors; that full professors in the department taught half as many hours as associate professors; and that many in the department believed that if the associate professors were promoted, the full professors would have to increase their teaching loads in order to maintain department productivity.

The faculty senate was asked to establish an intrauniversity committee to hear the grievances and to make a recommendation to the university president. The committee established by the senate consisted of four full professors and one assistant professor. In addition to the points already discussed, it considered the following counterarguments: the associate professors were hired as part of a quality improvement program that was designed to upgrade the department; they were involved in developing the changes in promotion and tenure criteria; and the allegations that the full professors were motivated by selfish, personal considerations were untrue.

The committee rejected the grievance. The grievants then threatened a lawsuit, alleging that the senate committee was stacked against them. To avoid an acrimonious public airing of the controversy, the university president agreed to promote two of the associate professors and to consider the third application the following year.

Grievance Heard before a State Hearing Officer

The following dispute occurred at a state university that had no collective bargaining contract. The case was eventually heard before a state hearing officer.

The university hired Howard Gibson to serve as director of the university art gallery and as assistant professor of fine arts. At the time the department chairperson, Roger Smythe, assured Gibson that an assistant gallery director would be employed within six months. The assistant director, however, was never employed. In addition to administering the gallery and teaching, Gibson was expected to create and display his own works on the same basis as other members of the art department. Some of his associates asserted that Gibson had the heaviest workload in the department.

Four years after Gibson's appointment, the art department evaluated its untenured faculty members. Gibson was not formally informed that this evaluation was going to take place; therefore he did not submit any of his material. He later indicated that he thought the session was being held only to review the files of those faculty members being considered for tenure. The committee voted 7 to 2 in favor of abolishing Gibson's position. The chairperson's report to the dean stated: "The position is simply too big for any one person to handle. Since the administration cannot provide the funds for the department to employ an assistant gallery director, we must do away with this aspect of our program entirely." Gibson's contract was then not renewed.

After the nonrenewal, several students circulated a petition that endorsed Gibson's retention and that received considerable student support. Four members of the department's evaluation committee, each of whom had voted to abolish Gibson's position, stated that they had never intended to recommend nonrenewal of his contract and would have voted against the measure if they had understood that it would result in his termination. Nevertheless, the university administration acted in accordance with Smythe's recommendation, and Gibson was sent a notice of nonrenewal. He filed a grievance that resulted in a formal hearing, with a state-appointed hearing officer serving as an umpire. The officer's decision was not binding but merely served as a recommendation to the president.

Smythe, the chairperson, was the administration's chief witness and the defender of his department's recommendation. The university administration depended on Smythe's verbal and documentary evidence in putting together its case. The chairperson was rigorously cross-examined by the grievant's attorney. Members of Smythe's department, some students, and some upper-level administrators attended the meeting. Charles Jones, university attorney, represented the administration in the hearing. Jones requested and received from the department chairperson evidence in support of Gibson's termination.

Gibson's attorney was extremely successful in buttressing the argument that his client had not been properly informed of the nature of the evaluation. He also had several committee members testify that their vote to abolish the position of allery director was not a vote to abolish Gibson, whose abilities they respected and admired. The hearing officer's decision was in Gibson's favor. He asserted that the grievant's rights to due process were violated in several ways and that even though the university had the right to abolish the position of gallery director, it did not have the right to terminate Gibson's employment in a manner inconsistent with established university practice. The university accepted the recommendation of the hearing officer and renewed Gibson's contract.

Potential Grievance at a Private University with No Collective Bargaining Contract

Mary Ellis, a member of the social work department, complained to her chairperson that she had been discriminated against. First, she had received no merit pay during the previous four years. Although she admitted that she had not published a great deal, Ellis pointed out that the department's thrust had been toward teaching and service and that she excelled in both areas. In addition, Ellis's publishing record was no weaker than those of other department members who had received higher salary increases. She therefore felt she was entitled to merit pay.

Ellis also protested that she had not been treated fairly in her teaching assignments. Although her course load was not heavier than that assigned to other department members, she was denied her request to teach late afternoon courses. Late classes in her department constituted an overload and provided extra pay. The late afternoon courses were applied courses taken by students already employed in the field, and Ellis did not have expertise in the applied area.

Ellis basically supported her department's democratic tradition of forwarding to the dean, directly and unchanged, the salary recommendations of an elected committee. An elected committee also determined the annual assignment. Ellis claimed, however, that faculty members with Master of Social Work degrees dominated all key department committees and received "high merit" raises at the expense of faculty members with Ph.D.'s in fields other than social work. Ellis holds a Ph.D. in sociology.

Discussing the matter with the dean, the chairperson asserted that since Ellis's degree was in sociology and her background was strong in research methodology, he expected her to have a stronger publication record than her colleagues. The dean suggested that the chairperson review Ellis's case carefully, since there seemed to be some merit to her argument. The dean further stressed the need for documenting the facts of the case in the event of a formal grievance, which could conceivably end up in court if the problem were not satisfactorily resolved. He urged the chairperson to advise Ellis about what she might do to upgrade her expertise so that she could teach some applied courses. He also suggested that the chairperson assign a research role as part of Ellis's workload.

The chairperson followed the dean's advice and met with Ellis several times to discuss her concerns. Ellis made an earnest attempt to heed the chairperson's suggestions and qualified for a merit raise the next year.

Potential Grievance under a Union Contract

Bosley Cowpens had been an assistant professor of history for five years. The department tenure committee voted 7 to 2 against his being granted tenure in the department, and he contemplated filing a grievance. Although the department placed a high priority on research, Cowpens had only a mediocre publishing record. His record showed improvement, but the improvement did not satisfy the department committee. He claimed that his publication record for the last two years was equal to the record of two senior tenured professors. The department had thirty members, sixteen of whom were tenured. On the basis of student evaluations, Cowpens's teaching record was below the department average. Moreover, on numerous occasions he had failed to meet his classes, and a letter of reprimand concerning his unexcused absences was on file. He did, however, have a small but loyal following among the students. His service record showed an enormous amount of time and effort spent on the United Fund campaign but very little service to the profession or department.

Cowpens claimed that the real reason for his failure to gain promotion was his iconoclastic behavior on committees. The promotion and tenure committee called his behavior abrasive and reported that he had withdrawn from committee work whenever he had quarreled with other members. The chairperson had discussed his previous unsatisfactory annual evaluations with him, but Cowpens had refused to accept the substance of the evaluation. He was kept on, according to the chairperson, in the hope that his performance would improve, but the degree of improvement had not been deemed satisfactory. The chairperson kept records of his discussions and his attempts to counsel Cowpens and informed him of his record keeping.

Cowpens insisted that he was being denied tenure because he was not a team player and because of personality differences with other faculty members. He also insisted that his community service deserved to be recognized and that his teaching was as good as that of many other department members.

The department union representative, a close friend of Cowpens, expressed his willingness to support the assistant professor if he wanted to file a grievance. The chairperson feared that Cowpens, if he were not granted tenure, would file a formal grievance and would receive union support. Nevertheless, the chairperson was determined to support the findings of the tenure committee. He felt confident that the department committee was properly constituted, had followed established procedures, and was justified in its decision.

The chairperson then met with the university (not the department) union representative to discuss the issue. Despite the fact that Cowpens was counting on union backing, the union, in this instance, decided not to support a faculty member whose case was so weak and informed Cowpens accordingly. Cowpens received notice of nonrenewal of his contract. A grievance was never filed.

By anticipating the kinds of personnel problems that are occurring in postsecondary education, by understanding the nature of grievance mechanisms and the chairperson's role in them, and by becoming familiar with the way rulings, recommendations, and settlements occur, chairpersons can prevent many potential grievances. Personnel problems, however, will be with us as long as there are bosses and workers, managers and employees, and administrators and faculty members. Thus there will always be grievances, whether a collective bargaining contract exists or not. Formal bargaining may result in a greater number of officially filed grievances, but unofficial grievances have always existed.

Chairpersons will no doubt see some changes in their roles as a result either of collective bargaining or of conscientious support of state law and institutional personnel rules. (The latter often emerges when a collective bargaining contract seems probable.) Chairpersons will give greater attention to formal evaluations and personnel decisions and will thus be faced with more paperwork. They will have to provide evidence and appear at various kinds of hearings, while administrators will be transmitting more rules and directives to the department level. Chairpersons will assume the task, often avoided in the past, of counseling less productive department members and suggesting ways to improve their work. If chairpersons avoid such tasks or attempt to reject them because they see themselves as faculty members and not administrators, the administration will shift the position of chairperson upwards into the management bureaucracy.

Such trends have not occurred solely because of collective bargaining. For example, institutions of higher education, with or without collective bargaining, have become increasingly centralized. In addition, chairpersons have always had both academic and administrative responsibilities; they were sometimes colleagues and sometimes bosses. Thus some chairpersons have always perceived themselves as centaur-like creatures—half man and half beast. Whether the beast is the management half or the employee half depends on the chairperson's philosophy.

Questions

1. The following questions are based on the O'Hara case:
   a) Distinguish between a grievance and a complaint according to the definitions given in the chapter.
   b) How was the union contract violated in O'Hara's case?
   c) What instructions should the department chairperson have given the tenure and promotion committee about its charge as well as about the contract?
   d) What might the chairperson have done in order to avoid the situation? What should have been his reaction to the 9–0 vote against O'Hara?
   e) What effect will the retention of O'Hara now have on the department?
2. The following questions are based on the Gibson case:
   a) How might Chairperson Smythe have countered the argument that the department committee members did not understand what they were voting on?
   b) If the university had no clear policy or rules regarding evaluation and review of faculty members, on what grounds could Gibson have filed a grievance?
3. The following questions are based on the Ellis case:
   a) As department chairperson, how would you have attempted to resolve this problem?
   b) What specific measures might a chairperson institute within a department in order to keep this type of problem from occurring?
4. The following questions are based on the Cowpens case:
   a) If Cowpens had filed a grievance, he probably would have

lost. If you were the chairperson, what arguments would you use to persuade Cowpens to resign?

b) Under what altered circumstances might Cowpens have won a grievance?

5. If a college or university has no faculty union and its board of trustees prefers not to have one, what can the administration do to bolster the faculty members' feeling of security so that they might not feel the need for union representation?

6. If a college or university has a faculty union and wants to keep grievances to a minimum, how should administrators and department chairpersons deal with faculty problems on a continuing basis so that faculty members will not feel the need or the urge to file grievances?

References

Benewitz, Maurice C., and Mannix, Thomas M. "Grievance Procedure in Higher Education Contracts." *Community and Junior College Journal,* December 1974–January 1975, pp. 22–24.

Bernstein, Merton C., et al. "Arbitration of Faculty Grievances: A Report of a Joint Subcommittee of Subcommittee A and N." *AAUP Bulletin,* Summer 1973, pp. 168–70.

Betten, Neil, and Oldson, William. *Contract Administration: From Grievance to Arbitration.* Tallahassee: UFF/Florida AFL-CIO Publications, 1978.

Edmondson, William Fred. "Grievance Arbitration and Its Role in the Settlement of Professional Negotiation Disputes in Higher Education." Ed.D. dissertation, University of Mississippi, 1973.

Ellis, John M. "Grievance Procedures: Real and Ideal." *New Directions for Higher Education,* Autumn 1974, pp. 63–76.

Ferguson, Tracy H., and Bergan, William L. "Grievance Arbitration Procedures and Contract Administration." *Journal of College and University Law,* Summer 1974, pp. 371–91.

Kelley, Edward P., Jr., and Rodriguez, Robert L. "Observations on Collective Bargaining: Implications for Academic Management." *Liberal Education,* March 1977, pp. 102–117.

Leslie, David W. "Impact of Collective Bargaining on Conflict Resolution Practices." Research Summary no. 2. Washington, D.C.: Academic Collective Bargaining Information Service, 1975.

Mannix, Thomas M. "Community College Grievance Procedures: A Review of Contract Content in 94 Colleges." *Journal of the College and University Personnel Association,* April 1974, pp. 23–40.

Plyler, Chris Parnell. "The Grievance Appeals Process in the State University System of Florida: A Case Study." Ph.D. dissertation, Florida State University, 1978.

Ruff, Raymond T., Jr. "A Description and Analysis of Faculty Grievances and Faculty Grievance Procedures in New York State Community Colleges." Ph.D. dissertation, State University of New York at Buffalo, 1972.

Satryb, Ronald P. "The Art of Settling Grievances: A Study in Campus Conflict Resolution." Special Report no. 27. Washington, D.C.: Academic Collective Bargaining Information Service, 1976.

————. "Evolution of the S.U.N.Y. Grievance Procedure from the First Contract to the Second." *Journal of the College and University Personnel Association*, July/August 1975, pp. 46–52.

————. "Faculty Grievance at S.U.N.Y.: The First Two Years under a Negotiated Contract." Special Report no. 10. Washington, D.C.: Academic Collective Bargaining Information Service, 1974.

Dealing with Conflict
and Maintaining Faculty Morale

||||| |||||||||||||||||||||||||||||||||||||||||||||||||||||||||||||||||||||||||||||||||||||||||||||||||||||||||||||||||||||||||||||||||||||||||||

Conflict, according to many department chairpersons, is something that happens in someone else's department. Academicians with preconceptions about harmonious campus life are often reluctant to speak or even think about discord and dissension in their immediate environment. Those who think of conflict as abnormal or aberrant tend to shun the subject. Some chairpersons view conflict in their department uneasily and feel that it is somehow their fault. Some chairpersons are unaware that conflict exists because they are so awe-inspiring that their faculty members conceal it from them. Even though conflict is a subject academicians do not like to talk about, they need to accept the idea that it can occur.

There seems to be an inverse relationship between the degree of conflict in a department and the level of morale: the more conflict, the lower the morale; the less conflict, the higher the morale. Although this discussion focuses primarily on types of conflict that may occur in an academic department, it also touches on promoting and maintaining good morale. Reducing conflict will not automatically raise faculty morale, but a good level of morale cannot exist in a department where energies are consumed by serious conflict.

The chairperson ought to be concerned about conflict within the department, because once it occurs, it tends to fester and grow. Conflict is divisive; it pits individual faculty members against each other and wastes time and effort that are best used in more creative endeavors. It often develops a dynamic and logic of its own. A conflict can polarize a department, forcing members into competing groups. In extreme cases, destructive and hostile behavior can destroy a department's effectiveness. Chairpersons who learn to identify and diagnose conflict at an early stage and who help their departments deal with it effectively fulfill one of the most difficult requirements of their role.

The term *conflict* is used here in a variety of ways. In psychology the term refers to the inner struggle between desires requiring immediate gratification and desires that can only be met by deferring the immediate in order to gain long-term benefits. For the purposes of this discussion, the term *inner conflict* will be used to describe tension, anxiety, turmoil, and frustration that can impair a person's activities but that do not emerge as interpersonal conflict. Webster's definition—"competitive or opposing action of incompatibles"—reflects a more common understanding of the term. Generally a disagreement becomes a conflict when it goes beyond the normal intellectual differences that characterize academic life. Serious conflict is often accompanied by feelings of fear, anxiety, or anger, and is often evidenced by intemperate or abusive language and overtly hostile actions.

Conflict may be defined either as an incident or as a process. As an incident, it occurs as a disagreement between two persons or parties in which the first acts in a way that the second perceives to be detrimental to the latter's interests and designed to force some undesired action. As a process, conflict is manifested in a series of actions by two persons or groups in which each person or group tries to thwart the other's purposes or prevent satisfaction of the other's interests. In essence, conflict is a struggle for control of another person's behavior.

Types of Conflict

Departments are made up of intelligent persons who are often ambitious, strong-willed, and competitive. Even though academicians are usually committed to the use of reason in problem solving and to the model of collegiality in interpersonal relations, conflict often arises either through personality clashes or as a result of institutional demands on faculty members. Conflict within departments can usually be categorized as one of four distinct types: (1) inner conflict; (2) conflict between employer and employee; (3) conflict among faculty members; and (4) conflict between faculty members and students.

Inner conflict concerns a person's feelings. It does not consist of a set of observable behaviors but has to do with frustrations and anxieties that a person feels and that can affect his or her normal functioning. For example, a faculty member who has long been a successful teacher but whose research skills are undeveloped fails to get promotions or merit increases as the department becomes more research oriented. He feels that the rules have been changed in the middle of his game and is angry and bitter. He withdraws from social contacts with other faculty members.

Disputes arising over matters such as promotion, tenure, merit pay, perquisites, work assignments, annual evaluations, and working conditions can usually be classified as employer-employee conflicts. These may involve faculty members and administrators, staff persons and administrators, or other types of employees and supervisors. Chairpersons who try to increase productivity by asking their faculty members to teach more or larger classes without discussing the matter with them beforehand can find themselves embroiled in employer-employee conflicts.

Conflict among faculty members can be the result of minor personality clashes or perceived inequities. Frequently such conflict arises when the egalitarian workload model is violated either by allocating varying awards for similar workloads or by allocating similar rewards for varying workloads. In the academic context, sorting out conflicting claims is extremely difficult, especially when the privileges of rank are considered. Many institutions have an uncodified, unwritten tradition that allows the senior faculty lighter course loads and more graduate courses. A more serious kind of conflict among faculty members is related to academic matters—e.g., what activities are worthwhile and what methodologies and techniques are best. Conflicts concerning the practice of the discipline are very difficult to resolve and sometimes lead to a kind of academic warfare in which entire factions are banished from the department.

Conflict between faculty members and students commonly begins either with student complaints about a faculty member's teaching performance or grading practices or with a faculty member's charge of cheating or plagiarism. Student complaints about faculty members sometimes grow into wholesale protests or demonstrations, especially when students feel that their right to due process has been violated.

In all types of conflict the disagreement can concern territory, clientele, and intergroup relations. Debates over humankind's territorial nature aside, conflict often does involve territory or "turf." Administrators, faculty members, and students at times all identify certain subjects, courses, or areas as exclusively their own and attempt to defend them against encroachment by others. Territorial disputes can break out over such seemingly trivial matters as the decision to assign some persons to windowless offices. Disagreements can arise when a new clientele is identified—as, for example, when a department adopts an off-campus program and faculty members argue with each other about who must teach in the program. Faculty members might also quarrel over a particularly able student, with whom they all may want to work, or a particularly poor student, with whom no one may want to work. Students may protest being assigned to particular faculty members.

Conflict in intergroup relations is often ideological. It may develop when various factions argue about what constitutes the proper methodology of a discipline. Intergroup conflict can occur when students organize and press demands. Student activism usually involves more than a department, however, and thus will not be discussed here. Other frequent sources of intergroup conflict in the academic environment involve relations between one department and another or relations between the university and the department. Neither of these sources of conflict is especially relevant to this discussion, but they are mentioned because the chairperson may be involved in such disputes. When departments are reviewed by policy councils or as part of accountability procedures, the chairperson may be thrust into the role of leading the struggle for the department's survival.

Attitudes toward Conflict

The way a person acts in a conflict situation may well be related to his or her attitude toward conflict. These attitudes vary considerably from person to person. Institutions in general and colleges and universities in particular also have "attitudes" toward conflict that are represented in institutional policy and procedure. Social theorists have, since antiquity, developed different views on the matter that are still with us.

Let us examine two extreme views and see how they are reflected in present-day approaches. The first, the "Rousseauian" perspective, assumes that men and women are innately good, but that this goodness is perverted by society. Hence, conflict is unnatural. If society's unjust conditions and institutions were removed and humanity's natural goodness allowed to emerge, conflict would disappear. The opposite view—which might be called an "original sin" view or, in a more secular context, a Hobbesian view—assumes that each person attempts to maximize his or her goods and opportunities until he or she is stopped by someone else who is doing the same thing. In this view, conflict is natural as well as normal. Improving social conditions will not reduce conflict and might even increase it. Conflict is regulated by strict rules and procedures and accompanying sanctions.

These two views are, of course, mutually exclusive. While neither is intended as an empirically verifiable description of reality, these and similar attitudes toward conflict are prevalent. From these examples we can say that a person's behavior in conflict situations is related to his or her attitudes and beliefs about the nature of conflict and its role in human affairs.

J. Victor Baldridge, in *Power and Conflict in the University*, identifies three models of university governance based on attitudes toward conflict. The first governance model, the *collegial model*, views conflict as abnormal. This view holds that a true community of scholars would eliminate conflict altogether. When disagreements arise, they are solved by deliberation and reason, not by negotiation and arbitration. Moreover, professors are civilized men and women, not brawlers, who prefer to live in an atmosphere of harmonious consensus.

The second model, the *bureaucratic model*, also views conflict as abnormal. This model of governance, however, assumes that conflicts will occur but that they will be controlled by bureaucratic sanctions. Although the bureaucratic model does not adequately describe traditional faculty behavior in most colleges and universities, it seems to be increasingly appropriate in large systems where collective bargaining is practiced and where guides to organizational behavior are increasingly codified.

The third model, the *political model*, accepts conflict as a normal part of organizational life. This model assumes that contention among competing interests precedes almost any policy change. In the language of the model, the social structure of the university is not a homogeneous community of scholars. Instead, the professional community is said to be pluralistic, fractured into subcultures and divergent interest groups, and composed of fairly autonomous professional practitioners. The general style of decision making and policy development involves negotiation, political influence, and bargaining (i.e., making trade-offs). Political influence is attained by persuading and mobilizing persons of like opinion into an interest group or faction. It assumes neither a community of professional interests nor agreement about the ends of higher education beyond the need to preserve academic freedom.

To view the collegial, bureaucratic, and political governance models as ideal types, abstracted from reality, is helpful. Most institutions have elements of all three models within them, and members of the institutions often behave in ways that are consistent with the model to which they personally subscribe. Comparing the governance models to the attitudes toward conflict, the collegial model seems compatible with the Rousseauian "natural goodness" attitude; the bureaucratic model, which assumes that people must be constantly watched and supervised, is compatible with the Hobbesian model, which sees people as inherently selfish.

The three models also emphasize communication and its role. The collegial model stresses the importance and value of communication in consensual decision making. The bureaucratic model emphasizes the need for clear channels of communication to avoid mistakes and get the messages through. The political model rejects the view that conflict is due to misunderstandings and communications breakdowns and labels such belief "the communications fallacy." Indeed, the political model, while admitting the desirability of authentic communication, denies that communication is in itself sufficient to reduce conflict. Even though two disputants may clearly understand each other, such understanding well may lead to increased rather than reduced hostility, as may a clear communication that one side is losing and the other winning. In fact, the perception of "them" winning and "us" losing almost always precedes conflict. The political model sees conflict resolution essentially as a trading off of advantages and favors in a process called "rational selfishness."

A continuum reflecting the various stages of conflict within a department—from an anarchic state of total conflict at one end to a bland and blissful state of total cooperation at the other—can easily be constructed (see figure 9.1).

| Total Conflict | Controlled Conflict | Competition | Collaboration | Total Cooperation |

Fig. 9.1. Department conflict continuum

One interesting aspect of this continuum is the central position of competition. Friendly competition lies to the right of center; unfriendly competition lies to the left of center. On the continuum, the balance point is the competitive state, and the implication is that life in an academic department goes on in a state of nonconflictual competition. Conflict can be constructive when it enables antagonists to make their beliefs and dissatisfactions explicit, thus clearing the air. In such a case, a step toward problem solving has been taken, and, it is generally agreed, conflict ought to be reduced to problem solving.

Stages of Conflict

Another way of understanding conflict is to view it as a series of stages that make up a conflict episode. This theory permits taking a developmental view of conflict and treating the separate stages individually. Each stage, it should be noted, contains the elements of the preceding stages as well as elements of its own.

The first stage is called *latent conflict*. In this stage the conditions are being set for future conflict. Common sources of conflict include competition for scarce resources, drives for autonomy, divergence of individual goals, incompatible role expectations, and the frustrations of a person or group resulting from events beyond its control.

Latent conflict, deriving from the causes mentioned above, exists in almost every department in every college and university in the country. We need hardly discuss competition for scarce resources, which has characterized academic affairs for the last decade. Drives for autonomy or independence can be interpreted in several ways: faculty members can become frustrated when they feel that they have no role in the department's decision-making process; a department chairperson may desire more authority than the administration is willing to delegate; a faculty member may claim the right to teach anything she sees fit, even while teaching a section of a colleague's course. (Faculty members who pursue their own goals without regard for others in the department are common figures, often creating dissension and frustration by their tactics.) Faculty members serve as teachers, researchers, providers of service, and, sometimes, as administrators, and the demands of these many roles can often lead to frustration and conflict. So too can the role expectations of the faculty of professional schools when it clashes with the liberal arts faculty at promotion committee meetings. Finally, of course, many academicians feel they are losing control of their professional lives.

This stage of conflict is called "latent" because the conditions that lead to conflict are present but, for a variety of reasons, are suppressed. Some persons avoid conflict, perhaps because it can be painful and threatening, and ignore or withdraw from a situation that promises to erupt. Clearly, within any department there are many examples of latent conflict.

The next stage of conflict is called *perceived conflict*. In this stage, one element from the latency stage emerges as problematic. The persons involved are aware of a disagreement but do not yet feel tense or anxious. This stage is sometimes called the "semantic" conflict stage, because the perception of conflict comes from information that may be erroneous or incomplete. At this stage, *if* the perception really comes from misinformation, improved communications may nip a crisis in the bud. If the information, once clarified, proves the perception correct, however, the conflict can rapidly move on to the next stage, *felt conflict*. Felt conflict moves beyond intellectual awareness to a personalized feeling of anxiety and tension. Some persons at this stage withdraw and become uncommunicative. Nevertheless, once tension, unease, and anxiety emerge, the progression to open conflict is simple.

The stage of open conflict, often called the *manifest conflict* stage, is marked by open aggression, generally verbal but occasionally physical. Instances of faculty members engaging in physically aggressive behaviors are few but not unheard of. Occasionally, a frustrated student will attack a faculty member whom he sees as having prevented him from achieving his goals.

The final stage is *conflict aftermath*. Every conflict ultimately comes to an end. The conflict may not have been satisfactorily resolved, but hostilities have simply ceased. Sometimes one side is clearly victorious. Sometimes an external party may intervene and impose a settlement. Sometimes a genuine solution satisfactorily to every party is achieved. Unfortunately, many a conflict aftermath merely sets the stage for a new conflict.

Understanding conflict as a process that encompasses several stages can help the chairperson recognize the importance of maintaining department morale. The subject of maintaining morale will be discussed in some detail here because low morale is often an indication that conflict is moving from the latency stage to a higher stage. Moreover, much conflict, especially inner conflict, comes from the perception that the interests of human beings are pitted against the interests of the system. The feeling that the system, whatever *system* means, is becoming larger, more powerful and more oppressive, and that the person is powerless to do much to oppose it contributes to the anxiety and frustration that lead to conflict.

Diagnosing and Dealing with Conflict

A number of factors that affect department morale have been identified. The chairperson has little control over many of these, but he or she can nevertheless try to minimize the feelings of dissatisfaction that lead to inner conflict. Two of these factors are the salary and working conditions of the department members. Faculty members can easily become depressed about the fact that their income declines in inflationary times. They also resent the imposition of heavier teaching loads or larger classes. Although the chairperson cannot magically produce salary increases for the entire department, he or she can reduce resentment by showing that, compared with departments elsewhere, the department is not doing as badly as its members think. If the department actually is in a poor position compared with similar departments in other institutions or other departments in the university, the chairperson can boost morale by showing that he or she is actively lobbying for a fair share of the funds available. Similarly, faculty members often feel that they are being discriminated against with respect to the allocation of travel funds. Again, the chairperson should be able to show them that they are no worse off than anyone else in the college or the institution.

Another factor that contributes to low department morale is the sense of ever-increasing bureaucratization—the proliferation of meaningless rules and regulations and increasing outside pressure on the department. The chairperson can raise department morale by showing that he or she opposes the proliferation of administrative trivia. When the chairperson is seen as the defender of the department's welfare, he or she helps create a climate of solidarity within the department. Faculty members will come to feel that by sticking together in the face of adversity they can overcome some of the difficulties that appear insurmountable.

A common source of frustration and inner conflict for faculty members is the feeling that they are losing control over crucial department decisions affecting their future. One way to reduce feelings of alienation and powerlessness is to establish a set of policies within a department that permit the faculty to participate in the decision-making process. There should be formal means for allowing debate over department policy and procedures, such as faculty meetings that allow open discussion and debate. Written reports on policy decisions should contain evidence that a variety of points of view have been reviewed. In this way, the chairperson can show that minority opinions have been considered and respected.

Conflict can be reduced when the lines of authority and responsibility in the department are clarified. For example, a chairperson assigned a faculty member the task of making up teaching schedules for the entire department but failed to inform the department members that he had given this responsibility to one of their colleagues. When the schedule was distributed, the faculty members were confused and resentful. Had the chairperson informed the faculty that he had delegated this task and had he instructed the schedule maker to consult with each member of the department, this conflict would have been avoided. Whenever a chairperson delegates administrative responsibility to faculty or staff members, the lines of authority must be clarified.

Department meetings should allow open confrontation over controversial issues. Confrontation need not lead to destructive conflict. Free debate and free expression can ensure a fair hearing for diverse viewpoints about significant issues. Debate can also bring out conflicts at an early stage of development, allowing them to be dealt with before they become critical. The chairperson can help develop an atmosphere of commitment to orderly change within the department. Autocratic methods should not be advocated, and both majority opinions and minority rights should be respected and upheld.

This discussion of minimizing latent and inner conflict has emphasized what a chairperson can do to identify conflict before it becomes destructive. Chairpersons are advised to establish an atmosphere that prevents conflict from escalating, since conflict is difficult to resolve once the department is polarized. A chairperson who does not hear of conflicts—particularly a chairperson of a large department, where the probability of their existence is high—should ask whether there is something about his or her administrative style that causes the faculty, staff, and students to avoid discussing difficult situations. Perhaps the chairperson is perceived as too authoritarian or unyielding. If so, the chairperson might begin to visit briefly but regularly with every member of the faculty and staff. These visits, which may be held once a month, should be on a one-to-one basis and should not be held in the chairperson's office. Meetings on neutral ground, such as a faculty club or restaurant, or on the faculty member's turf, such as his or her office or home, are much less threatening. The purpose of the meetings is not to solve problems but to listen and look for the emergence of latent or inner conflict.

One skill the chairperson can learn is the technique of "active listening," developed by Thomas Gordon, which is useful for discovering latent conflict. Active listening is an extremely effective communications technique that is used by many thousands of parents. Academicians have some difficulty with the technique because the listener does not lecture, teach, give logical arguments, judge, criticize, question, interpret, analyze, or diagnose. In other words, all the logical and conceptual skills that are indispensable to a university career are temporarily put aside. Active listening consists of the listener (or receiver) "feeding back only what he feels the sender's message meant—nothing more, nothing less."[1]

By listening patiently and "feeding back" the feelings of the speaker, chairpersons may promote a good relationship between themselves and their faculty, facilitate problem solving, and, in general, foster a cooperative spirit in the department. To be an effective listener, the chairperson must want to be helpful, believe in the speaker's sincerity, and be willing to accept the speaker as a fellow human being. A chairperson who gets good results by listening quietly, with an occasional empathetic grunt and a few gestures showing he understands the speaker's feelings, would be well advised to read Gordon's book in order to perfect the listening technique.

Occasionally, conflict in a department may be related to a faculty member's mental state. Recent research has examined and brought to the public consciousness the existence of "life crises" that most people undergo. The chairperson should be sensitive to each faculty member's state of mind. Reading some of the literature on life stages, such as Levinson's *The Seasons of a Man's Life* or Sheehy's *Passages*, can help the chairperson understand some of the personal crises that can lead to unhappiness and consequent strife within a department. Many personal crises, such as divorce or a death in the family, can temporarily impair or disrupt a faculty member's normal functioning. The chairperson can arrange for substitutes in the classroom and on committees. But how long can a chairperson cover for a faculty member? There are no hard and fast rules. Some persons take longer to recover from crises than do others. The chairperson who is thoroughly aware of university rules and policies on leaves of absence and sick leaves can support faculty members in times of personal adversity.

Academicians, like all professionals, may suffer from serious personality disorders or develop patterns of behavior that are disruptive or dangerous. The chairperson must be able to distin-

---

1. Thomas Gordon, *Parent Effectiveness Training* (New York; London; and Scarborough, Ontario: New American Library, 1970 and 1975), p. 53.

guish between a person who is frustrated or temporarily disabled and one who is chronically disabled. When a faculty member is in constant conflict with colleagues or students, the chairperson must exercise judgment. Sometimes the chairperson may wait patiently in the belief that the crisis will be temporary. At other times the chairperson may decide to suspend the person from work. A decision such as this is a painful one: it may ease or erase conflict in a department, but only at the expense of that faculty member's professional life.

The matter of faculty members who behave erratically is complicated by the legal and the psychological aspects of the issue. To suggest to a colleague that he or she is sick and needs help may result in a charge of character assassination and a lawsuit. Chairpersons must remember that they have no legal or professional authority to counsel a department member. When someone with no training attempts to counsel an emotionally unstable person who is incapacitated by inner conflict or actively engaged in a dispute, serious and unpleasant consequences may result. If a faculty member needs to be referred to a counselor or psychiatrist, the chairperson should discreetly discuss the matter with the dean and the legal staff before proceeding.

Thus far, we have discussed situations in which the chairperson has been dealing with inner conflict, latent conflict, and feelings of powerlessness against the system. We have not discussed in detail manifest or overt conflict. But conflicts, despite strenuous efforts to control them, do emerge and, in most cases, are destructive and costly. There is, of course, no clear blueprint of what to do when conflict occurs. The chairperson who is aware of the stages of a conflict episode and who has a finger on the department's pulse will not be surprised if conflict does emerge, because he or she will have been watching it develop. Yet there is more to dealing with conflict than simply not being surprised by it, since some persons who are not surprised by events are still unable to handle them.

Much department conflict can be managed effectively by an astute chairperson. What does *conflict management* mean? For our purposes, it means the shaping of conflict in such a way that it is reduced to a process of problem solving. In many cases, this transformation can be accomplished if the chairperson is able to develop a clear idea about the basic attitudes of the disputing parties toward, first, the conflict they are engaged in and, second, the stakes involved. This understanding is important because attitudes toward conflict influence persons' behavior and because conflict over low stakes is much easier to resolve than conflict over high stakes.

Analyzing the participating parties' attitudes to the conflict need not be complicated. The chairperson should know whether they feel that the conflict was avoidable and whether they feel that some agreement or compromise is possible. If disputants feel agreement is possible, they can generally be persuaded to convert their dispute into an opportunity for problem solving. If, on the other hand, they feel that an agreement is impossible, they may engage in a fierce struggle to the bitter end, especially if the stakes are high. Generally, if the stakes are high, the conflict will be much more vigorous, and the possibility exists that the conflict will not be settled amicably.

Chairpersons can settle a dispute if they can make the opposing parties believe that an agreement is possible or if they can get the parties to lower the stakes in their dispute. For example, an anthropology department was engaged in a bitter dispute between its structuralists and its functionalists. Each side was accusing the other of not being "real" anthropologists and was preventing the promotion and tenure of young faculty members in the enemy camp. The stakes were the survival of each faction in the department. The chairperson, even though a member of one of the factions, was able to persuade the groups that they could live with each other and that their ideological differences need not lead to the expulsion of half the department. In this case, the stakes were not lowered, but the attitudes were changed.

The question of what "high" stakes are, compared with "moderate" or "low" stakes, is somewhat subjective but certainly includes such matters as promotion, tenure, and status in the department. Low stakes might include a large office, allocation of a typewriter, and travel funds. Nevertheless, serious conflicts have erupted over the last three examples. Someone once said that the reason academic politics is so sordid is that the stakes are so small. Low stakes for one person may be high stakes for another.

The question of whether parties to a conflict think the conflict was avoidable is of little concern here. Some persons believe that conflict is avoidable but that, if it should occur, an agreement is impossible. Research indicates that such persons often tend to withdraw from the conflict when it occurs. Generally, however, if persons see conflict as inevitable, agreement as impossible, and stakes as high, they are likely to engage in the most bitter of conflicts. Sometimes attempts to lower stakes and change attitudes do not succeed, and the results can be serious indeed.

When diagnosing a conflict, a chairperson must exercise analytical ability. He or she must use good judgment in deciding whether to intervene and strive to reduce conflict or channel it creatively. If the chairperson can identify an emerging conflict, uncover the faculty's attitudes and beliefs about the nature of conflict, and assess the stakes involved in the conflict, he or she will be better equipped to decide what to do in a particular situation. Often, the best decision is not to act. When intervention obviously will not improve the situation or even make it worse, the chairperson's best strategy is to remain aloof from the conflict while staying alert to the situation and sensitive to the conditions that produced it. For example, two senior faculty members have been bickering for years. Their differences do not impede the operation of the department, and the chairperson does not attempt a peace-making role. On the other hand, if the quarreling department members attempt to pressure the rest of the faculty to choose sides and build up factions within the department, some intervention is called for.

As stated earlier in this discussion, the chairperson should try to transform conflicts into opportunities for problem solving. It may be useful here to make conceptual distinction between *conflicts* and *problems*. A problem exists when a set of expectations is not being fulfilled; a conflict exists when one or more persons is intentionally or unintentionally thwarting the needs or wants of another person or persons. For example, several faculty members taught an introductory graduate seminar on a rotating basis. Students who took the course from a particular faculty member had great difficulty passing the department qualifying examination. This difficulty caused conflict between the students and the faculty members, as well as among the faculty members themselves. The chairperson arranged a meeting of all the teachers of the course. Instead of permitting them to dwell on their differences, he limited the agendum to a discussion of what the students were expected to know at the completion of the course and what the examination should cover. By concentrating on the problem rather than on the dispute and by reaching a mutually satisfactory solution, the chairperson defused the conflict.

The chairperson can resolve some conflicts by acting as clarifier. An emerging conflict may be reduced if the chairperson can show the parties that their expectations are based on incorrect information. For example, conflict in a department over inequitable teaching loads may be reduced if the chairperson supplies precise information about who teaches what. On the other hand, such information, if it gives evidence of real inequities, may widen the conflict.

When the chairperson receives reports of a conflict, he or she would be wise to begin a discreet inquiry into the situation before taking any overt action. For example, two faculty members were engaged in a bitter feud because one believed the other had misrepresented her ability and record to a Washington funding agency and thus was responsible for its rejection of her grant proposal. By conducting a few interviews, the chairperson was able to clarify the situation. Discreet inquiry was also effective in a case involving rumors of sexual misconduct by a faculty member. When the chairperson met with some graduate students, he discovered evidence of a pattern of sexual exploitation in which the faculty member threatened the careers of students unless they granted him favors. In some instances when rumors of misbehavior were ignored, the university was later subjected to adverse publicity and legal action.

The department as a whole or committees within the department can be used to settle or reduce conflict. For example, a bitter quarrel over who was to teach a certain course threatened to disrupt the activities of a statistics department. The department referred the problem to a committee and asked its members to develop a set of criteria and procedures for determining who would teach specific courses in the department. The decision of who was to teach each course, including the one in question, would henceforth be made on the basis of established policy.

Some conflicts are caused primarily by problems that the chairperson may be able to identify but not be authorized or suited to address. In such cases, the use of an outside authority may be required. For example, a faculty member's alcoholism was ignored and even concealed by his colleagues and chairperson until a committee of graduate students spoke with an attorney about the man's chronic absenteeism and erratic behavior. The chairperson then discussed the matter with the dean, and they contacted a staff member who was an effective alcoholism counselor. Together they worked out a program of action that they offered to the faculty member.

Occasionally a chairperson will encourage an emerging conflict in the belief that getting things out in the open will help correct misunderstandings and ultimately result in a more positive relationship. Some chairpersons may even induce conflict in order to discover the intensity of feelings about a particular issue. Only a skilled conflict manager should attempt to introduce a dispute into the department. The potential for damage is high and the probable outcome too unpredictable.

When thinking about the kind of strategy to use to reduce a conflict, the chairperson should examine the values held by the opposing parties. He or she should be aware that intervention might unwittingly lend support to one party's values. Examining values is especially important when the department has no clear priorities or goals. In such instances, the chairperson, by supporting a value or goal, is causing a conflicting value to be downplayed or rejected. The chairperson then becomes a party to the conflict rather than a mediator, part of the problem rather than part of the solution. In departments that have no clear-cut goals, the value supported by the chairperson establishes priorities and creates a latent conflict situation. For example, in a department that had established no priorities concerning the value of research or teaching, the faculty members began to argue about the relative merits of generating large numbers of student credit hours rather than publishing research. The chairperson sided with the advocates of teaching large classes. By so doing, he established a priority that would later cause conflict between the disaffected researchers and the rest of the department.

Although it is often wise to adopt a neutral stance toward conflict in the department, the chairperson must sometimes become embroiled in a conflict because the role demands it. On such occasions, one of the parties in conflict may perceive the chairperson's action as partisan or punitive. Thus far we have emphasized the chairperson's role as a problem solver, but there are times when the attempted solution to a conflict requires that the chairperson make a decision that arouses someone's anger and hostility. Indeed, on occasion traditional ways of reducing conflict are not successful and a party to conflict must be warned, disciplined, or reprimanded. Chairpersons should know what authority they have to order persons to desist from certain behaviors. They should be aware of institutional rules and regulations and know the extent of their legal powers as chairpersons.

In some cases of conflict the best action is to intervene immediately. If equipment, students, or faculty or staff members are threatened with danger, the chairperson must act quickly and effectively. In the rare case of hostile or threatening behavior, the chairperson and the staff should know how to contact police or security officers. The chairperson should also know what to do in the case of fire, storms, and accident. Thefts should be reported promptly, since they may be part of an organized and systematic activity that the police might be able to identify and stop.

Some disputes can be settled only by consultation with a dean or other official. Such disputes include quarrels between departments, quarrels between a department and the administration, and quarrels between a department and a university committee. With chairpersons vigorously advocating the claims of their own departments, quarrels can escalate into conflict. In such an event, the dean or the academic vice president must try to settle the fight. For example, a school of education offered statistics courses to its own students, while a statistics department offered courses to the university in general. When many arts and sciences students began to take courses in the school of education, the statistics department pressed for a regulation that would prohibit crossing college lines for statistics courses. Each department began accusing the other of proselytizing, so the chairpersons decided to cool things down by taking the problem to the academic vice president. Another example: When the graduate policy committee suspended a department's authorization to grant graduate degrees, the department claimed it was treated unfairly. Again, the chairperson took the problem to the dean. In both instances, the chairpersons were part of the conflict, but they used their knowledge of the dynamics of conflict to arrive at a solution.

The chairperson is sometimes called on to appear as an expert witness or as an independent observer in proceedings that arise as a result of conflict. During grievance procedures and in the course of official hearings, the chairperson may be required to present evidence or give testimony about the conduct of department members. The chairperson should keep journals or records that recount in detail the actions of the parties in a dispute, especially if he or she intervenes in the conflict. The chairperson should take into account the legal aspects of building a case history or record and should comply with requirements of due process and with laws respecting privacy. Ordinarily, if a file is being kept, the person or persons who are the subject of the documentation should be informed of its existence. The file should not simply document the errors or misdeeds of persons or parties; it should also record the steps taken to resolve the dispute or transform it into an opportunity for problem solving.

A conflict poses a more difficult dilemma for chairpersons when none of the possible interventions seems likely to resolve the whole problem. On occasion a chairperson may hesitate to intervene in a conflict for fear of losing his or her effectiveness as chairperson, alienating powerful members of the department, or possibly losing his or her position. Suppose that two very influential faculty members who generally disagree about each other's principles and practices and who both are extremely vindictive have joined forces to deny junior faculty members the opportunity to teach certain courses and the opportunity for released time to do research. The two faculty members are politically strong enough to threaten the chairperson's position. The junior faculty members have approached the chairperson and asked for assistance in the conflict. What should the chairperson do?

Another hypothetical dilemma: The short-tempered dean of the college is a tenured faculty member in a certain department. He thinks of himself as a superb teacher and insists on teaching a required undergraduate course. In fact, he has the deserved reputation of being one of the worst teachers in the university. The students are outraged at the poor quality of instruction and the lack of organization in the course and are vigorously protesting. In addition, one of the younger faculty members in the department is upset because he feels he is more qualified than the dean to teach this particular course. What can the chairperson do about his own dean?

The chairperson's role in dealing with conflict and maintaining morale is crucial to the smooth operation of the department. He or she must be aware of the conditions in the department that might give rise to conflict and be prepared to use analytic ability, good judgment, and creativity in order to handle conflict effectively. He or she must be able to recognize and analyze a conflict when it occurs and to exercise good judgment when deciding whether or not to intervene. The kind of intervention depends on the facts and dynamics of the situation. The chairperson must be creative and deal with each situation individually. In the case of recurring conflict, the irrational and emotional elements of the situation can be defused if the chairperson can find or get the department to develop a regulation or policy covering that type of conflict. As a general rule, conflict that can be reduced to an opportunity for problem solving has the greatest chance of being settled. This transformation requires that the chairperson explore the limits of his or her own creativity. Although no formula exists that can be applied to all conflict situations, the following guidelines can be of help to the chairperson.

- Keep in touch with the feelings and attitudes of faculty members. Through frequent meetings, the chairperson can discover latent conflict situations before they emerge.
- Be aware of the four stages of conflict episodes in order to be able to deal with them at the earliest opportunity.
- Use techniques of active listening to raise morale and to understand the perceptions of faculty members who may be engaged in conflict.
- Structure the department in such a manner that conflicts can be discussed, aired, and dealt with through normal governance procedures.
- Be sensitive to faculty members with personal problems but do not necessarily get involved. Intervene only if the operation of the department is impaired.
- In cases of conflict, determine what conflicting values are held by the parties.
- Do not take sides in a conflict that does not concern the welfare of the department.
- Do not intervene in conflicts unless you have reason to believe that intervention can help the situation.
- Find out whether disputants perceive the stakes as high or low. If they are perceived as high, try to reduce them.
- Find out whether parties believe the conflict is amenable to solution. Try to persuade them that solutions are possible.
- Try to change any conflict to an opportunity for problem solving.
- Be prepared to make discreet inquiries about reported potential and actual conflict.
- When appropriate, use department committees to establish policies and procedures that govern situations in which conflicts have occurred and may occur in the future.
- As soon as possible, clarify misconceptions that may cause conflict.
- Communicate clearly with the faculty about any unprecedented action that might cause conflict.
- Be prepared to be called as a witness to or observer of a conflict. Keep records of action and involvement in conflicts.
- Do not violate laws or institutional regulations when dealing with conflict.

We have briefly discussed, from both a theoretical and a practical point of view, conflict as it occurs in academic departments.

Chairpersons of academic disciplines other than the social sciences may be unaware of the great amount of research conducted by sociologists and psychologists on the problems of identifying, analyzing, and resolving conflict. Knowing how to deal with conflict can be useful in managing families, schools, churches, businesses, legislatures, and international affairs. Chairpersons, in order to be effective, must continually be alert to the possibility of conflict in their departments. They must be sufficiently wise to determine whether they should get involved. If they decide to become involved, they must select the strategy that has the best chance of solving or diffusing the conflict.

Questions

1. What factors or influences outside the university have caused latent conflict among the faculty members in your department?
2. What factors or influences *within* the university but outside the department have caused latent conflict among your faculty members?
3. What kinds of issues, situations, or relationships that exist within your department have contributed to latent or emergent conflict?
4. *a*) Review one or more conflicts in your department or in another department that have been constructive. How were they resolved?
   b) Review one or more conflicts in your department or in another department that have been destructive. How were they resolved?
5. Do any serious conflicts exist in your department at the present time? What are they?
6. In this chapter we have discussed morale in general terms. Identify factors that at one time or another have lowered morale in your department. How did you react to those factors? Do you think your reaction was appropriate?
7. Identify factors that have raised morale in your department. Did you have any influence over these factors?
8. What elements in the governance structure of your department serve to minimize conflict?

References

Baldridge, J. Victor. *Power and Conflict in the University: Research in the Sociology of Complex Organizations.* New York: John Wiley & Sons, 1971.

Baldridge, J. Victor, et al. *Policy Making and Effective Leadership: A National Study of Academic Management.* San Francisco: Jossey-Bass, 1978.

Barzun, Jacques. *The American University: How It Runs, Where It Is Going.* New York: Harper & Row, 1968.

Bennett, Dudley. *TA and the Manager.* New York: The American Management Association, 1978.

Blake, Robert R.; Shepard, Herbert; and Mouton, Jane. *Managing Intergroup Conflict in Industry.* Houston: Gulf, 1964.

Gordon, Thomas. *Parent Effectiveness Training.* New York; London; and Scarborough, Ontario: New American Library, 1975.

Gordon, Thomas, and Burch, Noel. *T.E.T.—Teacher Effectiveness Training.* New York: David McKay Co., 1975.

Gouldner, Alvin W. "Cosmopolitans and Locals: Towards an Analysis of Latent Social Roles." *Administrative Science Quarterly,* December 1957, pp. 281–306; and March 1958, pp. 444–80.

Hersey, Paul, and Blanchard, Kenneth. *Management of Organizational Behavior: Utilizing Human Resources.* 3rd ed. Englewood Cliffs, N.J.: Prentice-Hall, 1977.

Hobbs, Walter G., and Anderson, G. Lester. "The Operation of Academic Departments," *Management Science,* December 1971, pp. B 134–44.

Jenks, Christopher, and Riesman, David. *The Academic Revolution.* Garden City, N.J.: Anchor Books, 1969.

Levinson, Daniel J. *The Seasons of a Man's Life.* New York: Alfred A. Knopf, 1978.

Loewenberg, Peter. "Love and Hate in the Academy." *The Center Magazine,* September-October 1972, pp. 4–11.

Luthans, Fred, ed. *Contemporary Readings in Organizational Behavior.* 2nd ed. New York: McGraw-Hill, 1976.

Luthans, Fred. *Organizational Behavior.* 2nd ed. New York: McGraw-Hill, 1976.

McConnell, T.R., and Mortimer, Kenneth P. *The Faculty in University Governance.* Berkeley: Center for Research and Development in Higher Education, University of California, 1971.

Pondy, Louis R. "Organizational Conflict: Concepts and Models." In *Contemporary Readings in Organizational Behavior,* edited by Fred Luthans. 2nd ed. New York: McGraw-Hill, 1976.

Sheehy, Gail. *Passages.* New York: Dutton, 1976.

Snow, C.P. *The Masters.* Lib. rep. ed. New York: Charles Scribner's Sons, 1960.

Tanter, Raymond, ed. "Why Fight? Conflict Models for Strategists and Managers." *American Behavioral Scientist,* July-August 1972 (special issue).

10

Department Accomplishments and Aspirations: Setting Goals and Developing Action Plans

The chairperson is frequently asked to describe the department's activities and accomplishments as well as its aspirations. Such requests can come from the central administration of the institution, from foundations and agencies that allocate grants and contracts, from accrediting associations, and even from other departments. The task of reporting department activities with clarity and precision can be irksome, but it can pay handsome dividends if done well. Although no one wants to spend valuable time describing what seems to be obvious and well known, the chairperson should remember that accomplishments taken for granted within a department are not necessarily noted or publicized elsewhere. The allocation of resources may be based on reports or documents that reflect the chairperson's skill in articulating the importance of the department's accomplishments and aspirations. Also, academic departments are being asked to justify their own existence with increasing frequency. Those who dispense funds for higher education usually try to give them to departments or programs that evidence a sense of direction and purpose and that show the greatest potential for achievement. Many potentially valuable activities have never been begun because the chairperson lacked motivation or was unable to report adequately the department's activities and goals. This chapter will focus on ways in which the past activities and the future direction of a department may be described.

Reporting Department Accomplishments

A chairperson is usually required to prepare and submit a report of the past year's activities to the dean or the central administration of the institution. A department that maintains adequate records of activities and files these in an orderly manner can compile its reports much more efficiently than a department that

196

must send its members scurrying about once a year to find information that might have been amassed routinely and easily. An honest and well-written annual report can help a department determine its strengths and weaknesses and may suggest measures for improvement. Furthermore, when a department has an updated report of its accomplishments, it can more easily state its desires and aspirations. Answers to the questions below are useful in evaluating a department, developing a good annual report, and creating a data base for planning future activities.

Information about students

- How many students are majoring in the department's field?
- How many students are enrolled in each course?
- How many degrees in the department's field have been conferred?
- How many students have received scholarships, fellowships, assistantships, grants, and gifts?
- How many students have won honors?
- How many new majors have been accepted for the coming year?
- How many minority students have been recruited, trained, and graduated?
- How are the students performing in terms of grade point average and national tests? How does student performance compare with that of past years?
- What theses, dissertations, or research reports have been completed?
- What percentage of the total number of lower-division, upper-division, and graduate students in the university is majoring in this field? Is the percentage increasing, decreasing, or remaining relatively stable? What accounts for the change or stability?
- What evidence indicates that students are receiving the courses and information necessary for the next stage of their academic or employment careers? How many and what percentage of graduating seniors in the department were admitted to graduate school? To what graduate schools were they admitted? How many and what percentage of graduates were employed in jobs for which they have been trained?
- What other schools and colleges within the university are sending students to this department? Are other departments asking for service courses? Has a systematic

needs survey been conducted? What are the past, present, and anticipated student demands for courses in this department? What are the past, present, and anticipated job market needs for graduates of department programs?

Information about degree programs, course offerings, and curriculum

- What courses were offered at each level during each term of the year and how many students were enrolled in each course?
- How many full-time equivalent students were generated by the department at each level?
- Have course syllabi been updated?
- Have courses been changed by using other media or more individual modes of instruction?
- Have new courses been added? How do these courses contribute to the program?
- Do the courses in the program meet the present and anticipated needs of the students and the job market?
- Has the program been reviewed? If so, by whom? A university committee? A state agency? Has the program been reviewed for accreditation?

Information about faculty members and their achievements

- How many full-time faculty members are in the department?
- Have new faculty members been added to the department?
- How many faculty members are on leave or sabbatical?
- Have any faculty members resigned?
- Have any faculty members been dismissed? Have any contracts not been renewed?
- Do any faculty members have reduced workloads?
- How many faculty members are temporary or part-time? Is the number of part-time or temporary faculty members increasing?
- Which faculty members have received professional honors or teaching awards?
- Have any faculty members received grants and contracts for research, development, or training?
- What is the record of publications by faculty members?
- Have any faculty members received awards for research or publication?
- What service activities have faculty members per-

formed? For the school or institution? For professional associations? For the community?

Information about equipment, facilities, and supplies
- Are resources adequate to meet demands?
- Do any programs not have adequate resources? Are additional resources needed?
- Has new or special equipment been acquired for the department?

Information about department governance and administration
- How is the department structured? What are the roles of department committees? To what extent do students participate in department affairs?
- Have any new policies been implemented for the department's operation?
- How is travel money allocated within the department?
- Is the level of faculty morale satisfactory?
- What other important activities or actions should be mentioned?

Aside from the official information that is required by the central administration and the dean, each department must determine for itself what data it wishes to collect and maintain on a regular basis. Answers to the questions above illustrate the kinds of statements that appear in annual reports, though requirements for these statements differ from one institution to another. Departments can obtain much information from the university's institutional research office, which collects and stores much of this data.

Most chairpersons see the advantages of using the previous year's annual report as a guide when preparing a report for the current year. This procedure has the positive aspect of ensuring that the most important continuing commitments and activities are given proper attention. The activities of most departments have an organic continuity, and it is not surprising that annual reports repeat a large volume of information from the year before. Since the annual report summarizes and reviews the department's history for a given year, it can be used to compare the year's accomplishments with those of previous years, thereby giving some indication of the state of the department. The report can show whether the department is growing or shrinking, flourishing or floundering, but the comparison will be based only on the standard of what the department has done in the past.

A department may designate a particular year as a normative

standard—for example, the year of the greatest number of undergraduate enrollments; the year of the highest graduate enrollments; the year of the highest number of degrees conferred; or the year of some significant achievement in research, publications, or grants awarded. The department can then compare its current activities with those of the normative years.

Alternatively, the chairperson might want to know how the department measures up to other departments. A department can be compared with departments representing the same discipline at other universities in the region or in the nation. The department may also be compared with other departments within the same institution or with a set of department standards derived by a professional or accrediting association.

When a department wishes to compare itself with departments of the same discipline at other institutions, nationally top-ranked departments are often used as the basis for comparison. First, the department might look at characteristics that are easily measurable, such as the number of faculty members, the number of students, admissions standards, funding per student, and so forth. One frequently cited standard of comparison is the student-faculty ratio, the assumption being that the smaller the ratio, the more contact a student will have with faculty members, resulting in education of higher quality. Another way of comparing accomplishments with those of other departments of the same discipline at other institutions is to count the number of times a particular author is cited in the professional literature. By noting the department affiliation of the most frequently cited scholars, the chairperson can gauge with moderate assurance the ranking of his or her own department in the areas of research, scholarship, and publication.

A crucial but questionable assumption underlying judgments based on this procedure is that the future creative activities of the faculty will be like those of the past. Furthermore, whereas this form of comparison is based on objective, quantifiable evidence, it is limited by focusing on research, which is only one of the three major functions of institutions of higher education. The national ranking of graduate programs also reflects this focus, but in a much broader way. Unfortunately, graduate school rankings are often based on judgments that are extremely subjective and that may at times be woefully out of date. Nevertheless, in the "professional status sweepstakes" some department chairpersons commonly make sweeping assertions based on these kinds of data. Chairpersons and faculty members have to guard against believing that their past productivity indicates something about the present; to confirm this assumption, they must examine the department's current activities.

Sometimes departments are grouped with others at the same institution. Usually a group includes departments from related or cognate disciplines, such as those in the social sciences. Since there are no uniform or national standards for grouping cognate departments, some interesting problems can result. For example, a history department, because of its concern with literary exposition, might find itself grouped with a humanities or language and literature group, or the same department, if it emphasizes historical data analysis, might be grouped with the traditional social science departments. Psychology departments have been grouped with the social sciences when social-psychological relations were most important, with the biological sciences when the emphasis was on animal studies and experiments, and occasionally with the health sciences area when a clinical program was preeminent. Some departments may find that they are being compared with other departments in their college or university with whom they feel they have very little in common. Most of these groupings are for administrative convenience in monitoring and controlling budgets and expenditures and analyzing cost data. The chairperson who is required to respond to comparisons of this kind needs as much knowledge as possible about the other departments in the group in order to defend the interests of his or her department.

A department may be part of a discipline that, through its professional association, has developed a set of normative standards by which a department can evaluate itself. Some professional associations conduct evaluations using such standards when preparing to credential degree programs. These standards frequently specify such details as the percentage of the faculty that should possess the doctorate and the minimum number of faculty members needed to set up and maintain a bachelor's degree program. The existence of normative standards usually indicates a high degree of professional consensus on the most valued characteristics in that discipline, the activities considered appropriate within it, and the quality of education and accomplishments expected of students enrolling in and graduating from programs within it. Departments that aspire to meet minimum standards within the discipline tend to look to the professional association's guidelines; departments that are interested in meeting or exceeding the accomplishments of the top-ranked departments in the discipline tend to compare themselves with those departments.

Most forms of comparison mentioned above have a growth bias built into them; that is, they incorporate an assumption that progress toward some desirable end or level of achievement is demonstrable by continued growth and expansion. In today's world the potentional for growth appears to be limited; the growth rate has slowed and, in many cases, is in decline. Many departments aspire to maintain their level of accomplishments despite declining resources, but such aspirations are difficult to achieve.

Describing Department Aspirations

An interesting question sometimes raised in academic circles concerns comparing the department not with other departments but with its own ideas of what it ought to be doing. How do the department's activities measure up to the purposes and aspirations of the university and the department? A department cannot compare deeds with aspirations unless it knows to what it aspires. Aspirations can be formally stated in writing or can exist only in the minds of the chairperson and the faculty. A written statement of purpose has certain advantages in maintaining stability and continuity as the department changes. Formulating such a statement also helps department members articulate their feelings about their proper roles and functions in the framework of the college or the institution. Ordinarily, such a statement is called a *mission statement*.

The term *mission statement* may seem a mildly absurd way to categorize an expression of department aspirations; for some persons the word *mission* has quasi-military or religious connotations. Nevertheless, those who control the purse strings, especially administrators and granting agencies, look for and expect to find mission statements in the proposals and requests they read and review. Stroking the hand that feeds you is hardly an intellectual justification for a mission statement, but the case can be argued on other grounds—for example, the need for a broad, covering statement of fundamental purpose. A hallmark of any intelligent activity, especially intellectual activity, is that the participants know what they are about. It is not unreasonable to expect a department to have a sense of what it is doing and where it is going. The mission statement serves as the foundation on which the department builds and justifies the grounds for its existence within the university. A department should forthrightly state its professional aspirations before making final commitments for an academic year. Then if it truly wants to take responsibility for shaping its professional destiny, it will, at the end of the academic year, compare its achievements with earlier aspirations.

Mission statements typically contain both abstract and concrete elements, which may range from the grandiose to the specific. They often contain ideological components representing widely held beliefs about the value of a college education, and they include societal as well as professional aspirations. The idealistic components of the mission statement have strong roots in American culture and continue to be affirmed, despite the odds against their being achieved. The mission statement is often based on two assumptions: that progress is an incremental movement toward some high aim and that the aim will not actually be achieved.

Many departments write their own mission statements, but not all do. Mission statements can be prepared by planning officials, external consultants, legislative committees, administrators, and, of course, faculty committees. Many mission statements have a formal aura about them; they often appear in master plan documents, budget request documents, long-range plans, and development grant applications. Mission statements often contain information and data that serve as guides for making appropriate decisions about a department's commitments. Often the statement about the department that appears in the university catalog stands as a mission statement. The chairperson, in conjunction with a faculty committee, should conduct an annual review of the mission statement and bring it up to date, if necessary. Systematic redefinition of the department's mission is appropriate at certain times—for example, after the departure of senior faculty members, when curricular changes are called for, and when resources become so scarce that the department's historic mission cannot be achieved. Listed below are some central characteristics of a good mission statement. Each characteristic is followed by an excerpt from a college or university catalog, but none of the excerpts is a complete mission statement in itself.

- A mission statement clearly identifies the department's overall purpose.

  The mission of the department is to train professionals who are capable of doing research in the methodology of biostatistics and to apply their statistical and quantitative knowledge to the solution of problems encountered in the community health field. [A biostatistics department]

- A mission statement describes the scope and character of the teaching, research, and service activities of the department. It identifies the persons or groups that the department serves, tells how it serves them, and describes the results of the service.

  ... to provide undergraduate instruction in physics for physics majors and to prepare elementary and secondary preservice teachers to meet state certification requirements. [A physics department]

  ... research is focused primarily on the pulmonary and cardiovascular system and the effects of environmental agents on human and animal health. [A physiology department]

  ... meets the needs of commercial fishermen in the southeast by providing extension services. [A fisheries department]

- A mission statement indicates the general direction in which the department is moving and furnishes a frame of reference from which department goals may be derived.

  ... teaches administrators and research workers to understand how to take advantage of modern computers in their work. [A computer science department]

- A mission statement should describe any resources or activities that distinguish the department from others and should emphasize any unique qualities the department may have.

  ... offers programs in bilingual-bicultural education, with special emphasis in Greek and Hispanic studies. [A foreign language department]

Chairpersons should beware of mission statements that are too broad and thus fail to show how the department differs from other departments. Other mission statements are too narrow and describe activities in too much detail. Following are two examples of complete mission statements based on actual statements found in university catalogs. The first is from a behavioral science department in a school of public health:

The Department of Behavioral Sciences is concerned with the application of social science theory, methodology, and empirical findings to the study of health and illness. The department serves as a resource to the School by providing the basis for systematic consideration and study of the social and cultural aspects of health problems and theories from the disciplines of sociology, anthropology, social psychology, and political science. Departmental students are prepared primarily for careers in research and teaching. The central focus of the department is in major areas of medical sociology and anthropology, including: individual motivation in health behavior; socio-cultural factors in disease; health organizations and professions; comparative healing systems; and comparative sociopolitical contexts of public health.

The next mission statement is from an English department in an urban university:

> The Department of English primarily serves the individual undergraduate student, the academic community and society in general. The department seeks to develop the students' reading comprehension and writing skills in order to help insure maximum realization of their potential. The faculty hopes to develop understanding of the humanistic heritage and at the same time to stimulate the students' imagination and sense of joy in life by familiarizing them with British and American literature and with other literatures which have contributed to the culture. Courses are designed to foster creativity, and the department offers specific courses for students with identified creative gifts. The department attempts to teach the fundamentals of research; to stimulate the use of scholarly methods and attitudes throughout its programs; and to encourage the individual scholarship of its members. Through the discharge of the responsibilities described above, the Department of English strives to prepare students for such professions as teaching, law, and medicine, and for an individually enriched and socially productive life.

These examples are not perfect. A mission statement that meets the criteria already discussed is difficult to write. Nevertheless, each statement attempts to describe the particular department in a way that shows its special characteristics. The first of the two statements is more precise and specific than the other, perhaps because of the nature of the discipline.

Departments should have statements of purpose for the reasons already described. Many departments that have such statements prefer to call them *goals* rather than *missions*. What they are called is relatively unimportant compared with the substance of the statements. This chapter suggests a progression of specificity of aims, using the terms *mission, goal,* and *objective* to delineate increasing specificity. Nevertheless, there are numerous nomenclatures for the different levels of specificity and the ways in which they may be elaborated. One purpose of this chapter is to discuss and clarify this conceptualization. The vocabulary used here should not necessarily be considered superior to others; it is simply one that is widely used.

Having discussed mission, we can move on to the next higher level of specificity—goals. A goal has a specified or implied end, whereas missions are continuous. This is not to say that all goal statements must indicate the period of time within which they must be achieved. Goals may be short-term or long-term, but they must be realizable sooner or later; the department ought to be able to tell when a goal has been accomplished. To predict when some goals will be reached is sometimes difficult. In such instances, intermediate goals may be set in order to help develop plans for achieving the goals.

In addition to specifying a certain end, goal statements have other characteristics: they represent a logical extension of the mission statement; they are oriented toward specific results; they are explicit; and they are supported by a series of objectives. A *goal*, therefore, is a statement of intention to achieve a specified result that is compatible with the mission or purpose of the department and institution. It is the end toward which one or more activities are aimed. An *objective* is a statement of intention to achieve a specified result, which, when achieved, will contribute to the realization of the goal.

These definitions are best understood as stipulations. *Mission* and *goal* can be interchanged without doing violence to the language, and indeed some persons interchange these terms while others interchange the terms *goals* and *objectives*. So goals as well as mission represent the department's aspirations. Goals are simply more specific and action-oriented expressions of the results that the department hopes to achieve. Some departments feel that goals must be expressed in behavioral terms; that is to say, the goal should contain a specific time frame and indicators of achievement so that at the end of the specified time the department can easily assess whether the goal has been achieved. Other departments do not insist on such a high degree of quantification in goal statements. Certainly some areas of endeavor are more amenable to behaviorally stated goals than others.

Can a department develop goals that are not immediately related to its academic or educational mission? If academic goals are to be realized, the department must pay attention to its resources and plan to use them effectively. In many cases, departments need to set goals that deal with the acquisition and management of resources. A distinction may therefore be made between what are sometimes called *primary goals* and *support goals*. Primary goals are directly related to educational mission— i.e., the familiar triad of teaching, research, and service. Support goals are advocated not for themselves but for establishing conditions or situations whereby the primary goals can be achieved.

Support goals within the department are concerned with the staff, students, physical facilities, department planning and management, record keeping and information gathering, and procurement of funding or support. For example, the goal of formulating department goals is a support goal that should lead to improvements in teaching, research, and service.

Following are examples of primary and support goals:

> To identify entering freshmen with deficiencies in reading and writing skills and to improve those basic skills. [Primary goal, English department]

> To produce graduates who will be eligible for admission to medical school. [Primary teaching goal, biology department]

> To maintain the department's level of publications in scholarly journals held during the past three-year period. [Primary research goal, any department]

> To provide advice and assistance to teacher education centers throughout the state. [Primary service goal, education department]

> To establish an internship program for seniors in law enforcement. [Primary goal, criminology department]

> To involve faculty in a faculty development program. [Support goal, any department]

> To establish a system of department record keeping consistent with university policy. [Support goal, any department]

> To obtain additional laboratory equipment. [Support goal, any science department]

Why should a department have goals? At a time when accountability is repeatedly used as a warning and a threat, department members should not only have a statement of their purpose but should be able to point to a set of goals that they expect to achieve. They should be able to express the professional aspirations of the department in ways that will allow those aspirations to be compared with actual accomplishments. The chairperson of a department that has stated its goals clearly and realistically and that has indeed achieved its goals within a certain period of time can make a good case for a fair slice of the economic pie that the dean keeps in the cupboard. Aside from the practical advantage of being able to say, "We said we would accomplish these things, and we have done so," goal setting serves another, more theoretical, purpose: it helps academicians not only know their purposes but also clarify their ideas about how those purposes can be fulfilled.

As mentioned earlier, goals must be realistic and attainable. The chairperson should try to avoid ill-conceived or badly stated goals. Following is a list of reasons that many goals cannot be realized or are flawed in other ways.

- Goals may be too specific, allowing for too little flexibility to take advantage of unforeseen opportunities or to deviate from a narrow path that may become blocked.
- Goals may be too broad or abstract, to the extent that the faculty cannot agree on what constitutes achievement.
- Goals may be too simple and trivial, to the point that even when attained they have little professional or political significance.
- Goals may be too grandiose to be attained given the existing faculty, student body, or resources.
- Goals may be too optimistic given the time or administrative support available.
- Goals may be overambitious in relation to the attitudes of the administration, the public, or the legislature.
- Goals may be too pessimistic or underambitious and may not reflect adequately the abilities and aspirations of the faculty.
- Goals may be contradictory and conflicting. When goals contributed by individual faculty members are not reviewed for consistency or realism by the chairperson or a faculty committee, the resulting set of goals may be contradictory.
- Goals may lack sufficient support from the faculty. If a chairperson develops a set of goals without faculty input and consensus, the goals may not be taken seriously or may be resisted or opposed.

The process whereby a department arrives at its goals is intimately related to the quality of the goals produced. An academic department is made up of persons who are likely to vary considerably in age, personality, style, and ability. Despite the stereotype of "the professor," anyone with academic experience knows that department members are rarely peas in a pod. Whereas it might be easier to get consistent and coherent department goals from a group of like-minded persons, the diversity of the faculty is probably a healthy thing, for a diverse faculty will have complementary skills. The problem the chairperson faces is how to derive a set of compatible expectations from persons whose styles and abilities differ. An unsatisfactory solution to the problem is to construct a department mold or procrustean bed that all members must fit. Such an approach is bound to stifle talent, creativity, and individuality.

Team building is a term much used in industrial management. Such language may rub academicians the wrong way, but the idea behind it is sound. The team metaphor may be applied to a university department; individuals with diverse strengths and talents may share a group of common expectations and aspirations, especially when those expectations enhance the careers of the individuals who make up the department. Although each faculty member rightly possesses individual goals, a department should be able to arrive at a set of expectations that are compatible and shared. Persons who have played on a team or in an orchestra know that it is possible to develop a solidarity of purpose that is very satisfying. A department that can come to agreement on goals can also develop esprit de corps and a sense of mutual support and interdependence. A chairperson can contribute to the well-being of the department by bringing its members together at appropriate times to review and clarify the aspirations they share for the department.

How can the chairperson encourage the department to develop its goals? No matter how appropriate the goals may be for a given department, they cannot be easily implemented without the support of the majority of the faculty. The chairperson, of course, should have some ideas concerning the direction the department might take, and he or she should present those ideas tactfully to avoid having them rejected out of hand. The chairperson's leadership style will influence the way the department arrives at its goals. Some alternative approaches to goal setting are listed below.

- The chairperson can prepare statements of department goals and objectives and circulate them to the faculty to stimulate discussion and input.
- The department chairperson can ask a faculty committee to discuss and recommend appropriate goals and objectives for formal review by the entire department faculty.
- The department can form a composite of the individual goals of the department faculty and make this composite the basic department statement of goals and objectives.
- The department can survey similar departments that have already established legitimate goals and objectives.
- The department can employ a consultant or a representative from an accrediting agency to review the department's strengths and support appropriate goals and objectives.

Whichever approach to goal setting is followed, the goals that the faculty ultimately adopts must be ranked. Thus, the faculty assigns priorities to its goals. This step is critical because it provides a guide for others who might attempt to evaluate the department. A priority list is also important when the faculty wants to reward members who make significant contributions toward achieving high-priority department goals. The department priority rankings of goals could be weighted and included in the annual faculty evaluation.

The department next needs to consider what must be accomplished in order to approach its goals. Activities and outcomes necessary to move toward a given goal should be specified. A statement that indicates an outcome and stipulates the activity leading to it can be called an *objective*. To speak of objectives is to speak of the concrete, the observable, the knowable. Although missions and some goals may be ambiguous and imprecise, objectives generally specify some observable product or result.

Objectives are, of course, closely related to the goals from which they are derived. For this reason, an objective taken out of context may be indistinguishable from a goal statement. Though some objectives in other contexts might constitute goals, objectives generally are more concerned with short-term effects than are goals and usually specify a time by which the result will be accomplished. Well-stated objectives have these characteristics:

- They are consistent with the goals from which they are derived.
- They are oriented toward specific outcomes.
- They identify activities by which the outcome or result is to be achieved.
- They are measurable in some way.
- They suggest an expected qualitative or quantitative change or accomplishment.
- They stipulate a time by which the result will be achieved.

As an example, let us reconsider the goal of identifying the freshmen whose English skills were deficient and improving those skills (see page 207). According to our criteria, the objectives derived from this goal should specify steps that must be taken to identify the freshmen and the measure of achievement or improvement that would be considered satisfactory by a certain time. Two objectives for this goal might be (1) administering and scoring Test ABC for all freshmen by October 30 and (2) raising the average score of deficient freshmen on Test ABC to the national norm of 540 by May 30.

Objectives that focus exclusively on results are often called *outcome statements*. The second objective could be converted to an outcome statement by rewording it in the following manner: "By May 30, 87 percent of all freshmen will score at least 540 on Test ABC."

Some faculty members resist stating objectives in quantitative terms because the numbers and percentages that are so often a part of those statements appear to be arbitrary. In some cases, such objections are justified. Why specify 87 percent instead of 83 percent or 90 percent or any other percent, for that matter? There may well be no reason for designating 87 percent, except that on the basis of past experience it seems to be an attainable percentage. Good judgment and common sense are needed when stating measurable outcomes.

Outcome statements contrast with *activity statements*, which typically describe what the students, faculty and staff members, and others *do*. Activity statements that are not linked to outcomes do not translate into good statements of objectives. Nevertheless, activity statements are frequently used as objectives, because the activities of educational processes are more readily observable than the outcomes. To observe a faculty member teaching and to specify what, where, and for how long he teaches is easy; to measure the long-term effects of that teaching is not so easy. When educational objectives are stated primarily as activities, too little emphasis is placed on educational outcomes. Although clearly specifying educational outcomes is an extremely difficult task, and in some disciplines may be well nigh impossible, faculty discussion of desired outcomes might be beneficial for all. The faculty should be able to distinguish between activities and outcomes and, wherever possible, should link outcomes with activities when formulating department objectives.

One further refinement of the planning sequence—mission, goals, and objectives—should be mentioned. In implementing an objective, list discrete tasks that must be accomplished. Developing a timetable for the completion of each task is sometimes useful. The term *milestone* is used to designate a task and the time by which it will be finished. Most granting agencies require that proposals for the funding of projects include a timetable with the designated milestones. A task that includes an activity, an outcome, and a timetable is a sort of mini-objective that is completed on the way to implementing the larger objective. In the same way, the completion of an objective contributes to the attainment of a goal. Objectives, then, can sometimes be seen as intermediate goals. For example, if one of a department's goals is to increase a specific research activity, an intermediate goal might be to obtain a grant for that activity. In another department, obtaining a grant might be considered an objective, a task, or even a goal. Whether a statement of department aims or intentions is called a task, an objective, or a goal does not matter as much as whether those statements can be expressed in a logical, orderly, and precise manner.

Developing Action Plans

The hierarchy of missions, goals, objectives, and tasks has been covered in some detail, but we have not discussed the process by which a department selects appropriate means for reaching goals. The careful consideration of how goals and objectives may best be reached is called *action planning*.

A hypothetical instance of action planning can be built around the previously mentioned example of the English department in an urban university. One department goal, which was related to its mission statement, was "to identify entering freshmen with deficiencies in reading and writing skills and to improve those basic skills." This goal, one of many recommended by a faculty committee appointed by the chairperson, was formulated in response to the faculty's general feeling that many incoming students were failing because they could not handle the material assigned. Some essay examinations did not contain a single sentence that was grammatically correct.

Since there was general agreement that freshman reading and writing skills needed improvement, a committee was appointed to develop an action plan for implementing the goal. The committee first prepared a clear statement of the department's status as it related to the goal. The department had a well-qualified, hard-working faculty that had no special training in remedial work. Some older faculty members were shocked at the idea that a university should concern itself with ill-prepared students and felt that the problem could be solved by raising admissions standards. Other faculty members were actively interested in working closely with students whose skills needed improvement.

The committee then prepared a list of alternative strategies and tried to specify for each strategy objectives and tasks that might help attain the goal. In this instance, three possible means to the same end were discussed. The first alternative was a set of objectives and tasks that focused on establishing a reading laboratory, with equipment acquired through external funding. The second alternative involved using prepackaged, pretested materials from the university's resource center. The third strategy suggested using undergraduates in a program of intensive tutoring. The committee leaned toward the idea of a reading laboratory but abandoned that notion when the department failed in its initial attempts to get a laboratory funded. The second strategy, using prepackaged materials, was chosen because it seemed a better way of doing things given the available data. A minority of the faculty members preferred the tutoring plan, but they could not convince their colleagues that it was feasible.

The next step in preparing the action plan was to describe in detail the objectives and tasks that, using prepackaged materials, would help reach the goal and to specify a means of evaluating whether the action plan had been successful. The project would be considered successful if one-third of the participants brought their skills up to the average level of entering freshmen based on national norms. The goal suggested two objectives: (1) to administer and score a test for all freshmen and (2) to take them through a program that would improve their performance.

With the help of colleagues in the education department, the faculty of the English department selected a standardized test, specified a plan for administering and scoring it, and drafted letters explaining the program to the incoming freshmen. The second objective was also broken down into discrete activities and thoroughly described. The department decided to hire two graduate students to supervise the distribution and use of the prepackaged remedial materials. The students also were to monitor the progress of the freshmen students in the program and keep records. At the end of two quarters, the students would be retested. Those whose reading skills had improved would transfer to freshman English. Those who did not improve to the specified point would continue in the program. Thirty percent of the students who participated in the program made significant gains and entered the freshman course. In this case, the program proved moderately successful.

This case has been presented to give an idea of what action planning is like. The steps of action planning can be briefly summarized as follows.

1. Start with a clear statement of a desired goal.
2. Describe the department's status as it relates to the goal—i.e., show in a quantifiable way the relationship between where the department is now and where it wants to be.

3. List alternative courses of action that might be a means to achieving the goal or objective.
4. Analyze each alternative course of action, listing the tasks required and attempting to anticipate the consequences. Specify a means of evaluating the success of the action plans.
5. Rank the courses of action in preferred order of implementation.
6. Begin to implement the top-ranked course of action. Be prepared to shift to the next-highest ranked course of action if serious problems arise.

Some administrators use a simple technique to evaluate suggested courses of action for achieving a desired goal. Each course of action is rated in terms of (1) potential for achieving the goal, (2) cost, and (3) feasibility. The rating scale can be a simple one, such as "high," "medium," or "low."

Figure 10.1 shows a table that a chairperson developed to help him choose among alternative courses of action.

Another hypothetical case may be helpful in pointing out the relationships among the statement of mission or purpose, the annual report, goals, objectives, tasks, and action plans. The department, a small physics department, provides the following statement for the college catalogue:

> The mission of the department is to provide undergraduate instruction in physics for physics majors and for elementary and secondary preservice teachers, and to fulfill some of the general education needs of the university in the physical sciences. In addition, the department shall contribute to new knowledge in physics and physics education and shall serve local and regional needs in this area through programs for in-service teachers.

The department's annual report shows that it has six faculty members, adequate office space, good facilities for instruction, and an annual budget of around $200,000. The department's assets include well-equipped teaching laboratories, two young fac-

PROPOSED ACTIVITY OR ACTION	————————— EVALUATION —————————		
	Potential for Achieving Goal	Cost	Feasibility
#1	High	Low	Medium
#2	High	High	Medium
#3	Low	Low	High

Fig. 10.1. Evaluation and selection of alternative courses of action

ulty members who are especially enthusiastic and recognized as excellent teachers, and other faculty members who have good theoretical capabilities in the field of physics. The report recognizes that the department members generally lack expertise and proven performance in experimental physics.

State law requires that faculty members teach a minimum of twelve hours per week or the equivalent, and the state college system has set minimum class size at twelve students. No significant college growth is anticipated. The need for general education will remain constant. The number of physics majors is expected to remain the same—i.e., about forty students. The need for elementary and secondary teachers is expected to remain constant or rise slightly, in contrast to the decline in teachers needed in other areas. In addition, there is a continuing need to upgrade the training of general science and physics teachers in the large regional school system.

Although this statement of the department's status is minimal, it will serve the purposes of this example. A greatly expanded information base would be essential for effective department planning and goal setting; for example, data about enrollment levels, number of majors, number of course offerings, faculty assignment patterns, and patterns of financial expenditures should be recorded over a period of several years. The resulting department "fact book" would be useful for planning and goal setting, preparing annual reports, writing grant proposals, justifying budget requests, and simplifying many of the department chairperson's other tasks.

At the urging of the chairperson, the physics department developed the following goals: (1) to increase the current level of faculty research and publications; (2) to train elementary education majors in physical science topics that are part of the public school curriculum; (3) to plan and implement a summer workshop for high school teachers; and (4) to improve the writing skills of undergraduate physics majors. Following are the goals with their objectives and tasks:

Goal 1: To increase the current level of faculty research and publications
  Objective 1:   Increase the amount of faculty time assigned to research
       Task: Increase each faculty member's research assignment by 5 percent per year, to a level of at least 35 percent per faculty member
       Task: To compensate for increased research assignments, increase class size to reduce the number of classes to be taught

Objective 2:   Seek and acquire funding for research projects from external sources
  Task: Conduct a proposal writing seminar in fall quarter
  Task: Supply clerical and technical assistance for proposal writing
  Task: Write grant proposals to potential donors
Objective 3:   Publish six articles in refereed journals over the next two years
  Task: Establish a biweekly research seminar for faculty members to discuss ideas and projects
  Task: Discuss and, if feasible, implement a reward structure for publications
  Task: Provide clerical and technical assistance for research projects

Goal 2: To train elementary education majors in physical science topics that are part of the public school curriculum
Objective 1:   Revise curriculum of general physics course to suit needs of education majors
  Task: Meet with science supervisors in public school system to outline topics emphasized in curriculum—October 1
  Task: Alter course curriculum to encompass desired change—December 1
Objective 2:   Teach and evaluate revised course
  Task: Teach revised course—February 1–June 15
  Task: Administer and score department evaluation forms—June 15–20

Goal 3: To plan and implement a summer workshop for high school teachers
Objective 1:   Prepare list of desired subjects for high school teachers
  Task: Appoint committee to study National Science Foundation recommendations—September 15
  Task: Meet with school board and curriculum supervisor to establish needs—October 15
Objective 2:   Plan and publicize new program
  Task: Develop curriculum and select faculty—November 15
  Task: Advertise workshop in educational journals and newspapers—December onward
Objective 3:   Conduct and evaluate summer workshop
  Task: Teach workshop as planned—July 1–July 26
  Task: Prepare and administer questionnaire to evaluate program—July 25
  Task: Prepare and administer follow-up questionnaire—December 1

Goal 4: To improve the writing skills of undergraduate physics majors
Objective 1:   Plan writing seminar for fall quarter
  Task: Contact English department and establish interdepartment committee—January 1

      Task: Develop course in technical writing—March 15
Objective 2: Teach and evaluate writing seminar
      Task: Announce course offering for majors, encourage students to register—September of next year
      Task: Read and evaluate students' efforts

Although the goals, objectives, and tasks are presented here in outline form, the outlines themselves are the result of action planning. After the physics department established its four goals, the faculty met to plan how these goals could best be implemented. Each goal became the focus of an action plan that encompassed the steps described earlier. The objectives and tasks were formulated after the department members considered a variety of possible ways of achieving the goals. For example, when discussing the revision of the course for education majors, the faculty members spent a great deal of time and effort considering the possibility of converting the course to self-paced instruction using the computer. The action plan called for a series of tasks (see figure 10.2).

According to the calculations presented in figure 10.2, the cost of implementing the program would have been more than $10,000. The results of the first task, however, revealed that computer-assisted instruction worked better with students who were already highly motivated than with students who had limited mathematical and scientific interests and skills. The goal of a computer-assisted course was abandoned before much money was spent. The experience of other institutions was sufficient to convince the chairperson and the faculty that the contemplated

Tasks	Timetable	Estimated Cost
1. Review experience of other institutions using a computerized system	Sept. 1–Oct. 1	$600 (faculty time and travel)
2. Develop baseline data of test scores of students taking the course by the conventional method	Sept. 1–June 1	$500 (faculty time, student assistant time, data analysis)
3. Write programs needed to implement system	Sept. 1–Jan. 1	$6500 (faculty time, programmer time, computer charges)
4. Test programs	Jan. 1–Mar. 1	$2500 (faculty time, computer time)
5. Evaluate achievement of students in computer-assisted programs	Mar. 1–Sept. 1	$500 (faculty time, data analysis)

Fig. 10.2. List of tasks, timetable, and estimated cost

innovation was not likely to succeed. Instead, the department decided to identify what subjects the schools wanted their prospective teachers to know. Then the chairperson assigned the department's most dynamic teacher to the course. The course requirements were tailored to the needs and abilities of nonmajors, and the evaluation showed its popularity. Some faculty members, however, thought that the new course was not quite rigorous enough, and the debate about its merits continues.

The idea to computerize the course, which was subsequently abandoned, actually came from the action planning that was undertaken while the first goal—to increase the level of research and number of publications—was being considered. Here the department was reacting to the fact that a member's application for promotion was rejected on the grounds of insufficient publications. The goal of increased publications was a result of the department's unease over the college's increasingly rigorous promotion and tenure policy. While the faculty was trying to conceive of ways to get more time to do research, the switch to computer-assisted instruction was suggested. Teaching through the computer would save faculty teaching time, which could be spent in research. Translating the idea of computerized teaching to a goal and an action plan, which included a description of how the objective was to be accomplished, led to the rejection of the idea. Implementing the idea would have required a significant amount of computer programming, storage of large amounts of information and test items, purchase of additional terminals for student use, and payment of staff to monitor the terminals for many hours every day. Evidence of the increased costs did not lead to the immediate abandonment of the tentative objective, though it did dampen some of the early enthusiasm. Proceeding with the action plan described above, however, the chairperson and department got enough information to warrant abandoning the plan.

To be able to distinguish between ideas and goals is useful. Computer-assisted instruction seemed to be—indeed, was—a good idea. When translated into a goal, with objectives and an action plan, the idea's flaws became more and more apparent. The university has been the repository of innumerable ideas that have devoured time and money for years. Usually no one has bothered to identify the goals, the objectives, or results associated with the idea. No one has identified the measurable and desired results that the idea is supposed to produce, and no time scale for accomplishing results has been established. That the idea itself endures is not surprising, for there is no way to assess progress or lack of progress of an idea. If programs are to be effective, however, they need to develop measurable goals and objectives that are oriented toward results.

Not every goal or objective can always be attained, but when a legitimate goal is not met, an active and strong department needs to review its activities and procedures seriously. The weak department is one that does not learn from mistakes and repeats useless routines year after year.

In this chapter, we have discussed ways in which the department can report its activities and pursue a rational course in attempting to chart its future. The need for a sense of purpose, the relationship of goals to the overall purpose, and the formulation of objectives that have measurable or observable outcomes have been detailed. Planning has been discussed here mainly in the language of behavioral objectives.

Although many academicians are put off by the language of behavioral objectives and its industrial counterpart—management by objectives—others are quite taken with these concepts. Some education planners seem to think that simply stating objectives in behavioral terms with clear specification of outcomes is all that is needed to clear up confusion in the university. Even if a department can state its objectives with clarity and precision, it still must be able to assess the quality of those objectives. Whether a department's objectives are good depends on much more than the form in which those aims are stated. This chapter has suggested ways in which some clarity in the statement of purposes and goals may be attained, but their qualitative assessment depends on the good judgment and insight of the chairperson and the department. A chairperson can help unify the faculty members by involving them in developing department missions and goals.

Department members who have been successful in obtaining grants from external sources know that to specify their plans using the terminology *missions, goals,* and *objectives* is useful and convincing. Stating the department's planned activities in ways similar to those described in this chapter can be a valuable tool for obtaining resources at a time of increasing competition for available resources. The chairperson must decide how much precision and quantification can sensibly be used in reporting and planing the department's activities. Effective leadership includes the ability to foresee the consequences of one's actions.

Planning a department's activities intelligently implies that the chairperson should have a good idea of what will happen to the department if the plans are carried out.

Questions and Exercises

1. List, according to the following categories, some of your department's more important accomplishments during the past year:
   • teaching, including curriculum development, new programs, and innovative methods
   • research and publications of individual faculty members
   • service to the university, region, and nation
   • important decisions related to department policies concerning faculty, students, and staff; curriculum; committee structures; governance; expenditure of travel funds; and so forth
2. List, according to the categories given above, your aspirations for your department for the coming year. Formulate goal statements based on these aspirations.
3. Select a specific, genuine goal that your department wishes to implement in the near future. Develop as comprehensive an action plan as you can, including objectives, tasks, and a time frame. Try to use the nomenclature suggested in the chapter.

References

Carnegie Commission on Higher Education. *Governance of Higher Education: Six Priority Problems.* New York: McGraw-Hill, 1973.

Gross, Edward. "University Organizations: A Study of Goals." In *Academic Governance,* edited by J. Victor Baldridge. Berkeley: McCutchan, 1976.

Gross, Edward, and Grambsch, Paul V. *University Goals and Academic Power: A Study in Conflict and Cooperation.* Washington, D.C.: American Council on Education, 1968.

Mager, Robert F. *Goal Analysis.* Belmont, Calif.: Fearon-Pitman, 1972.

Migatoki, Glenn K., and Byers, Maureen L. "Module 1: Identifying and Organizing Academic Unit Functions." *Academic Unit Planning and Management.* Technical Report No. 75. Boulder, Colo.: The National Center for Higher Education Management Systems, 1976.

Perrow, Charles. "The Analysis of Goals in Complex Organizations." In *Readings on Modern Organizations,* edited by Amitai Etzioni. Englewood Cliffs, N.J.: Prentice-Hall, 1969.

Peterson, Richard E. *College Goals and the Challenge of Effectiveness.* Institutional Research Program for Higher Education. Princeton, N.J.: Educational Testing Service, 1971.

————. *Toward Institutional Goal-Consciousness.* Princeton, N.J.: Educational Testing Service, 1971.

Trivett, David A. *Goals for Higher Education: Definitions and Directions.* ERIC/Higher Education Research Report no. 6. Washington, D.C.: American Association for Higher Education, 1973.

11

The Budget Cycle: Preparing Department Budget Requests and Persuading the Dean

||||| |||||||||| |||| ||||||||||||| ||||||||||||||||||||||| ||||||||||||||||||||||| ||||||||||||||||||||||||| ||||||||||

Obtaining appropriate university resources for the department is one of the chairperson's more sensitive responsibilities. Since the majority of the faculty tends to believe that departments are underfunded, ability to compete successfully for institutional funds is often seen as an important indicator of a chairperson's leadership quality. This perception appears to prevail even in departments that receive extensive external support from grants and contracts.

The budgetary procedures used by different institutions vary considerably. Many chairpersons, especially those who have been appointed only recently, may not be well informed about the budget process within their universities. Further, some tend to assume, often incorrectly, that the dean possesses extensive knowledge about their departments. Frequently, what may be an obvious problem to a chairperson is not so obvious to a dean whose academic home is in another department. Unless they have been briefed, deans are often unaware of department developments. For this reason, budget requests should include complete, updated information. Generally, the dean operates within a value system; consequently, the request should indicate how the requested resources will help meet college and institution priorities.

The purpose of this chapter, therefore, is to help chairpersons formulate department budget requests and prepare effective presentations about the department during review sessions with the dean. Formal budget requests may not be required of all departments. Nevertheless, the chairperson must be able to communicate department needs effectively when the opportunity presents itself.

The process of preparing a department budget is easier if the chairperson understands the broader aspects of budgeting within the academic context. This global view includes an appreciation of the budget review process within and outside the university, budget cycles, alternative budgeting systems, and the language of budgeting.

The Global View

Chairpersons who are responsible for preparing or supervising the preparation of budget requests should have a general understanding of the budget process at all levels and of the sequence of events preceding appropriation for the institution as a whole. Such awareness will not necessarily lead to an increase in department allocation. It will, however, provide an understanding of those political and economic realities that affect the budgetary process; it will also facilitate communication with a concerned faculty.

Many institutions begin preparing a budget request for the coming year's operation as much as a year in advance, and the chairperson must be able to communicate anticipated needs. The individual budgets may be reviewed at each level of the hierarchy, with each department chairperson meeting with the dean, each dean with the academic vice president, and then all the top administrators meeting with the president. The institution's board of trustees may approve the final budget request, and, in the case of a public institution, the request is submitted to the appropriate state agencies.

Private Institutions

In the case of private colleges and universities, budget requests are reviewed and analyzed within the institution, and approval by boards of trustees is the final action necessary before internal distribution of funds. In formulating budget requests, chairpersons in private colleges and universities should be mindful of the institution's general financial health. They should be aware of the status of the endowment fund and the recent pattern of gifts and bequests. Since tuition payments constitute a sizeable portion of the income of many private schools, chairpersons should be able to anticipate the effects of increased tuition on department enrollments. At many private institutions, faculty members are expected to participate actively in a variety of fund-raising activities, in addition to generating contracts and grants.

Public Institutions

Budget requests from public institutions, even if approved by boards of trustees, are subject to external review and analyses before being acted on by the legislature. The depth and complexity of the external analyses depend on the type of governance under which the institution operates. For example, the University of Michigan, because it is not a member of a university system, will transmit its institutional budget requests directly to the governor's state budget agency and to offices of appropriate legislative staff. On the other hand, Florida State University, because it is one of several members of a state university system under a single governing board, must transmit its institutional budget request to the central staff of the Florida university system for review and analysis. The central staff will examine budget requests from each institution in the system and submit a recommendation to the offices of the governor's state budget agency and to the appropriate legislative staff.

In other types of state systems, individual institutional requests may not be forwarded to external agencies; rather, an aggregated system request may be submitted to the funding agencies. In this type of system, the institution's top officials meet together with the system staff throughout the budget development process and before the aggregation of all institutional requests. The system staff interprets the state budget guidelines and prepares the combined budget request, which is submitted to the system coordinating or governing board for approval. It is then transmitted to the governor's state budget agency and the legislative budget staff, which often meets with institutional representatives and the system staff to ensure that the budget request meets the needs of both the executive and legislative branches of government.

Thus, the institutions in the system may be listed separately in the system request and appropriations act, or they may be aggregated by program or some other classification system without institutional identification. Because many state legislatures have developed their own priorities for higher education, the institutional or system budget requests may be submitted to the legislative staff when the request is sent to a governor's budget agency. In almost all states, however, the governor's state budget request to the legislature is still treated as the official budget proposal.

At the state level, the possibility for increased appropriations depends on the level of economic activity and the taxes collected.

Through the process of estimating tax revenues, state officials estimate the amount of "new" money that will become available. Legislatures almost always test budget requests against these estimates and against legislative priorities. Department chairpersons can obtain a ballpark estimate of "new" money for higher education by noting the priority given to education and relating it to the estimated percent increase in state tax revenues or moneys available for appropriation, an increase that is usually well publicized.

Within a bicameral state legislature, each chamber reviews budget requests and emphasizes its own individually determined state priorities. For this reason, the "super bowl" of the legislative appropriations process is the conference committee, created jointly by the two chambers to work out their differences. Because of the complexity and magnitude of the state programs, many important funding details are listed only in work papers or exist in "understandings" among state officials, legislators, and their staffs. Usually only a few items are of sufficient priority to be listed separately in the appropriations documents. Because the house of representatives, the senate, and the state budget agency each has only one or two persons functioning as higher education budget analysts, more unwritten rules and understandings about higher education budgets and appropriations may exist than are ever listed in the published appropriations act; there often is not sufficient time to spell out all details. Sometimes, as is the case in Florida, a "letter of intent" follows the appropriations act and gives supplemental instructions regarding the use of appropriated funds.

In recent years a few states have returned to biennial budgets in the hope that reducing the number of budget cycles will stimulate better planning and program analysis preceding preparation of the budget request. Double-digit inflation and rising energy costs, however, can also require supplemental appropriations in the second year. Furthermore, when legislators meet annually, they are tempted to "redo" portions of the budget in the second year. Nevertheless, the published two-year appropriation can provide some sense of continuity and confidence for department chairpersons, since actions in the second year of the biennium tend to involve supplemental funding.

In formulating department budgets, chairpersons in public institutions that are part of state systems should be aware of the process whereby a system budget request is formulated. They should know what the main issues at their institution are and what the system's priorities are. They should stay as informed as possible about the status of the request from start to appropriation. Knowledge of the schedule of activities at the legislative and system levels may help chairpersons plan functions at the department level. This type of information, as general as it may be, helps chairpersons put their department's priorities in a wider perspective and set their expectations at realistic levels. Department chairpersons in public institutions that are not part of university or college systems should be especially sensitive to legislative schedules and actions, which are transmitted directly to the institution rather than through the central staff of a system.

The chairperson, then, should take a more global view of the budget process and learn as much as possible about financial conditions and priorities at all levels. If the legislature uses a formula to appropriate funds, the chairperson should know what the components of the formula are. In the case of an institution that is a part of a system, the chairperson should be aware of the system's technique for distributing funds among the institutions; he or she should be especially familiar with the procedures used to derive the resources that concern academic areas.

The Budget Cycle

Each budget cycle begins with the preparation of a *budget request*. A series of decisions are then made at various levels, taking into account the budget request and the funds available. These decisions lead to the development of an *operating budget*, which is an expenditure plan covering the period, usually a single year, for which funds are made available. At the end of each year a *financial statement* is prepared, showing the financial status at the start of the year, the activities during the year, and the financial condition at the end of the year. Finally, an *audit* is performed to verify that established rules and regulations have been followed. Budget cycles may overlap at some institutions—for example, a university could be preparing a budget request for a coming year at the same time it is preparing an operating budget for the current year. Chairpersons should be aware of budget cycles, since they affect institutional decision-making processes.

Preparation of a Budget Request. This activity is usually begun well in advance of the time period for which resources are being requested—for example, the budget request for fiscal year 1983–84 may have to be prepared during late 1981 or early 1982. In the case of public institutions, the date for submitting a budget request depends on the dates of legislative sessions. The Florida legislature, for example, meets annually during April and May and considers the governor's spending plan, which was presented in late February; thus, the institutional budget request must be prepared during the summer of the previous year and submitted in October of that year. Because of recently adopted biennial budgeting, the budget request submitted in October 1980 covered the years 1981–83.

Universities take different approaches to the preparation of budget requests. For example, in the case of some private and public institutions, the department request may be the first step in a continuous planning process that eventually results in the allocation of an operating budget. At the University of West Virginia, department budget requests are submitted and priorities established at the college level, and college requests are then arranged in priorities at the institutional level. During the allocation process, these institutional priorities serve as the basis for distributing resources. At many public institutions, especially those funded through an enrollment formula, department requests may serve as the basis for distributing resources among departments within a college.

Thus, in the first approach, department requests are used in a continuous process to describe the institution's needs. In the second case, department needs are not aggregated and the distribution of resources to the institution and sometimes even to the school or college may depend on some other variable, such as enrollment. A third approach, which combines the two methods and which is becoming more widespread, is to distribute resources by expenditure categories to implement defined institutional priorities.

Regardless of the approach to generating an institutional budget request, chairpersons should involve themselves in the process as much as possible. The process provides one of the few opportunities for the department to describe its past successes and future objectives. Generally, the more that is known and understood about the complex activities of an academic department, the greater the possibility that positive decisions will be made. At the same time, however, chairpersons should be careful to keep their expectations at a reasonable level. Departments often request an amount that would be sufficient to accommodate all their needs. The funds to meet such requests are rarely available, however, and the chairperson should be prepared to receive fewer resources than were sought.

Allocation and Control of the Operating Budget. Allocation and control of a current year's budget occur after the state legislature has appropriated the funds, the college or university has received its allocation, and department operating budgets have been authorized. Chairpersons and deans exercise budget control by signing approval for proposed expenditures. They may find that, although their annual budget has been approved, the funds are not made available all at one time. This situation occurs in states that operate on a funds release schedule other than an annual one—for example, the state of Florida releases funds on a quarterly basis. If the state is on an accrual accounting basis, the accounting at the end of the fiscal year includes all obligations made during the year, and funds are "certified forward" to the next fiscal year to cover these obligations. This type of year-end activity normally occurs in states where unspent or unobligated funds "revert" to the state. Not all states operate this way, however.

Budget Close-out. The budget for the academic year is closed out in the last month of that fiscal year, at which time there is usually an end-of-the-year rush to complete authorized transactions and to prepare final annual reports. In states where state funds revert, chairpersons must be aware that any allocated funds not spent or encumbered during the allocation year will be lost to the department.

Expenditure Audit. The record of expenditures is generally audited by internal auditors during the current year or thereafter. Expenditures may also be audited by external auditors, who conduct audits of the institution for its board of trustees or for the state. Colleges or universities with large federal grants and contracts may have auditors present from different federal departments much of the year. Some foundations conduct audits simultaneously with reviews of programs they fund.

In any current budget year, all or most of these activities may be occurring at the same time, although they may be grouped variously and performed by special offices or service departments. For example, at the beginning of a new fiscal year, an institutional budget office may be allocating funds to departments, authorizing the payroll office to increase the salaries and benefits of persons receiving pay raises, compiling cost data for the budget request for the subsequent year, estimating the current and future revenues from student tuition and fees, helping close out last year's budget, and beginning planning for the future. Budget responsibilities may be centralized or decentralized within the institution. In the decentralized model, the activities may be distributed so that the planning office is concerned with the budget request, the controller's office with the implementation of current-year decisions, and the academic vice president's budget office with all budget-related activities pertaining to academic areas.

The chairperson, aware of the complicated activities of the budget cycle, should maintain accurate records of expenditures, even though such records may also be kept in administrative offices. He or she should plan department expenditures wisely and systematically to avoid last-minute scurrying about to purchase supplies and services before the budget close-out.

Since the budget requested for a given year is usually prepared one or two years in advance, the department needs to know what activities it intends to pursue in the next year or two in order to request appropriate funds. Plans for the department's general future are linked to budget planning. The timetable and deadline dates established for completing the various stages in budget preparations are often used by chairpersons as a basis for scheduling academic planning sessions. Some chairpersons feel that planning is a wasted effort unless additional funds are expected to be made available. Such persons are not sensitive to the possibility that a department may be required to change or modify some of its academic activities to accommodate new societal needs or that at times such changes will have to be made without additional funding.

Academic planning is necessary whether anticipated funds for the coming year are more than, less than, or the same as the amounts allocated in the previous year. Departments can plan alternative courses of action to meet whatever situations occur, such as implementing new, unfunded projects in the event that unanticipated money should become available. Just as budget preparation is continuous, so should academic planning be continuous. Regular assessment of current positions and identification of key activities to be pursued will keep the department from straying too far from its missions and goals. Ideally, the planning process should take alternate possibilities into account. In reality, the tendency is to get the resources first and make the plans afterwards, especially in the case of annual appropriations.

Budgeting Systems

Institutions of higher learning use a variety of budgeting systems. When preparing budget requests, departments should follow the instructions distributed by the appropriate office of the institution. Specifically, the chairperson should be familiar with the budgeting approach used by his or her dean. Administrators who review budget requests may not attach sufficient importance to items that are not presented in a familiar format. The following summary of commonly used budget systems is presented here to expand the chairperson's language of budgeting.

Incremental Budgeting. The system of incremental budgeting usually uses last year's expenditures as a base; it estimates and justifies an increase, or increment, above the base. This system does not require an extensive analysis or review of goals. It is widely used in colleges and universities, mainly, no doubt, because it is easily comprehensible.

Usually, each category within a budget—such as faculty salaries, expenses, travel, and so on—is increased by some percentage or flat amount of dollars. The guidelines for preparing the budget request may identify the maximum percentage increases that will be considered. When the economy becomes unpredictable and tax revenues uncertain, the budget guidelines for public colleges and universities may direct each institution to prepare and submit several different budget requests, one with perhaps a 5 percent decrease, another with no increase, and still another with a 5 percent increase. The guidelines from a state budget agency may include such specific instructions, even when an institution uses a different budgeting system. The budget request selected for approval will depend on the actual amount of state funds that will become available for higher education.

One major advantage of the incremental system is that the base is already agreed upon; further agreement is needed only on the amount of the increment. Moreover, the incremental system does not preclude the review of programs during the decision process, nor does it preclude subsequent resource adjustments to the base. Not inherent in this system, however, is a complete examination of program objectives and outcomes during each cycle.

Zero-base Budgeting System (ZBBS). This system assumes that a department's objectives should determine its budget and that an assessment should be made of how well objectives are reached. Zero-base budgeting starts from the premise that each time a new budget is prepared, it must demonstrate that it includes the best combination of costs and benefits for achieving each goal or the effective operation of each program. Sometimes, even the alternatives that were considered and rejected have to be specified. The base of the incremental system discussed earlier is not taken for granted in the zero-base system. In the ZBBS only demonstrable needs are to be funded. The ZBBS involves the use of "decision packages" (programs described at various funding levels) and the ranking of these "packages."

When the zero-base system is attempted annually, administrators often take the documents prepared for the previous year, reread them, and add the information provided and the funds requested. Such practice leads the system away from its emphasis on objectives, nullifies the rationale for zero-base budgeting, and leads toward a reintroduction of an incremental system. An academic department's objectives do not vary significantly from year to year, however; consequently, the complete review suggested by the ZBBS may itself be questioned on the grounds of cost efficiency. The exercise of evaluating achievement of objectives at different funding levels becomes too uncertain, and generally organizations using ZBBS arrive at set percentages to be used.

The major problem with using zero-base budgeting in academic departments is the nature of faculty costs. Faculty salaries, which are a major portion of department budgets, remain constant or increase with the longevity of faculty members, regardless of changes in department, college, or university objectives.

Line-Item Budgeting. Most institutions use organizational units and expenditure categories, rather than defined programs and activities, as the basis for budget planning. An organizational unit is an academic department, center, institute, school, or college. Expenditures include such categories as salaries, expenses, equipment, and so forth. Salaries and expenses to be budgeted for an academic department, for example, would include the cost of programs in the department, such as instruction, academic support, and advising. This itemizing is called *line-item budgeting.* By adding the budgets of all organizational units in the institution, the total institutional budget can be determined.

Planning, Programming, and Budgeting System (PPBS). This system uses "programs" rather than organizational units as a basis for budget planning. A *program* is defined as a collection of related activities and services that together constitute the achievement of the goal. Theoretically, PPBS involves identifying objectives, listing alternative courses of action (showing cost benefit), choosing one alternative, and, finally, implementing the alternative through funding. Generally, funding (or at least the request) is related to workload measures for each activity.

In higher education, reaching a consensus on what constitutes a program is difficult. Following are examples of what some instructional programs include. If a stated goal is to provide instruction to all students in an institution, the program of instruction might consist of all courses offered by the institution. If the goal is to provide undergraduate instruction to all students in an institution, the program would include all undergraduate courses offered at the institution. The difficulty in defining *program* is so great that the term remains undefined in several state statutes governing higher education.

The National Center for Higher Education Management Systems (NCHEMS), a federally supported research agency, has developed a sophisticated budgeting model that defines a program of instruction as a discipline major or any collection of courses designed to satisfy curricular requirements for a degree or certificate.[1] This concept recognizes that each department makes only a partial contribution to the education of a degree-seeking student. The modern computer, with the aid of computer technology, can divide the cost for each student among all the departments in an institution, a calculation based on the level of student enrollment. The total cost for producing a degree in a given major can be estimated by adding the costs of the educational services provided to a student in that major by all contributing departments over a four-year period.

In addition to different types of programs of instruction, some institutions using PPBS have designated "academic support" and "student services" as separate institutional programs. Each program includes all the related activities and services that together contribute to the achievement of its respective goal. "Academic advising," including all activities related to this function, is sometimes designated as an institutional program in its own right and sometimes as a separate component of a larger program, such as "instruction," "academic support," or "student services." Occasionally, academic advising activities are decentralized—i.e., an advisor may be placed in each department—in which case they become an integral part of a program of instruction.

Basically, PPBS incorporates the idea of the zero-base system that an organization's goals and objectives should determine its

1. *Procedures for Determining Historical Full Costs: The Costing Component of NCHEMS Information Exchange Procedures*, Technical Report no. 65, 2nd ed. (Boulder, Colo.: 1977), p. 16.

budget; in addition, however, it includes a long-range planning component. PPBS is strongly influenced by the rationale and techniques of systems analysis and represents an attempt to bridge the gap between planning and budgeting. PPBS also involves attaching cost estimates to the multiyear planning goals and objectives after the most efficient and effective means for achieving the programs' objectives have been identified. The selection and number of component activities contained in a program depend on the scope of the stated goal and the preferences of the person who is developing the system.

A budget plan that assigns moneys to organizational units usually focuses on resources as input to the instruction process rather than on output and goals, whereas a program budget plan that assigns moneys to defined programs provides the means to relate program activities to output and goals. Institutions using organizational structure for budget planning find managing and accounting for resources easier than do institutions that use program classification based on activities.

The statements of goals and objectives for several years and the resources required to achieve them become extremely tenuous during periods of rising costs and double-digit inflation. The need to revise five-year projections during each annual budget preparation, for example, may lead to incremental adjustments of the kind mentioned in connection with zero-base budgeting. In colleges and universities, long-range projections are subject to extensive revisions, partly because the turnover rate for chairpersons is high and because program priorities within departments change as frequently. Whenever new administrators, regardless of level, search for ways to implement fresh ideas within the department, school, or college, the probability is high that older goals and objectives will be changed. Rather than trying to follow a fully developed comprehensive plan to bring about change, most administrators adopt a strategy of shifting budgeted funds gradually from one set of programs to another. Some of the analytical techniques developed within the PPBS approach, however, have value in department planning. For example, the planning for a new program will be much improved if objectives, alternatives, workload measures, and resource requirements are estimated before the program is implemented.

Individual departments should not attempt to implement a PPB system solely for the purpose of facilitating data compilation for the budget request, especially if the dean or administrator is not familiar with or sympathetic to the system. PPBS, properly implemented, provides a great deal of detail and clarity, but the hard work of developing a system may be wasted if the department's priorities clash with the institution's priorities. In some institutions, experience has shown that when departments attempted five-year plans, much effort was devoted to projecting needs for adding new specialty courses in the face of declining enrollments. This kind of expanded need may be inserted in any budget request, regardless of the budgeting system in use. A department has a much greater chance of being successful in its requests, however, if it fully, accurately, and realistically justifies its needs, regardless of the budgetary system used.

Formula Budgeting

Formula budgeting uses formulas as a basis for preparing budget requests and for determining allocations. One purpose of formula budgeting is to provide equitable funding for all competing units, such as institutions in a state system or academic departments within an institution. The uniform application of formulas to colleges and universities in a state system tends to reduce conflict among presidents and, when applied uniformly within an institution, helps reduce conflict among deans, provided, of course, that the formulas have been agreed on and accepted by all concerned. Various formulas can be used for education budgets. Zero-base formulas, for example, derive resources based on estimated full-time equivalent (FTE) enrollment and the agreed-on cost per student. Some formulas, on the other hand, may address only increases or decreases to the existing base.

One formula, for example, involves multiplying the projected number of FTE students by the cost per FTE student. When applied to an institution across the board, regardless of discipline or student level, the formula can provide an estimate of the total cost for operating all academic programs in the university. The formula can also be applied separately to departments and programs, as well as to graduate and undergraduate students within programs. For example, estimates of operational costs can be calculated for lower-division students in biology, upper-division students in psychology, graduate students in chemistry, and so forth. The sum of the separate costs for each category will be the total operational cost for all academic programs in the institution. Before the formula can be used, however, a determination must be made of what constitutes a FTE student in each of the above categories, how many FTE students are expected to enroll in each category, and the cost per FTE student. (A more detailed definition of *full-time equivalent* appears later in this chapter.)

Another formula for developing budget requests involves multiplying the estimated number of needed faculty positions by the average faculty salary. This formula, when applied to an institution as a whole, will provide an estimate of the total faculty salary cost for the university. Before the number of needed faculty positions can be estimated, however, a determination must be made, for budgetary purposes, of what constitutes a faculty workload.

Several state university systems have, for a number of years, used workload formulas to determine the number of positions needed. "Normative" workload factors were estimated originally from turn-of-the-century teaching load data. For example, a faculty member who taught one 3-credit-hour course with 25 students in the class would generate 75 student credit hours (3 × 25). If the instructor taught four such courses during a term, the total number of student credit hours generated that term would be 300 credit hours (4 × 75). The workload factor for this instructor, therefore, would be 300.

The number of student credit hours generated by a course may vary, depending on its assigned number of credits and the number of students enrolled in it. At many institutions, as late as World War II, faculty members were expected to teach four courses each semester. For budgetary purposes, the average faculty workload per semester was described not in terms of the total number of courses taught, but in terms of the total number of student credit hours generated. Originally, workload factors were calculated only for the different levels of enrollment without consideration of discipline. Because many lower-division classes are taught by lecture and generally have larger enrollments than advanced classes, the average number of student

Educational Status	"Normative" Workload Factor (Equivalent of One Faculty Position)
Freshman or Sophomore	400 student credit hours
Junior or Senior	300 student credit hours
Beginning Graduate	200 student credit hours
Advanced Graduate	100 student credit hours

Fig. 11.1. "Normative" workload factors, by educational status of students

credit hours generated by an instructor teaching the lower-division courses was expected to be larger. Figure 11.1 illustrates this type of approach.

The number of faculty positions needed at each level is estimated by dividing the faculty workload factor assigned to a level into the total anticipated number of student credit hours to be generated by the institution at that level. The total number of faculty positions needed by the institution can be estimated by totaling the faculty positions needed at all levels. Multiplying that total by an average faculty salary, regardless of rank or discipline, results in an estimate of the institution's total cost for faculty salaries. By constructing ratios between faculty positions and support or administrative positions, the number of support positions can also be estimated—for example, ten faculty positions might generate one support position. Thus a budget request can be built for all authorized and needed positions covering all functions within an institution.

The workload factors described above represent averages that do not differentiate disciplines. In reality, workload factors vary in size from one discipline to another because of the nature of the discipline. The number of students in music and art classes is much smaller than that in social science classes, thus making the workload factors in music and art smaller than that in the social sciences. The availability of the large computer makes possible the calculation, using documented or anticipated student enrollment, of workload factors for each discipline or department and for each enrollment level within each department. When data about disciplines from several previous years are averaged, more realistic workload measures can be derived. Table 11.1 contains a standard list of specific and broad discipline areas often used by institutions in reporting data to the federal government. Illustrated in the table are the workload factors in the State University System of Florida for 1976, adjusted according to those disciplines and the enrollment levels within each.

Thus far, we have discussed ways in which formulas can be used in the preparation of budget requests. Rarely is the same formula used both to prepare a budget request for an institution and to allocate resources within the institution. Most formulas in use are zero-based and have no variable that accounts for college or institutional priorities. Therefore, more faculty positions may be assigned to some programs than would be generated according to formula. On the other hand, this excess must be balanced by assigning fewer positions than are earned to certain programs

TABLE 11.1
ADJUSTED BASE-YEAR PRODUCTIVITY (WORKLOAD) FACTORS,
STATE UNIVERSITY SYSTEM OF FLORIDA, 1976–77

DISCIPLINES	LEVELS			
	Lower	Upper	Graduate	Dissertation/ Thesis (Combined)
Agriculture & Natural Resources	420.00	240.00	108.00	60.00
Architecture & Environmental Design	300.00	240.00	120.00	45.00
Area Studies	240.00	240.00	84.00	60.00
Biological Sciences	360.00	240.00	132.00	45.00
Business & Management	480.00	360.00	192.00	60.00
Communications	360.00	240.00	168.00	60.00
Computer & Information Sciences	420.00	360.00	216.00	45.00
Education	360.00	380.00	228.00	75.00
Engineering	360.00	240.00	120.00	45.00
Fine & Applied Arts	180.00	120.00	84.00	75.00
Foreign Languages	240.00	180.00	84.00	75.00
Health Professions	360.00	180.00	108.00	45.00
Home Economics	300.00	300.00	180.00	60.00
Law	0.0	0.0	480.00	60.00
Letters	240.00	300.00	168.00	75.00
Library Science	540.00	300.00	228.00	60.00
Mathematics	420.00	360.00	96.00	45.00
Military Science	0.0	0.0	0.0	60.00
Physical Sciences	420.00	240.00	168.00	45.00
Psychology	540.00	360.00	204.00	45.00
Public Affairs & Services	540.00	300.00	168.00	60.00
Social Sciences	540.00	360.00	192.00	60.00
Technology	300.00	180.00	0.0	60.00
Interdisciplinary Studies	300.00	240.00	144.00	60.00
Continuing Education	0.0	0.0	0.0	0.0

SOURCE: "Derivation of Productivity Levels (Student Credit Hours) by Discipline and Course Level," Interinstitutional PPB Committee for Appropriation and Allocation of Academic Positions, Florida Board of Regents, September 20, 1976.

NOTE: Each factor represents the number of student credit hours that will generate one FTE faculty position at the different levels in each of the listed disciplines per term.

with high student-credit-hour productivity. Thus, even though the formula for a budget request may be based on the number of FTE students generated by each department, each administrative level in a university may follow a completely different system for allocating funds to units at the next lower level. Chairpersons would do well to familiarize themselves with the formulas, priorities, and procedures used in both the requesting process and the allocation process.

Despite their usefulness, student-weighted funding formulas are creating problems for many colleges and universities today. The formulas are disliked because they usually rely on averages and because they reward high enrollments in the absence of other considerations. Moreover, in times of declining enrollments, the amount of funds generated by the formula may not be sufficient to continue some academic programs of an institution. Such insufficiency results because most formulas are linear and do not consider that departments have fixed costs—i.e., a class of nineteen students may cost as much as a class of twenty-one students. In addition, formulas do not take into account the difference in costs due to faculty seniority, rank, and labor market rates. Thus, some formulas fail to provide the equity that was the very rationale for their initial application.

Most funding formulas are based on a cost analysis of some kind in which data are stated in terms of cost per FTE student. The availability of the electronic computer makes it possible to process the large volume of data needed to conduct cost studies. In *A Study of Cost Analysis in Higher Education*, the American Council on Education reports that none of the existing costing systems was useful to institutional administrators in improving or managing higher education. Nevertheless, many state-required formulas continue to rely on these cost data.

Formulas that use averaged data derived from several institutions in a system generally tend to reward the teaching institutions at the expense of the research universities. Some states, like North Carolina, have different funding systems for different kinds of institutions. State budgeting systems that vary according to the mission, role, and scope of each institution in a system are now gaining much attention. Should such a system emerge formally, it would quite likely be applied to the departments within a college or university. The congruence of a department's goals and objectives with those of its parent institution would then become much more important for internal funding purposes.

The Language of Budgeting

The budgeting process is often perceived as mysterious and esoteric. Some persons find it dry and boring, and those who find it fascinating frequently choose some facet of it as a vocation. To the layperson, the jargon used by finance experts seems to be incomprehensible except to a chosen few, and those who understand it are thought to be "important." In actuality, the budget process is part of planning and is frequently less precise than it may appear. Although we may not demystify the entire process by explaining some of its intricacies, this discussion will help chairpersons become familiar with the more common terms related to budgeting. Let us review some of these terms.

1. *FTE* is a commonly used abbreviation that stands for "full-time equivalent" and refers variously to students, faculty, and staff. This concept is often used in formula-base budgeting.

a) FTE student. Let us assume that a full course load for a typical undergraduate has been designated as 15 credits per term. For budgeting purposes, therefore, one undergraduate student enrolled for 15 credits of course work is considered to be one FTE student. Similarly, three students enrolled for 5 credits each, or a total of 15 credits, are considered to be one FTE. The number of credit hours designated as equaling one FTE may change according to the level of the courses or the level of the student. At many institutions, one full-time equivalent graduate student is 12 credit hours.

b) FTE faculty and staff. A faculty or staff member may be appointed on a full- or part-time basis for an academic or calendar year, depending on the institution's policy. Faculty members on full-time appointments are generally expected to devote 100 percent of their professional time and effort to the job to which they are appointed. What constitutes 100 percent of time and effort of a faculty member's professional life has not been clearly defined, however. Those institutions and departments who need a definition must stipulate their own.

For salary purposes, a faculty member who receives 100 percent of a salary for a designated period of time is considered one FTE faculty member for that time period. Some faculty members are appointed to two or more departments or offices simultaneously, and their salaries come from different budgets. For example, a person may receive 75 percent of his or her salary from a department and 25 percent from the dean's office. The fraction of the total salary that comes from each budget also indicates that fraction of FTE faculty assigned to each department or office. Similarly, a person who receives 25 percent of his or her salary from a contract or grant is considered to be 25 percent FTE "on the grant" and 75 percent FTE "in the department."

A faculty member whose full salary comes from a department budget and who is considered one FTE faculty member, as far as that department is concerned, is usually assigned a variety of activities, each of which is expressed as a percentage of full-time effort. For example, a faculty member's teaching effort may be assigned 50 percent of a FTE; research, 30 percent; and service, 20 percent. An institution may determine the total number of FTE faculty involved in research by adding all the individual percentage FTEs assigned to research and thereby estimate the total salary costs of the institution's research effort. Similarly, the total number of FTE faculty involved in the teaching of undergraduate lower-division courses can be estimated by adding all the individual percentage FTEs assigned to teaching lower-division courses.

A faculty member whose formal appointment is 25 percent FTE in the dean's office and 75 percent FTE in a department may devote 50 percent of his or her department effort to teaching and 50 percent to research. In this case the total teaching assignment of FTE is 37.5 percent (50 percent × 75 percent). Similarly, the total research assignment of FTE is 37.5 percent. Many urban colleges and universities employ a considerable number of part-time faculty members, each of whom is appointed to a fraction of one FTE position and is paid accordingly. If an institution hires three part-time faculty members, appointing one to a 0.5 FTE position, another to a 0.6 FTE position, and the third to a 0.3 FTE position, the three will constitute 1.4 FTE positions (0.5 + 0.6 + 0.3). Despite the many ways of calculating FTEs and their percentages, however, one faculty member can never be counted as more than one FTE, regardless of how hard or how many hours he or she works.

The FTE concept is also applied to nonacademic staff. In the case of staff, however, the percentage of FTE is based on the relationship between the number of assigned hours of work during a given period and the number of hours that constitutes a full workload for that period.

2. *SCH*, another common abbreviation, usually refers to "student credit hours." One student taking a 4-credit-hour course per term generates 4 student credit hours. Fifteen students enrolled in a 3-credit-hour course per term generate 45 student credit hours (3× 15). SCH may also refer to "student *contact* hours," the number of clock hours spent in contact with faculty members. One contact hour in a lecture class per week per term is usually equivalent to 1 credit hour. In the case of laboratory classes, however, 3 contact hours per week per term will often equal only 1 credit hour.

3. *Expenditure categories.* Resources may be allocated to institutions and departments in expenditure categories. The purpose of allocating funds in categories is to exercise control over how the money is spent. In many states and institutions, transfer of moneys from one category to another is not permitted or is permitted under restricted circumstances, such as a 5 percent limitation on transfers. Categories may vary from state to state, but the most common ones are listed and defined below.

   a) *Salaries*—Includes the funds required to pay salaries of persons in permanent or regular positions.

   b) *Benefits*—Includes funds for additional commitments made to employees, such as retirement, social security matching funds, health insurance, and so forth.

   c) *Temporary personnel*—Includes funds for temporary help, such as student assistants and peak load supplemental employees.

   d) *Graduate assistantships and fellowships*—Includes funds for teaching and research assistantships and fellowships.

   e) *Expenses*—Includes funds for supplies, travel, telephones, postage, equipment lease, rent, and so forth.

   f) *Equipment*—Includes funds for equipment, such as typewriters, duplicating machines, laboratory equipment, furniture, and so forth, which become the property of the institution. Sometimes equipment that costs less than a designated amount may be purchased with funds from the expense category.

   g) *Capital funds*—Includes funds for construction of new buildings. In some states, funds from this category may be used to pay for building renovations.

   h) *Lump sum*—Institutional funds are sometimes allocated in "lump sums"—i.e., the funding agency does not constrain institutional expenditures by category. In such cases, the institution makes its own decisions on the percentage of funds to be spent on salaries, supplies, equipment, and so forth. Institutions with this flexibility may provide the same flexibility to individual departments.

4. *Sources of institutional support.* Institutions usually get their funds from a variety of sources. Some of these funds are for general institutional support, while others may be directed toward specific purposes. The most common sources are listed below.

   a) *State funds* are obtained from the general revenue of the state and usually make up the major source of a public institution's operational funds.

b) *Incidental funds* come from student tuition payments, library fines, application fees, and so forth. Sometimes contract and grant overhead funds are included in this category as well.

c) *Contract and grant funds* are obtained from foundations and government agencies for the purpose of financing specific projects and research activities.

d) *Auxiliary funds* come from revenue generated by institutional auxiliary activities, such as bookstores, housing, health center, duplicating services, and so forth. These operations are designed or mandated to be self-sufficient. Generally, normal operating funds from the university may not be used to support them. Profits generated by an auxiliary activity may be used for institutional purposes such as scholarships.

e) *Agency funds* are funds that the institution holds and disburses on behalf of an agency. A university service fraternity, for example, is in this category.

f) *Activity fee funds* are collected as supplements to tuition and are used to support such activities as student clubs, intercollegiate athletics, and other student-related activities. Although often included within agency funds, they may be handled separately. How these funds are controlled and regulated varies from institution to institution, but there seems to be a trend toward student involvement in activity fee control.

g) *Investment earnings* are generated by investing funds from the above categories if their immediate expenditure is not required. The investment earnings are generally used as discretionary funds by the institution. Sometimes state statutes prohibit public institutions from investing state funds.

h) *Other discretionary funds* may be obtained from the profits of concessions and vending machines and are generally retained by the institution for discretionary purposes.

i) *Scholarship and loan funds* may come from government or private sources. Included, usually, are funds to support the federal College Work-Study program.

j) *Foundation funds* include gifts and donations; generally these are not administered by the university but by a university or college foundation that is incorporated as a separate entity. *Restricted funds* are those given for a special purpose, such as for a particular school, college, or activity; *unrestricted funds* are those that have not been specifically designated. Usually, the foundation board decides how to use them.

k) *Athletic funds* are the revenues from the intercollegiate sports program. Usually, these funds are also external to the institution and are controlled by an athletic board.

Allocations within the Institution

When an institution is informed of its level of resources for a given budget period, it begins the process of internal distribution. Before moneys are disbursed, however, the institution sets aside the dollars needed to pay for continuing commitments and expenses. These costs are generally determined by an office in the central administration, such as the budget office or controller's office.

The total cost of the faculty and staff is one of the first determinations that must be made. The related question of how to deal with unfilled positions is answered in various ways by different institutions. In some cases, unfilled positions are treated as if they belong to the departments where the vacancies occurred, while in other cases all positions are reclaimed by the central administration, which reallocates them to the same or different departments on the basis of demonstrated need.

Regardless of the differences among position control policies, the computation of total institutional personnel costs is the first step in the allocation process. Next, the central administration must decide how much to take "off the top" to fund mandated expenditures. Money must be reserved for liability insurance, workmen's compensation, and continually increasing utility payments. Third, some funds are reserved in order to cover revenue shortfalls or unanticipated expenses. Fluctuating enrollments do not allow dependable projections of income from tuition, and in times of unstable enrollments the funds to be reserved may have to be increased.

After the necessary funds for the purposes described above have been reserved, the remainder of the budget, usually called "operating funds," is distributed to the vice presidents, often on the advice of a university budget committee. Each vice president, in turn, must distribute the funds to the units in his or her division. The vice president for academic affairs allocates money to the academic deans, who subsequently make disbursements to the departments.

Early Commitments and Interim Requests

Appropriation schedules for state legislatures are often out of phase with institutional deadline dates for making and implementing planned distribution decisions. Some state universities never know for sure what their fiscal-year budgets will be until after the fiscal year has already started. Because of the number of administrative levels involved in making budgetary decisions, departments are usually the last to be informed about what resources they will have for the new budget year. For a part of the year, therefore, most chairpersons will be uncertain about resources and must make tentative decisions without exact budget information.

Even under biennial budget conditions, when the legislature appropriates funds for two years at a time, there is still bound to be a period of uncertainty while departments wait for distribution decisions to be made within the institution. This uncertainty increases the difficulty of administering a department under any sort of plan or set of priorities. For example, a chairperson cannot wait until late August to learn whether a new faculty position has been allocated; March is about the latest time to begin recruiting a new faculty member for the fall term. Similarly, the chairperson of a department with a graduate program, to avoid losing prospective graduate students because of uncertainty about available support, needs to know by February what to expect for the next year in terms of allocations for assistantships and fellowships. The chairperson should be informed as early as possible whether requests for new positions will be approved, whether he or she will be authorized to recruit for positions that will be vacated because of resignations or retirement, and what the level of support for graduate students will be. A strategy used by many chairpersons is to prepare and submit an interim request to their deans and academic vice presidents asking them to make certain commitments in advance of the normal allocation cycle. Chairpersons may also seek early commitments for summer school operation.

The *interim request* is a procedure whereby the academic vice president or dean, prompted by sound arguments from the chairperson, makes commitments in advance of the actual receipt of funds. Important results of early commitment may include a rise in faculty morale, improved planning for summer courses, and recruitment of good faculty members. The major effect, however, is the well-being of the department chairperson, whose uncertainty level is reduced because planning for the summer and fall quarters can proceed in a timely and appropriate manner. Everyone concerned should understand the potential for problems and the risks involved in making decisions based on early commitments, for it is possible that the anticipated funds may not become available. The chairperson must then be ready for the consequences and be prepared with contingency plans.

Although early commitments could be made quite easily in the early 1970s, when continuous enrollment increases generally assured the dean of additional resources, times have changed. Relatively stable enrollments, allocations increasingly earmarked for special purposes, and special constraints for the use of resources have caused uncertainties for the deans and vice presidents nearly equal to those that chairpersons face.

The chairperson's ability to recognize the new uncertainties, communicate that understanding to the dean, and demonstrate willingness to share the risk with the dean can result in optimal resource planning and allocations if the dean and academic vice president are able and willing to make early commitments. As in all high-risk situations, the chairperson must plan for and be able to deal with unanticipated consequences. In any event, when critical situations arise, the dean should be informed of the negative effect of any delay in decisions. A successful chairperson is likely to be one who is aggressive and tenacious in pursuit of a decision from a dean.

Comprehensive Fiscal-Year Requests

In times of decreasing enrollments and diminishing resources, the system of distributing funds to departments and programs according to enrollment may no longer serve the institution's best interests. This distribution process may have worked well in the late sixties and early seventies, when enrollments were continually expanding and institutions were generously supported by legislatures and patrons. When scarce resources are divided among departments according to their relative enrollments, however, some programs with high priority within the institution or the college may not receive sufficient funds to maintain or achieve quality. Although enrollment cannot be ignored when allocating funds, many institutions are beginning to place more emphasis on demonstrated relative need within the context of structured priorities. Consequently, clear and effective documentation justifying programs and purposes for which funds are being requested must accompany each budget request.

Academic departments compete for funds not only with each other, but also with other administrative units within the university. In the central administration the vice president for academic affairs represents academic departments, just as the vice presidents for administration and student affairs represent departments and units in their respective divisions. In making the budget case for academic programs, the academic vice president uses the aggregation of documentation prepared by department chairpersons and deans. Unless the academic vice president has sufficient and useful information at hand, he or she may be placed in an inferior negotiating position when participating with the other vice presidents in the initial process of resource distribution. Chairpersons required to prepare comprehensive department budget requests, therefore, must give serious attention to the task of providing strong supporting documentation.

Before and during the process of preparing a budget request, the chairperson should reflect on how best to present the department's needs and what information would be most pertinent and persuasive. He or she should also make a realistic appraisal of the funds expected to be allocated to the institution for the coming year. During budget preparation time, and perhaps at other times as well, the chairperson should keep informed of legislative actions and of amounts previously allocated to higher education in general and, specifically, to his or her university for each of the last several years. If the university's allocation or expected allocation compares favorably with the previous year's allocation, there is a reasonable chance that a department's request for funds to cover basic needs, program changes, and improvements will be granted.

If the university's allocation does not compare favorably with the previous year's allocation, the chances for success in obtaining major increases are slim. Such circumstances are discouraging to the entire academic community, especially to chairpersons of departments whose programs command high enrollment and high visibility. These chairpersons feel that, without adequate funding, their departments will be unable to maintain their academic status and reputation for quality. In such instances, some chairpersons may propose that funds within the college or university be reallocated and that their departments be given additional funds, even at the expense of other departments. In theory, reallocation of resources to accommodate shifts in enrollment and changes in program priorities should be possible; in practice, major reallocations seldom occur.

The allocation patterns within universities reveal that few moneys are available for immediate reassignment. Usually, approximately 70 percent of university funds are expended for salaries; the filled positions supported by those salaries are really not susceptible to reallocation because they are held by specialized and often tenured professionals. Approximately another 10 percent of university funds is reserved for items that the university cannot control, such as utilities, leaving 20 percent to be used for operating needs. Realistically, however, only a small portion of the 20 percent is available for redistribution. Even departments whose programs have low enrollment and low priority require a minimum level of support. Any reduction in their budget could result in their demise.

One indicator of a university's ability to fund new or expanded department activities can be derived by comparing the overall increase in the university budget from one year to the next with the increase in average salaries over the same period. If the overall institutional increase is at least 2 percent greater than the salary increase, the university is in a relatively good position to meet department requests for additional operating funds. This type of situation exists, for example, when the institutional allocation has been increased by 10 percent over last year and the increase in average salaries is only 8 percent. On the other hand, if the overall institutional increase is less than the average salary increase, the university is hardly in a position to consider even minor requests for additional funds. Such would be the case with an institution whose overall allocation is 5 percent above last year's but whose increase in average salary is 8 percent. Obtaining information regarding the university's current allocation and how it relates to the previous year's allocation may take some effort. Occasionally, local newspapers will carry the information; or a call to the dean or to the budget office may produce results. Knowledge of the university's situation will help the chairperson maintain realistic expectations and see the final allocations in proper perspective.

Budget-Planning Strategies

In preparing a comprehensive budget for a department, the chairperson should construct a schedule of critical events for which plans must be developed and budget needs identified. The following list of questions may serve as a guide for making such a schedule.

- What is the probable retirement date of each faculty and staff member?
- When will any faculty members be eligible for tenure evaluation? For an "up-or-out" review?
- Which faculty members will become eligible for sabbaticals

in the next five years? Which are likely to apply for them?
- Which faculty members are likely to obtain external support and seek release time from teaching and other regular assignments in the next several years?
- Which faculty members will develop sufficient visibility to be recruited by another institution during the next five years?
- Which faculty members are likely to leave voluntarily within the next few years?
- Which faculty members are changing their career emphases from professorial to administrative roles?
- Which college or university administrators whose academic home is in this department are likely to return in the next several years?
- Given current enrollment trends and reasonably reliable forecasts of jobs for graduates and so forth, what is the probability for change in the number of student credit hours generated over the next several years?
- Is it possible, given the available data, that the department will have a surplus of faculty members in the next five years? A shortage?
- If program changes are planned for the next few years, are these likely to cause increases or decreases in enrollments?
- When is the next department self-study due? When is the next professional reaccreditation scheduled?
- Is the number of students who graduate likely to change? Will the department initiate new degree programs at existing levels? At different levels?
- Will competition with other educational institutions prove detrimental? If so, when?

Flexibility in Transferring Funds from One Expenditure Category to Another

Chairpersons should be familiar with the degree of flexibility permitted the department in transferring funds from one expenditure category to another. Such flexibility—or lack thereof—will influence the presentation of a budget request. For example, the chairperson of a department that has a justifiable need for additional instructional personnel wishes to ask for funds to meet this need. He or she can ask for salary funds, which can be used to fill permanent positions, or for temporary employment funds, which can be used to hire part-time instructors. The chairperson would prefer to add permanent positions, because once allocated they tend to remain in the department. The request for funds, however, may not be approved in time for the department to recruit adequately for new faculty positions by the fall term. If the salary line dollars can be easily converted to temporary employment funds, the funds for the new positions can be used to hire adjunct instructors. If this flexibility is not permitted, the positions will have to remain unfilled during the long recruitment period and there will be a delay in meeting instructional needs. The chairperson, if he or she knows the degree of flexibility allowed, can then decide whether to request funds for permanent positions or for temporary positions. In the latter instance, the dean should be informed of the need for additional faculty lines in the subsequent year.

Similarly, if the department is permitted to transfer money from the expense category to the equipment category, the chairperson is sometimes able to make more efficient use of moneys available. For example, a department that is paying annual leasing fees from its expense category for a duplicating machine may find buying the machine cheaper in the long run, thereby precluding the yearly outlay of expense moneys. Purchases of equipment, however, must be paid for out of the equipment expenditure category. If the department's equipment expense fund is low, the only way the purchase can be made is by transferring funds from the expense category, provided that such a transfer is permitted. By knowing in advance how much flexibility for transfer exists, the chairperson will know the best strategy for obtaining the equipment in question.

Unanticipated Availability of Reserve Funds

As mentioned previously, universities often keep reserves to offset possible shortfalls in incidental income. When and if a university establishes that the funds kept in reserve are not needed, these funds may be distributed to departments. Most often these reserves are held for the equipment category; thus, additional equipment needs can be accommodated late in the year. The chairperson should be aware of the department's unmet needs so that he or she may respond quickly to inquiries by the dean when unused reserve funds become available. Since the turnaround time for expending the reserves may be short, the chairperson with available information stands to gain the most.

The Department's Role in Meeting Institutional Commitments

All departments should have a firm idea of the institutional purposes and goals they are expected to meet. Further, the chairperson should be aware that the type and condition of the department determine the nature of the budget request to be submitted to the dean. The department chairperson should be able to associate his or her budget request with department, college, and institutional goals and identify those strengths that specifically fit in with the institution's priorities. Different departments meet different institutional needs and commitments. Following are examples of five types of departments whose activities include performing specific functions needed to meet the institution's commitments.

1. *Departments that exist solely because of the university's commitment to an academic discipline.* Examples are classics and humanities departments, which generally do not attract large numbers of students or generate large amounts of contract and grant moneys. These departments often have stable enrollments and do not rank high in the institution's priorities for resource allocations. Nevertheless, they have traditionally been identified as indispensable components of the liberal arts, and their contribution to the university is felt to be important. In documenting their budget requests, such departments should stress the quality of their programs, since their enrollment figures may not be impressive.

2. *Departments that offer large numbers of service courses.* Many English and mathematics departments belong in this category. The budget requests of these departments should use official enrollment figures as a basis for demonstrating the need for personnel and instructional support funds. Even though these departments might also have good graduate programs, their requests should emphasize service to other departments and relate needs to anticipated enrollment increases.

3. *Departments that are heavily involved in community needs.* Examples are education departments with a large number of inservice teacher training activities. (Note that these types of activities are not associated with enrollments.) Budget requests from such departments should emphasize past achievements and ask for funds to expand or improve their programs.

4. *Departments that are able to obtain outside contracts and grants to support expanding research programs.* Departments of natural and physical sciences frequently belong in this category. Budget requests should show how the outside funding augments internal allocations, as well as the extent to which the benefits derived outweigh any overhead or matching funds that the insti-

tution must provide as a condition for obtaining the contract or grant.

5. *Departments that are closely tied to professions.* Schools of law, nursing, and social work are examples. Budget requests of these departments or schools should clearly state societal and professional demands and pressures to maintain quality programs. The requests should also emphasize the added instructional costs necessary to accommodate changing certification requirements, professional regulations, and so forth.

The preceding list has been compiled to show that all department budget requests should not be developed according to the same strategy.

A further consideration is the department's perception of itself. A department that already has or is striving for a national reputation will want to emphasize its gains or losses during the current year and note the effect its national exposure has had on the university. Federal and state grant awards, prestigious publications, and improvement in student quality are developments that should be included as background in the budget request. If the department perceives itself as regionally oriented and has no serious intention of competing in the national arena, it should present information that shows its local influence. If the department is basically a service department, the budget request should include information about current faculty loads, as well as a statement of the positive effect that additional resources would have on generating credit hours.

We have discussed alternative strategies that a chairperson might use when preparing a budget. Deans, however, have their own personal styles and react in different ways to various requests. Moreover, some have their own ideas about the nature of department goals. Because the priorities that the dean has in mind are not always apparent, the chairperson should not try to outguess him or her but rather present department needs in a straightforward manner. The chairperson must maintain credibility with the dean. Overstatements and inaccuracies in budget requests may rapidly erode the chairperson's credibility. Annual budget requests that contain well-developed, accurate documentation and that reinforce department objectives and priorities will have a cumulative beneficial effect over the years in shaping the dean's perception of the department.

Preparing a Budget Request

The comprehensive budget request should include relevant

background information to update the dean's knowledge about the department. The information used should be "official" information, so that precious discussion time is not wasted in disagreements over facts and figures. University fact books, published financial reports, and information that has been widely distributed should serve, as much as possible, as the sources of the data presented. Each institution has an office of institutional research, which is responsible for providing accurate information to external agencies. Therefore, if published information is unavailable, that office should be consulted for data or for verification of the accuracy of unpublished data.

Several indicators of the department's workload and its relative standing within the university should be compiled and kept current. These indicators include department trends and comparative data. A recommended way of showing *department trends* is to compile the following types of data for each of the last three years and to project figures for the next year:

1. number of credit hours produced by the department
2. number of students majoring in the department's discipline
3. number of service courses offered
4. average class size of service courses
5. number of faculty members and percent distribution of faculty effort in instruction, research, public service, and other areas
6. number of teaching and research graduate assistants
7. number of nonacademic staff persons, such as secretaries and technicians
8. effect of federal and state funds

The presentation of *comparative data* should show rates of change, ratios, or statistical averages:

1. percent change in credit hours for the department compared with percent change for the university
2. faculty-student ratios compared with those of similar departments
3. average faculty instruction loads compared with those of similar departments
4. faculty-support staff ratios compared with those of similar departments

Drafting the Request

The budget request should review, as concisely as possible, the various programs within the department, stressing the program's age, its relative academic and professional standing, and its strengths and weaknesses. The presentation should be clear, logical, and brief.

The request should include a summary of how the department is organized. Faculty members' names should be associated with department functions wherever possible. Faculty members who have served on recognized university-wide committees should also be mentioned, as well as those who are active in state and national professional groups.

After providing the background information, the chairperson should present the department's precise needs for the coming year. This section of the budget request should incorporate appropriate strategies, such as those discussed earlier. Once the background information has been clearly presented, then programs and indications of desired activities may subsequently be referred to by title.

The favorable effect of funding the proposed budget request should be described, along with the negative effect of not funding the requested improvements. If partial funding can provide some reasonable progress toward the stated goal, this information should also be stated, accompanied by a phased schedule for obtaining the remainder of the resources needed in future budget years.

A table should be provided to serve as a summary that communicates the essence of the budget request. It will further serve as a visual aid in budget discussions with the dean. The dean will become more familiar with the department and its requests if the chairperson frequently refers to the data table during budget discussions.

Budget-Related Discussions with the Dean

Much is to be gained and nothing lost by frequent discussions with the dean concerning the resources needed and the problems faced by the department. Chairpersons tend to review developments only at annual budget meetings, but they should take the initiative to call the dean's attention to problems as they occur. Conferences with the dean should be requested during the year, and matters to be discussed at these conferences should be well documented and should clearly indicate a continuous pursuit of department goals. The chairperson should provide the dean—in advance of any meeting, if possible—with facts and figures, estimates of the budget's effect, and the statement of needs. Oral presentations and face-to-face discussions should amplify, further explain, or emphasize the points set forth in the written documentation. This procedure allows for improved communication and better understanding of the request; it also helps bring about optimal results at allocation time. Consistency is necessary in describing department needs. In essence, the chairperson may help shape a dean's behavior by fostering a more rational approach and increasing the quantity and quality of the dean's response.

If the chairperson has some question about the results of a meeting with a dean, he or she should prepare a memorandum that sets down the details of the discussion, including points of agreement, action to be taken, and dates for future decisions. When shared with the dean and the department faculty, the memorandum may serve as a basis for department planning during the upcoming fiscal year.

Well-documented budget requests presented in a logically organized format will provide deans with information that may be helpful in the rational allocation of funds. The approaches described here may not always result in an improved resource allocation. They should, however, build credibility for the department. Further, they may help clarify the dean's perceptions of the department and his or her expectations about its future achievements.

Setting explicit goals—no matter how desirable for an institution, school, or department—is a difficult process, for goals are not usually formulated until the amount of available resources has been established. This process is a reversal of the rational planning model and results from increasing economic constraints placed on education. A chairperson should understand the major commitments that, in effect, are the implied goals of the school, college, and institution. Then he or she can better target the available funds for appropriate areas, programs, and components. The budget request presentation described above can elicit responses from the dean that should help the chairperson better understand the dean's philosophy. Furthermore, this presentation should improve the dean's understanding of the department.

Questions and Exercises

1. *a*) Is your department expected to prepare and submit a budget request, formal or informal, describing resource needs?

b) If not, how are the resource needs of your department made known to the administration? Who makes the request for you?

c) If yes, how detailed a budget request are you expected to prepare?

2. *a*) Within the administrative hierarchy of your institution, how many levels must review the budget request submitted by or for your department?

   b) What external reviews, outside of your institution, are conducted? Who conducts them?

3. Speculate on the special political, social, and economic factors that might, in the next two to five years, have an effect on the funding for your department.

4. At your institution, who decides the institutional priorities? Who decides the department priorities? Who decides how many resources your department will receive?

5. How successful were you in obtaining resources for the department last year?

6. *a*) What calendar must your department and institution follow in preparing a budget request? What is the rationale for using this calendar?

   b) What specific deadline dates must be met by your department in preparing a budget request? How do these deadlines fit in with the other activities that must be conducted in the department?

7. What is the primary role of your department in helping the institution meet its commitments? Is the primary role to conduct research, train graduate students, train undergraduate majors, teach courses, provide community service, or provide professional training? Does it have some other role not listed?

8. *a*) List, in decreasing order of priority, your department's five to ten most important resource needs—such as personnel, equipment, space, supplies, services, and so forth—during the next three years.

   b) In requesting funds for each of the needs listed, what strategies would be most effective in persuading your dean or academic vice president to provide the necessary funds?

9. Estimate the likelihood that all the needs listed will be funded.

10. Which needs have the greatest likelihood of being funded?

Which have the least? List the needs in decreasing order of likelihood of being funded.

11. Would your chances for obtaining funds be increased if you included in your budget request some mention of how the department's role helps the institution meet its commitments?

References

Adams, Carl R.; Hankins, Russell L.; and Schroeder, Roger G. *Literature of Cost and Cost Analysis in Higher Education.* A Study of Cost Analysis in Higher Education, vol. 1. Washington, D.C.: American Council on Education, 1978.

Budig, Gene A., ed. *Dollars and Sense: Budgeting for Today's Campus.* Chicago: College and University Business Press, McGraw-Hill, 1972.

Caruthers, J. Kent, and Orwig, Melvin. *Budgeting in Higher Education.* AAHE-ERIC/Higher Education Research Report no. 3. Washington, D.C.: American Association for Higher Education, 1979.

Colleges and Money: A Faculty Guide to Academic Economics. New Rochelle, N.Y.: Change Magazine Press, 1976.

Confronting the New Depression in Higher Education. Washington, D.C.: Academy for Educational Development, 1973.

Green, John L. *Budgeting in Higher Education.* Athens, Ga.: The University of Georgia Press, 1972.

Halstead, D. Kent. *Statewide Planning in Higher Education.* Washington, D.C.: Government Printing Office, 1974.

Jellema, William W., ed. *Efficient College Management.* San Francisco: Jossey-Bass, 1972.

Kaludis, George, ed. *Strategies for Budgeting.* New Directions for Higher Education, no. 2. San Francisco: Jossey-Bass, 1973.

Millett, John. *Resource Reallocation in Research Universities.* Washington, D.C.: Academy for Educational Development, 1973.

National Association of College and University Business Officers. *College and University Business Administration.* Washington, D.C.: NACUBO, 1975.

Procedures for Determining Historical Full Costs: The Costing Component of NCHEMS Information Exchange Procedures. Technical Report No. 65, 2nd ed. Boulder, Colo.: National Center for Higher Education Management Systems, 1977.

12

Assigning and Reporting Faculty Activities

||||||||||||||||||||||||||||||||||||||||||||||||||||||||||||||||||||||||||||||||||||||||||||||||||||||||||||||||||||||||||||||||||||

Department chairpersons differ greatly in the way they perceive their roles and responsibilities in assigning activities to faculty members. Some believe that the professional nature of university teaching and research forbids the formal assignment of faculty duties. Others hold that a chairperson is a manager of resources, especially human resources, and that he or she is responsible for the department's success or failure in helping achieve the university's mission and goals. The latter view clearly requires that the chairperson take an active role in assigning faculty duties. In recent years, legislative demands for accountability and union demands for explicitness in faculty-administration relationships have strengthened the view that the chairperson must play a role in assigning faculty activities.

The trend is for chairpersons to assume *more* rather than less authority and responsibility in faculty assignment. The State University System of Florida, for example, has for several years required a formal assignment of faculty activities; it even requires a periodic audit of such assignments. Further, the collective bargaining agreement between the United Faculty of Florida and the Florida Board of Regents specifically requires faculty assignments. Many other public and private colleges and universities have similar kinds of requirements.

Finally, college and university budget models may be based on minimum or average workload data of this kind; some multicampus university systems also have such standards. In some states the legislatures have passed laws establishing minimum workloads for faculty, such as 12 student contact hours per term for university faculty and 15 for junior college faculty. Some departments wrongly implement this policy by treating the established minimum workload as if it were a maximum workload. A chairperson may not believe in the worthiness of such laws, but where they exist, legislators expect faculty activities to reflect the laws' intent. Compliance with the law, however, does not mean that the university should use the 12-hour law as the framework within which all assignments are made. Assignments should be based on the department's goals, objectives, priorities, and policies, including the needs of the faculty and students. In implementing these goals and policies, every effort must be made not to violate the 12-hour law, should one exist.

Benefits and Purposes of Explicit Assignments

The chairperson has extensive responsibilities for assigning faculty duties, and this task is directly related to faculty evaluation. Most college and university administrators now understand that evaluations should be based on the performance of specifically assigned activities. They realize that individual faculty members and the groups who represent them wish to ensure that faculty members are not denied promotion, tenure, or salary adjustments because of failure to perform tasks they were never explicitly assigned in the first place.

Explicit assignments serve other important purposes in addition to evaluation. The development of equitable workloads among the department faculty almost demands a record of the particular assignments made to each faculty member. Systems for equalizing workloads are sometimes included in department policies. On the other hand, some faculty members believe that workload equity is a matter that they themselves must determine, rather than some absolute institutional standard of equivalency that they must follow. Such policy statements as those passed by the American Association of University Professors recommending numbers of teaching credit hours on the basis of the number of new and old preparations have been helpful guidelines in this matter. By making formal, explicit assignments, however, the chairperson is able to adhere to the department's policy, implement its goals and objectives, and maintain data to explain his or her good judgment in managing human resources.

Similarly, as students' needs are assessed and changes required, the chairperson can modify faculty assignments, thereby shifting faculty effort to cover these needs. If some subject areas are not covered or developed, the department can undertake some long-range planning so that it can do more than just fill the gap at the last minute. An analysis of the extent to which explicit assignments are completed may show the need for new faculty resources or professional career and development counseling.

Policies governing formal assignment of faculty duties generally include statements such as the following:

> Faculty members should be assigned duties and activities in writing. These assignments must be clearly stated, and those receiving them should acknowledge them as understood.

> The department chairperson, by virtue of his or her responsibility for attaining department goals and objectives, is the person who should make faculty assignments.

> Effective faculty assignments require clear statements of department goals, objectives, and workload policies. The proper functioning of the department depends on the chairperson's maintaining adequate records and consulting extensively with faculty members before and after the assignments are completed.

Preparation of Assignments

What are the essential requirements of an assignment of duties? How detailed must the assignment be? How often should an assignment be made?

The department chairperson who tries to understand the many conflicting requirements for faculty assignments can reach several conclusions. A chairperson may conclude that the best procedure is to make assignments as brief and as general as possible. In this way maximum flexibility may be preserved, thereby ensuring that all bases are covered, no matter what needs may come up during the year. Unfortunately, assignments that are brief and general are usually vague and subject to broad interpretation by the faculty member as well as the chairperson. Vagueness can make it impossible to determine whether the assignment has been completed successfully. In the event of a faculty grievance over tenure or promotion, the chairperson may be hard-pressed to substantiate any judgments made if he or she can present no clear evidence of duty assignment and performance criteria.

A chairperson who has faced only one grievance resulting from an assignment that is too vague or general is usually convinced that highly detailed assignments are necessary and justified. Even so, endless arguments may ensue, depending on how the assignment is worded, about the degree to which the various assignments were completed. In some cases, faculty members may demand tenure, promotion, or salary increases, claiming they have completed all the detailed assignments given them and then submitting evidence to support their claims. A problem may also surface if a faculty member refuses to complete a task that needs to be done but that was not listed as part of the agreed-upon detailed assignment made earlier in the year.

The two problems described above might have been avoided if the assignments had been precise. An assignment must be general enough to provide some flexibility for both the chairperson and faculty member, and it must be detailed enough so that both understand what performance is expected and what will serve as a basis for evaluation.

Chairpersons should be particularly alert to the information about assignments contained in the various documents that must be acknowledged by each faculty member. Some institutions notify faculty members of their next period of employment by means of a salary letter; it may contain general language indicating, for example, that for the fiscal year the person will be paid a specific sum for teaching, research, service, and other such functions as assigned. A person may be appointed for only part of a year or as a part-time employee during a school year; the assignment for a part-time faculty member may be more specific than for the full-time faculty member, e.g., the teaching assignment may consist of one specific course.

As the formal employment relationship between faculty members and the institution evolves, however, the salary letter often becomes merely a notification of salary award, whereas the contract document becomes the actual instrument of notification of employment and salary level. The contract document may contain a variety of other information, including a detailed statement of requirements in legal terminology. The assignment in the contract still may be given in functional terms—i.e., teaching, research, and service—but it may also list specific tasks—e.g., teaching one graduate course off-campus. In preparing a contract, the dean's office may solicit information from the chairperson about any special assignment terms to be entered in faculty contracts. At the same time, a chairperson should check with the dean's office to make sure that a faculty member is not assigned activities that are not likely to be required or performed—for example, a faculty member who has been assigned teaching as a full-time workload should not be assigned any research or service activities.

A chairperson might be required to solicit from each faculty member a projected work plan for an entire academic year. This plan might be the basis for the annual contract and the assignment of workloads each term. Note that institutions operating on the quarter calendar sometimes attempt to spread the annual department workload as evenly as possible over the four quarters. In such instances, full-time faculty members may have an opportunity to work during the summer quarter in lieu of another quarter. This type of arrangement, if approved by the chairperson, would be indicated in the work plan. Because plans of this kind are developed in early spring for the subsequent academic year, they are subject to change. Regular consultation with each faculty member should enable the chairperson to anticipate any changes and to make the necessary adjustments to the plan.

The chairperson usually is not required to agree to faculty members' requests concerning workloads; nevertheless, the assignment of a faculty member's workload or schedule should not be arbitrary or capricious. Consultation is a standard of collegiality; to impose a work assignment on academic professionals may be a denial of their expertise. In emergencies, of course, faculty members must be assigned certain tasks to ensure coverage.

In some universities, the annual projected work plan for each faculty member may be converted to an official document, and as such it will often include the details for each term of the contract year. The plan is not always implemented as originally prepared, however: the chairperson may change an assignment before it is fulfilled; the faculty member may undertake one or more activities not included in the assignment; or the faculty member may not perform an assigned activity. The alert chairperson will discover the existing discrepancies during periodic consultation each term and take appropriate corrective action. A consultation before a term begins, specifically to confirm and adjust the assignment as needed, should reveal the changes a faculty member is planning or anticipating. Such preterm conferences also inform the faculty member of possible changes that the chairperson may request to meet changing conditions in the department.

The chairperson should adjust the assignment planning or workload projection records to reflect the activities actually performed. Similarly, he or she should obtain explanations from faculty members as to why certain assigned activities have not been performed, especially when nonperformance represents a breach of agreement or a failure to support important goals, objectives, and priorities of the department. It is equally important that faculty members be commended, in writing, for tasks well done, new activities successfully undertaken, and so on. The chairperson should communicate to the dean and other appropriate university officials any extraordinary achievements by faculty members.

Equitable Assignments

A chairperson must be concerned not only with each faculty member but also with the department's total functioning and how its workload can be distributed equitably among all the faculty. He or she must not only keep in mind the needs of individual faculty members but must also assess the effect that a person's assignment may have on the other faculty members in the

ACTIVITY	POINTS
Teaching	
Course Teaching	
One lecture course	8 points
One seminar course	5 points
One lab course	3 points for first 25 students; 1 point for each additional 25 students
*One-on-one supervision**	
Director of master's thesis	4 points
Member of master's committee	1 point
Director of doctoral dissertation	6 points
Member of doctoral committee	2 points
Directed individual study, supervised research, or supervised internship	1 point per student; maximum 4 points per term; maximum 2 points per student
Research**	
Sponsored research project:	
Under $10,000	4 points
Over $10,000	10 points
Other activities	
Member of department or university committees Chairperson of department or university committee Administrative assignments within the department	The number of points allowed for each activity is determined by the chairperson based on the time and effort involved and the importance of the work to the department.

* The maximum number of points allowed for all one-on-one supervision during any academic year is 30. Points for the first four classifications listed in this section are given on completion of the graduate degree.
** The maximum number of points allowed for sponsored research during any academic year is 40.

Fig. 12.1. Point system in which points are assigned for specific tasks included in faculty assignments department. If, for example, a faculty member is assigned to teach a course for the first time and is given some released time from other teaching responsibilities for course development, who will assume the teaching responsibilities of that faculty member?

When assignments are shifted among the faculty members to distribute the workload equitably, the chairperson may have a difficult time trying to find the proper combination of activities for each person. The chairperson will have to assess each faculty member's skills and competencies to make sure the workload is spread equally among those who can best perform it. In some departments, the faculty may decide to assign priority factors for various activities. Some activities have higher priority than others, depending on the effort required and the comparative importance of the activity as perceived by the department. The priority factors expressed as points are used in calculations that result in the assignment of equitable workloads to the faculty.

Very few departments find a priority system either necessary or desirable, but some have used it successfully. Figure 12.1 shows a system used by one large, research-oriented social sci-

	POINTS
Faculty Member A	
Six lecture courses (8 points each)	48
One-on-one supervision	19
No grants	0
No committees	0
Total	67
Faculty Member B	
Three lecture courses (8 points each)	24
One lab (3 points each)	3
One-on-one supervision	22
Two grants (10 points each)	20
Total	69
Faculty Member C	
Four lecture courses (8 points each)	32
One lab (3 points each)	3
One graduate seminar	5
One-on-one supervision	13
Committee assignment	5
One grant	10
Total	68

Fig. 12.2. Sample of workloads and point allocations

ence department in a major university in allocating points for specific activities.

The department that used this system listed all its activities, regardless of who carried them out, and allocated to each activity the number of points designated. The sum of all the points was divided by the number of department faculty members to determine the average point load. The workload for this particular department amounted to 1056 points. Since the department contained sixteen faculty members, the average, or equitable, load was 66 points per academic year. Figure 12.2 shows three examples of faculty workloads and point allocations.

This point system was not used for evaluation purposes but only to help equalize the assignments given to individual faculty members. Any point system is cumbersome, and the result may not be much different from the result obtained by means of another system. Faculty members with heavy teaching loads continue to be assigned heavy teaching loads, and productive researchers are allowed reduced teaching loads. Some faculty members, however, feel more secure with a point system of this nature. Quite often, a faculty member will challenge the point values that the chairperson has allocated to certain activities.

Equitable faculty workloads can be accomplished in two ways: (1) by assigning workloads that are equitable term by term; or (2) by assigning workloads that are equitable when averaged over the academic or fiscal year. Averaging workloads over an academic year allows the chairperson to assign heavier teaching loads during terms when enrollment is unusually high and lighter teaching loads during terms when enrollment is usually lower. Moreover, faculty members may be willing to undertake an extra heavy load one term in order to have a light load the following term, during which they will have more time to concentrate on their own professional interests.

The first step in preparing teaching schedule assignments for a given term is to review the teaching schedules of previous years for the same term. This information—together with information from the faculty and an awareness of personnel changes, curriculum changes, changing student interests, and so forth—can serve as the basis for developing teaching schedules for the current term.

In assigning teaching activities, the chairperson should ask the following questions about each faculty member's assignment:

- Has this faculty member taught this particular course be-

	FACULTY MEMBER A	FACULTY MEMBER B
Example 1		
Teaching 67%	2 classes (8 hours)	4 classes (16 hours)
Research 20%	Research Grant	Research grant
Service 13%	1 committee	3 committees
100%		
Explanation of Example 1		
Teaching	*Graduate classes; 2 in-depth preparations*	*Same course; no additional preparation*
Research	*Self-explanatory*	*Self-explanatory*
Service	*University committee*	*Routine department committees*
Example 2		
Teaching 75%	3 classes (12 hours)	3 classes (9 hours)
Research 20%	No funded research grant	Research grant
Service 5%	2 committees	1 committee
100%		
Explanation of Example 2		
Teaching	*2 sections of same class*	*3 different classes*
Research	*In process of preparing a grant for funding*	*Funded grant*
Service	*Routine department committee*	*College committee*
Example 3		
Teaching 67%	5 classes (20 hours)	3 classes (15 hours)
Research 18%	No research project	No research project
Service 10%	No definite service activity	1 committee
Advisement 5%	Advisement	Advisement
100%		
Explanation of Example 3		
Teaching	*Undergraduate sections of same class; 4 activity classes; 1 lecture class*	*3 large classes (different course taught each term requiring preparation and work outside of class)*
Research	*Needs to develop some research and creativity pursuits*	*Needs to develop some research and creativity pursuits*
Service	*Chairperson will make a definite curriculum assignment prior to the beginning of the term*	*Department work*
Advisement	*Assigned students*	*Assigned students*

Fig. 12.3. Sample of equitable faculty assignments

fore? Does he or she have more than one new course to teach?

- How many new preparations does this faculty member have? Will special assistance be needed for labs, computer usage, and so forth?
- Do these courses require any special activities, e.g., field trips, demonstrations, and so forth?
- How much evaluation of student work will be required?
- What is the mix of level of courses? The size of the estimated enrollment?
- How many thesis and dissertation projects is each faculty member directing? How many committees is each serving? How many students is each counseling?
- How many undergraduates are being advised by each faculty member? What other undergraduate activities is each supervising or sponsoring?

Clearly, the chairperson must be flexible in assigning percentages of effort for each faculty activity. He or she should move away from rigid formulas and toward individual judgments about the workloads assigned to each faculty member. The examples given in figure 12.3 indicate that a wide range of assignments may be equivalent and, hence, equitable. Note that two faculty assignments can appear quite disparate and yet be considered functionally equivalent. The explanation following each example presents the factors used by an academic vice president of a major university to determine that the percentages assigned each category of activities were in agreement.

The number of credit hours of teaching, generally, is not a good measure of workload. For example, a 16-credit-hour load that consists of teaching the same course to four different undergraduate classes of twenty students each might be a light load for an experienced faculty member who has taught that course many times before. In contrast, an 8-credit-hour load that consists of teaching two entirely different courses to two different classes of forty students each might be a heavy load for a new, inexperienced faculty member who has never taught either course before, especially if the two courses required more themes and reports from the students than did the first faculty member's course. The chairperson should not hesitate to assign the same courses to two faculty members, giving one a 50 percent teaching assignment and the other an 80 percent assignment if the faculty members' relative experience and qualifications warrant the difference in assignment and would result in a similar "real" workload for each faculty member. To be more consistent, the chairperson may wish to assign the faculty member with less experience to 80 percent of full time for teaching a course that includes time for course development. Clearly, department needs and course workloads—not some requirement for a report—should determine the most efficient and effective use of faculty resources.

The equitable assignment of faculty duties systematically allows the chairperson to formulate and implement plans for attaining department goals while assisting faculty members in reaching some of their personal goals. This harmonizing, after all, is one of the purposes of assigning activities. The chairperson's success in this activity may well determine his or her effectiveness as an academic administrator and leader, since personnel assignment activities and decisions constitute a major function of the chairperson's role. Chairpersons who are inadequate personnel managers could become liabilities to their departments. Some chairpersons find personnel decisions so disturbing and distasteful that they resign. On the other hand, chairpersons who are interested in these kinds of problems and learn to cope with them may find rewarding careers in university administration.

Performance Criteria for Functional Assignments

For the busy chairperson, the task of assigning faculty activities commonly becomes a chore that must be done hurriedly. All too often the task is performed by making a simple list of the things the faculty member will probably be doing in the next few months. An even more unfortunate situation occurs when the faculty member is allowed to complete the assignment form without consulting the chairperson. In neither case has a real assignment been made, and the chairperson is forfeiting an opportunity to manage valuable human resources for the improvement of the department. Yet making periodic term assignments can sometimes be a distasteful waste of time. Assignment schedules that consist of a simple listing of the same set of duties each term are basically useless.

How can assignments be transformed into useful aids to the chairperson's already difficult task of resource management? A few suggestions about activities for each performance area should provide an indication of the essentials of a good assignment and should stimulate further thinking about the subject. The key is to think of each assignment in terms of how a chairperson should evaluate success in completing the assignment, i.e., what criteria should govern each assignment in each area?

Teaching Assignments

The assumption that teaching assignments should consist only of a list of courses to be taught is invalid. About the only thing that can be evaluated with such an assignment is whether or not the courses have been taught! More important, the performance of such an assignment must certainly be evaluated as "average." What could be the basis for an above- or below-average performance when everyone completes the assigned courses?

At the very least, a teaching assignment should rest on a clear understanding that the *quality* of the teaching will be evaluated. Further, a clear statement, preferably in writing, should be provided as to the types of evidence, such as student evaluations or peer review, that will be used in making the evaluation. It is the chairperson's responsibility to ensure that clearly stated criteria for evaluation are established by the department and are understood by all the department members.

Teaching assignments can be made with a degree of sophistication. The success of a teaching assignment should probably be measured in terms of what students learn, either in absolute terms or in relative terms (such as student growth). But have you, as the chairperson or as a department member, defined what is expected of a student who completes a given course? If so and if the learning outcomes are stated in measurable terms, successful course instruction will be measurable in terms of student learning. Of course, many faculty members will object to this method of measuring teaching success, citing inaccuracy of tests, differences in student ability or motivation, and a variety of other arguments. Admittedly, precise measurement of affective outcomes, such as attitude changes, does lag behind precise measurement of cognitive outcomes. Nevertheless, student learning is the primary goal of teaching and can be taken as one measure of successful teaching.

Other activities that might be included in the teaching assignment are developing courses; revising syllabi; updating laboratory experiments; converting courses to computer-assisted instruction; training, monitoring, and evaluating graduate teaching assistants; and other related activities. To avoid misunderstandings, the department faculty should agree that these teaching assignments are appropriate.

Research and Creative Activity Assignments

Research and creative activities seem to play an increasing role in the assignment process and, in many departments, are necessary conditions for promotion and tenure. Again, the necessity of specific assignments and the insistence on clearly stated criteria for evaluation are essential. Probably everyone can think of faculty members who have been talking research for years but have yet to produce a successful grant proposal, research report, publishable paper, or anything else that might be considered a significant contribution. These "wheel spinners" could write books of excuses and reasons for their failure to finish various projects—if only they had a little more time!

If research or creative activity is to be included as part of a faculty assignment and if it is to be evaluated at a specific time, the faculty member should be able to provide a documented plan of action with some sort of time schedule for completing various parts of the research activity. This action plan might include such information as the title of the project; whether a library review of the literature is required; when the project will be completed; whether a proposal for outside funding is planned and when it will be completed; whether laboratory equipment must be acquired and assembled and how much of the laboratory effort can be completed this term; and what efforts at data collection and processing are required. If the faculty member is writing an article for publication, he or she should note whether a rough draft can be completed this term. If a graduate student is scheduled to complete a thesis, note what must be done to assure that he or she will be able to complete the research.

If the faculty member cannot provide a detailed action plan, perhaps the research should *not* be assigned! If the plan can be stated clearly, the assignment should indicate that the research effort will be formally evaluated in the future. Failure to accomplish set goals means that the assignment has not been completed, and this failure should be reflected in an evaluation. Of course, the faculty member may have good reasons for failing to complete an assignment. The chairperson has the responsibility for ascertaining and assessing the validity of these reasons, converting this information to appropriate evaluation judgments, and adjusting the assignments for the next term accordingly.

The term *failure* may be considered unduly harsh when assignments are being evaluated; perhaps *noncompletion* would be less grating. Regardless of the term used to describe this unfortunate situation, the chairperson must make sure that failure is not rewarded or allowed to slip by without appropriate reaction.

Service Assignments

Service is an assignment activity that may include a range of activities, such as attending local service club meetings or serving as a member of campus or interinstitutional committees. For example, a faculty member may be assigned to develop and deliver off-campus presentations designed to alert the public to services offered by the university, gain support for an on-campus program, or attract students to the campus.

Again, the chairperson should think seriously about the real purpose of making such assignments and how their success can be evaluated. If a faculty member is assigned to a university committee, is regular attendance at meetings expected? Is regular attendance considered "outstanding" or just "average" performance of this assignment? Should the department chairperson ask the head of this committee to provide an evaluation of the faculty member's performance? If the faculty member was assigned to contact local high schools and explain new department programs, is the mere making of the contacts sufficient for successful completion of the assignment? Or does success require that a larger percentage of students in the schools contacted attend the university? Just why is this assignment being made? Will it really benefit the department, college, or institution?

Another kind of service assignment is holding office in a state or national professional society. Most chairpersons will insist that such activities bring "honor" to the home university. No doubt they do, but the effect is difficult, if not impossible, to measure. Fortunately, a chairperson is seldom called on to explain such benefits to taxpayers or legislators. Although service assignments can be made considerably more specific than most currently are, it is difficult to assign these types of activities in a way that makes objective evaluation possible. On the other hand, membership in professional societies has traditionally been considered a part of the academic life, and holding office in those societies has traditionally been deemed worthwhile. Some public institutions now require a written report from faculty members about the benefits—academic and other—of attending regional and national conferences.

Reporting of Faculty Activities

The discussion so far has focused essentially on the distribution of the department workload. The formalization of these assignments has come about because of such developments as collective bargaining, increased disagreement with tenure and promotion decisions, and, in some cases, state statutes.

The reporting of faculty activities, however, is a result of the quest for increased accountability. Specifically, any university that accepts federal or state contract and grant funds must be able to provide proof that the contracted amount of effort has indeed been expended on the contracted activity. Payroll certifications that would satisfy accountability requirements are often deemed too cumbersome; therefore, a quarterly or semester report on activity is generally substituted. Universities that have recently been audited by federal agencies have been told that the effort of the support personnel, as well as the effort of the faculty, must be certified. In the absence of clear federal guidelines, universities have developed their own reporting systems. Many of these systems not only satisfy federal agencies but also provide chairpersons and deans with pertinent information and allow cost studies to estimate costs more closely. Thus, many colleges and universities have developed detailed categories of activities, coupled with standard definitions, in order accurately to record data about faculty workload. The amount of detail reported on these activity forms seems to be increasing; the forms all focus on standardized reporting techniques and rely on computer processing for handling the increasing volume of data.

Recommendations for the data elements and counting procedures, as well as for the activities to be reported, can be found in relevant technical reports of the National Center for Higher Education Management Systems and in circulars. Following is a list of broad categories adopted by one state:

A. General academic instruction
   1. Lower-division instruction
   2. Upper-division instruction
   3. Graduate instruction
   4. Thesis supervision
   5. Dissertation supervision
   6. Department research
   7. Academic advisement
   8. Other instructional activities
B. Community education
C. Preparatory and adult basic education
D. Institutes and research centers

    E. Individual or project research
    F. Patient services
    G. Community services
    H. Cooperative extension services
    I. Academic administration—management
    J. Academic administration—governance
    K. Curriculum development
    L. Academic personnel development

The data recorded for each category are the percentages of effort a faculty member has spent on each activity. When compiled, the data are circulated through the organizational hierarchy to state budget, legislative, and federal officers. Academicians almost always view these reports negatively, seeing them as yet more bureaucratic encroachments on their lives.

The requirements for reporting faculty activities can have a significant effect on a department, however, and the chairperson should be sure that the reports accurately reflect not only the assignment but also the actual work accomplished. Accurate and complete reporting is essential for a number of reasons. First, the reported activities must not violate previous contractual agreements with a federal agency. For example, a faculty member who, for a given term, has contracted to spend 100 percent of full time on a research project funded by a federal agency cannot teach a course or otherwise share in the department workload during that term. If he or she does teach a course and therefore does not provide 100 percent of full time to the research project, the university may be required to repay a portion of the funds secured. Thus the chairperson must be familiar with faculty commitments when making assignments and reviewing reports of actual activities.

Second, many universities, under state legislative directive, annually conduct a cost study across all disciplines. These cost studies use information about faculty workload data as primary data. Cost-study reports, now being published across the nation, show instructional costs and cost per credit hour by discipline for each university. Since information about faculty workload may be the primary data for these calculations, the assignments made by the department chairperson can significantly affect the cost results in his or her discipline. The cost study could become the basis for legislative funding in future years and thus takes on major significance.

Third, faculty activity reports are used internally by institutions for various studies of costs and faculty workloads, and, sometimes, for collective bargaining purposes. Again, the accuracy of these data may have some effect on the department in terms of the allocation of financial resources and faculty positions and in possible grievance actions.

FTE Assignments

Faculty activity assignments are generally reported as fractions of a full-time equivalent (FTE) faculty position. The chairperson usually specifies the fraction of a full-time workload (1.00) for each assigned set of activities for each faculty member. For reporting purposes, each assignment is specified in terms of a decimal fraction of an FTE position, e.g., 0.50, or as a percentage (50 percent) of an FTE workload; the total of the fractional assignments must not exceed 1.00 FTE.

Many chairpersons, however, have difficulty accepting this concept because *full time* cannot easily be defined in terms of hours per week. Some chairpersons insist that their faculty members work sixty hours per week and should, therefore, be assigned more FTE, perhaps 1.50 FTE. An exception to the 1.00 limit may occur when a faculty member is assigned a full load, whatever that happens to be, and then is also assigned some overload activities, such as teaching in a division of continuing education. On the other hand, part-time faculty members are always assigned some fraction of an FTE, e.g., 0.50 FTE. Thus, what constitutes an overload, or a workload greater than 1.00 FTE, is determined by circumstances and by policies of institutional offices and divisions other than the department.

Although some chairpersons would argue to the contrary, full-load assignment cannot exceed 1.00 FTE for full-time faculty members, regardless of the number of credit hours taught, the total hours worked per week, or the "extra" activities that the faculty member may plan to do during the term. Previous examples (figure 12.3) have shown that functionally equivalent percentages of an FTE for two faculty members may not necessarily reveal the great differences in their patterns of activities. Furthermore, the same activity for two persons, each teaching a section of the same course, may result in significantly different FTE percentages. Accurate assignment of FTE fractions for each faculty member's activities depends greatly on the chairperson's understanding and experience in reviewing assignment reports and in questioning faculty members about their actual efforts with different assignments. Consulting with an experienced chairperson and with the technical staff processing these data can also be helpful.

In colleges or universities where minimum workload standards are important policy matters, chairpersons must be extra cautious not to use the minimum standard as the definition of a 1.00 FTE or as a basis for assigning fractions of FTEs to faculty activities. As repeatedly stated, the standard is a minimum, not a maximum, and usually refers only to the minimum number of class contact hours expected of a faculty member. This minimum number of class contact hours, be it 12 or 15, may constitute whatever percentage of an FTE workload is deemed appropriate by the chairperson and the department. A faculty member complies with the law or policy by satisfying the minimum contact hour requirement, but the law or policy does not tie the required minimum number of contact hours to any particular percentage of FTE workload assignment.

Chairpersons who misinterpret the minimum workload policy and make assignments on the basis that 12 class contact hours is a maximum load and thus represents 1.00 FTE often complain that no time is left for teaching, research, or service. This misunderstanding creates problems at those universities where every faculty member has been instructed by contract to perform some research and service in addition to teaching. Moreover, a faculty member who is teaching more than 12 contact hours may or may not be overloaded. As indicated in the section dealing with equitable assignments, a 20-contact-hour load may not be heavy at all, while an 8-hour load for a new faculty member may be a weighty 50-hour-a-week job. In sum, the workload standards should not be a basis for making assignments per se but should be implemented by ensuring that the faculty members perform their assigned activities and that the total department effort complies with the workload policy.

Sometimes workload policies may be satisfied by the compliance of a complete academic unit, such as a department or college, rather than by the compliance of each person in the unit. In such cases, workloads are averaged for each unit; that is, all instruction hours are totaled for a given unit and divided by the aggregate FTE faculty. A related problem concerns the interpretation of the differences between workload standards expressed as contact hours and as credit hours. For example, 3 contact hours in a lecture class per week per term are considered 3 hours of credit, but 3 hours of laboratory class per week per term may be considered only 1 hour of credit. Lecturing for one hour supposedly requires more effort on the instructor's part than supervising a laboratory class for one hour. The concept of the contact hour is also used to measure counseling and advising time with students. In any event, the chairperson should know precisely what is required for each particular FTE reporting category.

Faculty activity is generally reported in terms of percentage of effort. For example, a faculty member might report 75 percent of his or her effort in instruction and 25 percent in research, regardless of whether the total effort constitutes a 1.00 FTE appointment or any fraction thereof. To reiterate, assigning a specific portion of a 100 percent effort to each of the categories of teaching, research, and service is a distributive measure. Federal authorities no longer recognize the concept of "donated time." A faculty member cannot, within a given term, expend 100 percent of his or her effort within a research project and also "donate" the time required to teach a course.

In addition, the concept of "loans and borrows" is no longer accepted by federal authorities. Thus, a faculty member paid 100 percent from a contract during a given term cannot teach a course that term and be released from teaching during a following term to work on the contracted activity. If federal auditors observe this type of arrangement, they will recommend that the university repay the federal agency for the portion of time the faculty member did not expend on contracted activities during the term of the contract and will ignore the effort of the following term.

"Donated time" and "loans and borrows" are just two concepts that chairpersons must fully understand. A knowledge of external commitments is extremely important in making assignments and reviewing activity reports.

A General Assignment Strategy for Chairpersons

Clearly the chairperson's task of making faculty assignments is complex. It requires an understanding of many rules and regulations; it depends on a clear understanding of department goals and objectives; and it requires a significant number of judgmental decisions. A convenient and useful strategy by which to establish term assignments is outlined below. This strategy assumes that the chairperson already has department goals, objectives, and priorities clearly in mind; that the faculty has consented to these; and that the chairperson is fully aware of the department members' interests, strengths, and experiences. The strategy comprises eight major steps.

1. Establish the instructional, research, and service workload

that the department as a whole can be expected to accomplish during the term. Questions to be answered include these: What total FTE can be assigned? (That is, how many full-time equivalent faculty members, including graduate assistants and faculty adjuncts, are available to accomplish the department's work?) What relative effort among the categories of instruction, research, and service would best serve department interests and contribute to department goals?

2. Identify the courses to be taught during the term and the courses that are optional. Consult with faculty members, students, and other department chairpersons to assess the needs and demands here.

3. Determine the special requirements that have been imposed on faculty members for the term. Ask the faculty for this and other pertinent data. Which faculty members will have released time on research grants? What institution, college, or department committee assignments have already been committed for the term? (Note: If you as chairperson find these "external" commitments heavy, remember that *you* have control over most of them! If you do not, it is time to get your data together and have a long talk with the dean!)

4. List, for each faculty member, adjunct, and graduate assistant available to your department, the activities to which you tentatively expect each person to be assigned, without reference to time or fraction of FTE for each activity. Your choices of assignment should reflect both the department's needs and each faculty member's professional development (tenure, promotion, research, and so forth). The total listing for all faculty members should include each area and activity identified in items 2 and 3 above.

5. Determine how much effort, preferably in terms of fractions of FTE, you expect the faculty member to devote to each activity listed; double-check this with the faculty members as needed. If you use fractions of FTE, remember that the total FTE must equal exactly 1.00. If you use hours, the total hours assigned are not too important since, for reporting purposes, hourly assignments for each activity will ultimately be converted to the appropriate fraction of the total hours assigned (i.e., to a fraction of a 1.00 FTE). However, be aware that a 20-hour teaching load, if otherwise equivalent, may be 0.50 FTE for the 40-hour-a-week person but only 0.36 FTE for the 55-hour-a-week person. If hours are to be taken seriously, some standard hourly effort rates may have to be developed to ensure that persons do-

ing equivalent work share the same workload report fractions. For these and other reasons, the standard fractional FTE (plus or minus x percent) for particular activities may be the best understood and simplified measure of assigned (and reported) effort.

The crucial issue is whether or not the final assignment is realistic in terms of what a faculty member can be expected to accomplish and perform well. In making the FTE assignment, the chairperson's judgment on such matters as faculty experience and department needs in teaching, research, and service activities is extremely important.

6. Assess the reasonableness of each faculty assignment both in terms of the activities assigned and the time or fractional FTE allowed for the activity. If inequities exist, adjustments among the faculty or in the total effort assigned may be necessary, but note that some equity adjustments may be moved to another term.

7. Identify evaluative criteria that you will use to assess each assignment being made; these activities typically are faculty activities but may include expected outcomes. Be as quantitative as possible. Both you and the faculty member must share an understanding of how the level of success in completing the assignment will be determined.

8. Discuss each assignment with the appropriate faculty member. Consultation may be required by a collective bargaining agreement or state laws. A consultation may reveal new information or become a negotiation session, making further assignment changes necessary. The final assignment decisions, however, should remain in the hands of the chairperson.

These steps provide a reasonable and sound strategy for assigning faculty duties. The chairperson will want to involve the faculty in as many of the steps as possible but particularly in steps 1 and 2, where the department's goals, objectives, and priorities are established and form the basis for the planned quarterly activities. In addition, the chairperson should consult with each faculty member after the start of a term to make sure all is going as planned.

Questions

1. In your department, what is considered a maximum teaching load? Is it a certain number of courses or course credits taught per term, a certain number of contact hours per week, or something else?

2. If a person is assigned a maximum teaching load in your de-

partment, does this teaching constitute a full-time workload? If it constitutes less than a full-time workload, what other assignments do you give to make a full-time workload?
3. Is the teaching load of your department divided equitably among the faculty members, or do some members have larger teaching loads than others? Do faculty members who have the same size teaching loads receive the same percentage of FTE for teaching? In your department, what constitutes the workload of one FTE faculty member?
4. Have you ever reduced a faculty member's teaching load in order to assign him or her to other activities?
5. In making assignments, do you follow any special procedures to ensure that the assignments are equitable? For example, do you assign a faculty member a specific number of points for each activity, and is he or she considered to have a full workload when the sum of all the earned points reaches a predetermined number? Or do you have some other method for ensuring equitable assignments among your faculty?
6. In making faculty assignments last year, what factors did you take into consideration?
7. Have any of the teaching, research, or service assignments to your faculty members ever been tailored to help them develop a special competency or overcome a weakness?
8. During the past year, has your department had any problems related directly or indirectly to assignments?

References

Adams, Walter. "Faculty Load." *Improving College and University Teaching*, Autumn 1976, pp. 215–18.

Bossenmaier, Monica. "Faculty Perceptions of Academic Advising." *Nursing Outlook*, March 1978, pp. 191–94.

Brown, Stephanie. "Approaching Faculty Productivity as a Mechanism for Retrenchment." *New Directions for Institutional Research*, Winter 1979, p. 45–54.

Creswell, John W. "Faculty Acceptance of a Workload Survey in One Major University." *Research in Higher Education*, May 1978, pp. 205–26.

Dyer, James S., and Mulvey, John M. "Computerized Scheduling and Planning." *New Directions for Institutional Research*, Spring 1977, pp. 67–86.

Fawcett, Jacqueline. "Integrating Research into the Faculty Workload." *Nursing Outlook*, April 1979, pp. 259–62.

Feasley, Charles E. "Faculty Workload Formulas in Competency-Based Programs." *Education Technology*, November 1978, pp. 30–32.

Harper, Ronald L. "Faculty Activity Analysis." *New Directions for Institutional Research*, Spring 1978, pp. 73–81.

Nelson, Thomas Morgan. "Instructor Judgments of Classroom Assignments in Teaching Psychology." *Higher Education*, February 1978, pp. 83–86.

Sommers, Alexis N. "University Productivity." *Educational Record*, Winter 1977, pp. 251–56.

Swofford, Ronald. "Faculty Accountability Workload and Evaluation: A Synthesis." *Community College Frontiers*, Spring 1978, pp. 51–53.

Walker, John E. "Research First, Teaching a Distant Second." *Journal of Thought*, January 1979, pp. 11–14.

13

Managing Department Resources: Time, People, and Money

In these times of budgetary restrictions, declining enrollments, and fiscal instability, the need to stretch department resources to obtain maximum benefits becomes increasingly important. The chairperson must be aware of the resources available to the department and the various ways they may be managed. Although no blueprint for successful management exists that can be uniformly applied to all departments, some common allocation problems can be addressed, and the following discussion suggests various approaches to solving these problems.

In general, the resources that the chairperson must allocate, or manage, are time, people, and money. One important way of maximizing the use of time is to manage the curriculum efficiently. A well-managed curriculum can free valuable time for faculty members to pursue creative and scholarly interests. The faculty, students, and staff constitute the department's human resources. These human resources must be carefully nurtured and cared for if the department is to achieve its goals.

A more obvious resource is expense money. Departments find that the amount of money available is never sufficient for every desired activity. For example, choices sometimes have to be made between the amount to be allocated for travel for faculty members, the number of telephones, and the duplication of papers and documents. Once again, no master plan is offered beyond the general dictum that the department's welfare is the criterion to be used when allocating or managing its resources.

Management of Curriculum and Time

By efficiently managing its curriculum, a department can often effect savings in faculty time and instructional materials without compromising the quality of instruction or causing undue inconvenience to students. Conversely, if little or no planning time is devoted to the curriculum, the department may overextend its faculty, compromise its goals, and create morale problems that may be difficult to resolve. In other words, without planning, the teaching program may become inefficient, costly, and obsolete.

Departments must take the time to look at their offerings objectively. For example, the information about the department contained in the university catalog may be incorrect or out of date; some courses listed may no longer be offered, and the content of others may have been altered. The chairperson should ensure that the department's course offerings are appropriately and accurately described. Courses also must be related to the task of providing a coherent and sequential program of studies within the discipline and should not be offered only to satisfy the desires of individual faculty members.

Scheduling classes and assigning rooms are important activities that are sometimes carried out without consideration either of department goals or of data derived from a systematic analysis of needs. Sometimes scheduling duties are carried out by a staff assistant without adequate faculty guidance. Clearly, curriculum management is an important task that should be supervised by the chairperson, who should analyze past experience, examine complaints, and review suggestions for improvement. In effect, he or she should develop and implement reliable and relevant procedures for dealing with the curriculum. The task of curriculum management consists of making such decisions as which new courses will be offered, who should teach particular courses, and which courses might be canceled. All these responsibilities are part of the task of managing instructional resources.

One method of monitoring the curriculum is through a department curriculum committee. In many departments, such a committee may already exist, though it usually has only the responsibility for evaluating proposals for new courses. The committee's task, however, could be expanded to include many other aspects of curriculum management. Following are some suggested responsibilities for an active curriculum committee in the areas of approval of new courses, elimination of existing ones, course schedule and sequence, and curriculum review and analysis.

Approval of New Courses

Before approving any new course, the committee must take into account certain consequences. First, the committee should ask whether the new course will add to the content or perspective of the subject matter of the current offerings or whether it will substantially duplicate another course offered by this department or another.

A second consideration is the possible effect of the new course on other courses in the department. Will it draw enrollment away from department courses currently offered, or will it generate additional enrollment? If it generates new enrollment, will the enrollment in other university departments be affected? Is the course to be a core, elective, or service course? Will it primarily serve majors, nonmajors, undergraduates, or graduate students?

A third consideration is the effect of the new course on faculty members' teaching assignments. Will some department members have to assume an additional workload, or will a course currently offered be canceled so that its instructor can be assigned to teach the new course?

Finally, the committee should consider the effect of the new course on current physical or financial resources. Will the new course require materials and physical facilities that are not available to the department? Will the new course require an internal reallocation of funds or the acquisition of new funds?

When considering a new course proposal, then, the committee should analyse it in terms of, first, its educational contribution, e.g., course content, methodology, and prerequisites; second, its effect on enrollment, e.g., shifting enrollment and additional enrollment; third, its effect on workload, e.g., effect on current faculty and courses; fourth, budgetary limitations, e.g., faculty positions and the cost of new materials; and fifth, availability of space, e.g., laboratories, classrooms, and special requirements. The committee should also examine the place of the new course within the current sequence of courses and its probable effect on the student. For students, the proliferation of courses may not only allow but even encourage early specialization. In some disciplines, specialization may narrow the opportunity to obtain a well-rounded higher education, but in other disciplines specialization may be desirable.

The department, when considering a course proposal, may need to revise its curricular goals. Such goals and objectives often include specifying the kinds of knowledge a student should obtain while majoring in the department's discipline, the competencies that the student should be able to demonstrate successfully, and perhaps even the kinds of problems the student should be able to solve. Such information may be necessary for courses currently offered as well as for proposed courses to show how the courses relate to the department's curricular goals.

The decision to approve a new course should be based on careful consideration of the information obtained during the review of the proposal. Often, a committee will not consider the effect of a new course on department enrollment. Frequently, adding a new course only disperses students majoring in the field among a greater number of courses offered by the same department. In such a case, the average class size would be reduced and the faculty workload would be increased, but the total department enrollment would remain unchanged. The effect of a new course on department enrollment, while not the major factor in deciding whether to approve the course, remains an important consideration.

Elimination of Courses

Eliminating obsolete courses allows more efficient use of available resources and reduces the amount of misleading information appearing in catalogs and counseling manuals. Some researchers have even suggested that a course be dropped when a new course is added. Such a mechanical approach, however, may be indicative of unimaginative planning or desperation caused by declining resources.

A periodic review of enrollment in all courses is a systematic way for the curriculum committee to begin the task of designating courses to be eliminated. The ability to conduct an enrollment review depends in large part on the records kept by the department staff or on the availability of these types of data from the college or university institutional research office.

Such a review opens up at least three alternatives for the committee. First, a course that generates a minimum number of students might be retained if it were determined to be beneficial to the students enrolled in it. Enrollment could be enhanced, perhaps, by changing the meeting time or by offering the course less frequently. Second, the review could result in a course being eliminated because the committee determined that the content was no longer of interest or that another course was meeting student needs and drawing enrollment away. Third, the reviewing committee could recommend that course content, methodology, or emphasis be changed to revitalize the course. These decisions, when made well in advance of registration, enable the chairperson to allocate instructional resources wisely. Courses that continue to be offered but that are ignored by students should undergo stringent scrutiny.

The course offerings should be revised as little as possible during the registration process. Some departments allow university policies about minimum class size to determine which courses are to be dropped. The obvious drawback of this approach is that the reassignment of faculty members whose courses have been dropped is not determined by careful review of curricular or other department needs. Such inadequate curriculum planning and management usually results in ad hoc assignments, last-minute switching of instruction obligations, and "default" research or public service assignments. In addition, the department loses the opportunity to support student needs.

Some departments announce more courses than will eventually be taught and wait to see which courses actually attract the most students and which attract the fewest. Courses with few students are then dropped. The difference between this approach and the "no planning" approach is that in this case an alternative assignment has already been worked out should enrollment be insufficient to justify the course.

Course Schedule and Sequence

When developing a schedule of classes, the department must consider the needs of students, the availability of appropriate classroom space, and the times preferred by students and faculty members. A review of past experiences and careful scheduling of core and elective or service courses may lead to an improvement in class schedules and faculty workloads. The schedule also must take into account special characteristics of the department's students; for example, if a large number of the students are working full time, scheduling morning classes makes little sense.

The department would be wise to review its courses annually. Information such as the number of approved courses, the number and frequency of courses actually offered, the enrollment gathered, and the number of students who dropped each course affords the department an opportunity to exercise control over its course offerings. Perhaps examining records of students majoring in the field as to courses taken, sequence, and so forth may help determine whether the recommended sequence is being followed.

Following are four examples of hypothetical situations that would require in-depth analysis. In each case, the academic year is based on the quarter calendar.

1. Course A was offered all four terms and had the following enrollment: fifteen students during fall quarter; eighteen during winter quarter; fourteen during spring quarter; and seventeen during summer quarter. A review of student course sequences may indicate that no disruption would occur if the courses were offered only in the winter and summer terms. (The assumption here is that faculty resources would be available in the summer.) Furthermore, because the course is required for students majoring in the field, the total annual enrollment may not be substantially reduced. Thus, by offering the course only twice a year, the department has decreased its instruction workload without substantially decreasing enrollment.

2. Course B has been taught during three terms, and each term its enrollment has been low. Examination of the situation reveals that the course has always been offered in the late afternoon. If increased enrollment is desired, the course might be moved to "prime time," e.g., late mornings at residential universities, or evenings at universities with a large number of part-time students.

3. A department has 127 approved courses, but only eighty-seven of them were offered last year and eighty-three were offered the year before. Twenty-five of the approved courses had not been offered in either of the last two years, while two of the offered courses (four sections each) accounted for 75 percent of the department's total enrollment. This situation suggests that a curriculum review, including a close examination of the department's curricular goals, is in order.

4. During the past few years the enrollment in an upper-level undergraduate course has consisted mostly of graduate students. Perhaps this course should be offered as a graduate course.

Curriculum Review and Analysis

The importance of periodically reviewing courses before adding, eliminating, expanding, or revising them cannot be overstated. The periodic review should encompass enrollment data, revised course syllabi, statements of course objectives and student objectives, and any other special or relevant information about the courses.

Another form of curriculum analysis can be conducted using data showing department interrelationships. A given department may list all its courses and indicate the number of students majoring in other fields who are enrolled in each course. Knowing the extent to which other departments provide students for each

TABLE 13.1
SAMPLE OF AN INDUCED COURSE LOAD MATRIX: STUDENT CREDIT HOURS GENERATED FALL TERM 1977, BY PROGRAM MAJOR AND BY DEPARTMENT, SAN LUIS STATE COLLEGE, DOMINGO, FLORIDA

DEPARTMENTS	PROGRAM MAJORS, LOWER LEVEL										Total Student Credit Hours by Department
	Undeclared	Arts; Humanities	Biological Science	Science; Math	Social Sciences	Agriculture	Business	Health Sciences	Food Science Technology	Ornamental Horticulture	
Business	803	185		44	527	33	2514	38	35		4,179
English and Foreign Language Literature	261	1287	139	405	1206	314	784	442	146		4,984
Fine Arts	276	1153	14	84	230	8	149	63	20		1,997
Life Sciences	184	472	227	93	1174	1067	273	1492	53		5,035
Physical Sciences	249	786	198	1608	805	505	923	847	161		6,082
Social Behavioral Sciences	228	841	118	189	2116	99	595	331	104		4,621
Vocational Tech.	203	12	7	31	8	22	3	756	1927	870	3,839
Total Student Credit Hours by Major	2204	4736	703	2454	6066	2048	5241	3969	2446	870	30,737

NOTE: 15 student credit hours generate 1 FTE student

course may be the basis for adjusting course content or method of presentation. Table 13.1 shows how such information can be arranged in a matrix. By collecting this type of data from other departments, a given department may also discover what courses are serving its own majors. Therefore, the effect of referring students to courses outside the department can be estimated. A department that offers service courses to students majoring in other fields can estimate the effect of curricular decisions by these other departments.

Almost all universities that have computerized student data files have the capability to construct such a matrix, which is usually called "the induced course load matrix." Chairpersons should contact their institutional research offices for help in obtaining the data.

Data and Information Requirements

Institutional research offices amass a large body of data, often for purposes of program evaluation. If the chairperson feels that such information would be useful, even if no formal review is scheduled, he or she should contact the office of institutional research and request the information. The chairperson should understand that the data received are only as good as the data submitted to the centralized information sources. If there is a discrepancy between the data provided by the office and the chairperson's own knowledge, the chairperson should determine the reasons for the discrepancy and attempt to correct the data.

An improved curriculum, then, helps the students and the department alike. A system of curriculum management may be a departure from the common practice of allowing individual faculty members to determine the courses they want to teach. But a planned approach may be preferable to a situation where courses are frequently cancelled at the last minute, contracts must be revised, and students are unable to progress systematically through their programs of study. Planning is not synonymous with inflexibility, nor need it cause a decline in academic quality. By the same token, proliferation of courses is not synonymous with improvement in academic quality. By assigning time to a faculty member to revise a course or two, the chairperson may be making a short-term investment leading to increased student satisfaction and reduced faculty workload.

Management of Human Resources

As enrollments stabilize or decrease and enrollment-based

funding drops, the number of constraints on the institution will increase at all levels. Effective use of human resources will become essential but can be accomplished only if the chairperson is fully aware of the department's workload and can project assignments over the whole academic year. In general, he or she needs to know the department's workload, understand the faculty members' professional and personal concerns, and then be able to interpret and communicate department needs while negotiating assignments with the faculty and staff. Clearly stated department goals and reliable historical data about all department resources will allow the chairperson to justify assignments in terms of the department's objectives. The ability to estimate requirements for an entire year, rather than treating each term as a unique entity, will help stimulate acceptance of heavier workloads during some terms.

Faculty

Very few departments have enough faculty members to do everything that needs to be done for the university, the community, and other constituents. A department chairperson may need to juggle academic assignments to ensure that sufficient effort is expended on instructional activities to cover student demands while at the same time providing appropriate research and service time for the faculty. Careful planning of teaching assignments is required to allow time for research and service, particularly for younger faculty members, who must make reasonable progress toward promotion and tenure. Typical complications arise when established faculty members accept outside contractual obligations and have to find substitute teachers for the classroom. In addition, faculty members going on sabbatical may leave gaps in the teaching program and require replacement. As suggested in the preceding section, curriculum planning and management can provide a degree of flexibility. In any event, the chairperson must be able to show the faculty that each department member is treated fairly.

An equitable distribution of the department workload may be achieved by several methods. Some chairpersons make all assignments, while others depend on a committee process. A recommended technique is participatory planning. This method is not always the most efficient planning tool, since it requires extensive communication among faculty members.

Several arguments can be made in favor of the participatory planning model, however. An open discussion among faculty members who are familiar with the courses they teach can facilitate decisions about the sequence of courses, the frequency with which they are offered, the level of performance that can be expected of students following the sequence, and so on. The faculty can devise equitable procedures for assigning introductory courses as well as those courses with unusual workload requirements. Workload policy governing the balancing of large and small courses with new and old preparations can be most readily developed through participatory planning. Moreover, peer pressure tends to reinforce policies developed in an open manner.

The chairperson sometimes has the difficult task of determining whether particular faculty members are competent to teach certain courses. In a period of expanding resources and enrollment, a department may have added specialists and specialized courses. When these specialists leave, their specialized courses, having become a part of a subcurriculum, remain.

The chairperson must then choose among several possibilities: convincing another faculty member to step in temporarily; reassigning the course to another faculty member and allowing course development time; recruiting a part-time teacher; replacing the course with one that is already being offered either within or outside the department; or, with the approval of the faculty or students, dropping the course. Other considerations may include the graduate faculty status of the proposed substitute instructor or even a strong expression of preference by the dean or academic vice president for one of the alternatives. In any event, the chairperson needs to know about the faculty members' specialty training, their current specialty interests, their reputations for teaching effectiveness, and other characteristics that are relevant to the assignment process.

If the chairperson decides to retain the course offering, he or she will usually have to persuade the most able candidate from among the faculty to accept this new responsibility. The chairperson must proceed cautiously, however, so as not to give a "proprietary deed" for the course to the substitute teacher until and unless the other faculty members concur. "Ownership" can be a prime motivating force for the teacher to develop and enhance a course. On the other hand, a faculty member who regularly teaches the same courses, year after year, may become bored with them and become ineffective in the classroom.

The middle ground between ownership and boredom can be attained through a system of rotation. Even the specialized courses in many departments can be taught by more than one professor. Every faculty member might be required to be prepared at least to take responsibility for additional required or specialized courses. These arrangements can be worked out cooperatively, with the approval of the chairperson, after vitae and teaching records of each faculty member have been reviewed. The chairperson's genuine concern for faculty development will be tested in such cases. Finding the right opportunities for growth and improvement for each faculty member is a challenging task.

The problem of reassigning and revitalizing courses also occurs when enrollment in two related courses declines so markedly that they have to be combined to meet minimum enrollment standards. Prior "ownership," expertise in the subject matter, and rank and seniority in the department may complicate efforts at reassignment. The new activities required of faculty members who will have smaller teaching loads is a topic that ought to be discussed before or during the time that courses are being combined, not afterwards. A clear statement of department goals, as well as an inventory of research and service activities for each faculty member, would be helpful to those involved in reassigning courses.

Declining budgets and an increase in faculty grievances may well lead to a squeeze on human resources, which will, in turn, retard a department's progress toward achieving its teaching and research goals. In such situations the department's mood and productivity may depend more heavily on the manner with which faculty workload assignments are handled than on the assignments themselves. Perhaps greater involvement by the department faculty would be helpful. In essence, by using open planning to make teaching assignments, the chairperson can help change the faculty's perception of administrative capriciousness and promote unity of purpose within the department. This method, even though the results may not be ideal, may be perceived as more fair and, therefore, more palatable.

Understandably, the participatory process can create numerous problems for the chairperson. Moreover, there may be insufficient time to implement the process. Sometimes a chairperson will not know until July what the department's allocation will be for the upcoming academic year, which begins in August or September. Yet faculty assignments for a given calendar year must be made much earlier than July. One solution to this dilemma is to implement the planning process in the preceding February or

March. At the least, information from the faculty can be obtained and feelings aired. An estimate of instructional resources with alternative assignments can be made, and the result can be fine-tuned in the fall.

Essentially, planning with 90 percent of the information available is superior to no planning at all. Also, decisions that are generally understood and that are accepted by the majority of the faculty are more easily implemented. An open planning process that relates operational necessities to department goals is one technique for achieving important objectives. Furthermore, a process by which all faculty members can identify their contributions and feel productive will tend to minimize friction within the department.

Most descriptions of the planning process give the impression that it is a smooth, well-oiled operation, when in actuality it is usually a fitful and uneven affair. Planning consists of the working out of tensions among various opinions and ideas, and often occurs as a result of pulling and pushing by various factions within the department. Integrating differing opinions into a working and realistic plan requires a great deal of effort.

Support Staff and Graduate Assistants

Clerical, administrative, and professional employees, known as support personnel, are invaluable to the chairperson in carrying out the department's functions. Since staff members are often the first persons whom a visitor to the department encounters, the chairperson should insist that courtesy be shown to everyone, especially students, whether in person or on the telephone.

The effectiveness of staff members, of course, is determined by the quality of their training. New secretaries and staff assistants are often assigned duties and responsibilities for which they have had little or no previous experience. Many new employees are at a disadvantage because they do not know how to operate within the university network. One way to solve the problem is to arrange a meeting between the new staff member and his or her counterpart in another department and to allow the experienced employee to discuss duties and responsibilities with the newcomer. A new secretary must learn not only what to do and how to do it, but also whom to ask for help—for example, whom to call when a payroll error occurs or whom to contact when a purchase order needs special handling. This type of information is not usually found in procedural manuals, but it is nonetheless important. Time can be saved and department efficiency improved if the department staff knows the informal "people" network within the university.

Further, the chairperson should encourage the department staff to meet the staff of the dean's office as well as the staff of administrative offices with which they have frequent contact. Even though the university system abounds with rules and regulations, having good interpersonal relations and knowledge of who can expedite matters will help get the job done more easily.

Although competent clerical staff members frequently perform their duties with little direct supervision, at times they must be closely supervised, and registration is one of these times. The chairperson should see that the staff has the necessary information, that student flow has been considered, and that the appropriate persons are available during the registration process. The chairperson should also communicate clearly to all staff members precisely what is expected of them. Staff members should be included in department activities such as picnics and social events, for inclusion in such events stimulates loyalty and understanding.

The chairperson should try to keep abreast of personnel rules and regulations, especially those that govern recruiting, promotion, appointment, advancement, and termination. In times past, a chairperson who was authorized to hire a secretary simply went out and hired one. This approach is no longer possible. A bewildering variety of rules and regulations governs the process of announcing vacancies, interviewing candidates, meeting equal opportunity criteria, and choosing which candidate to hire. Failure to follow established procedures can result in a lot of problems, not the least of which might be legal action. Furthermore, the chairperson should not make promises of advancement unless he or she intends to keep them.

Regulations regarding personnel may vary from one institution to another. Therefore, the chairperson would be wise to consult with the appropriate institutional personnel officer for guidance.

New chairpersons may not be aware of the fact that terminating the employment of a secretary or other member of the support staff is no simple matter. In addition to causing great trauma, termination involves a host of established procedures that must be scrupulously followed to meet the requirements of due process. Some chairpersons may find it easier to tolerate a secretary's inefficiency or ineptitude than to go through the complicated process of termination. Occasionally, a department has been forced to retain an unwanted employee because of its failure to follow the rules. Consequently, the chairperson should be very selective when hiring.

Our discussion should not be taken to mean that the dismissal of employees whose performance is unsatisfactory is impossible. The task is indeed a difficult and onerous one, but knowing and following the rules makes it achievable. Here again the chairperson should consult with the institution's personnel officer even before discussing the contemplated action with the employee.

Departments that employ graduate assistants for instruction and research support must treat the students fairly and humanely. The chairperson should make sure that the process of awarding assistantships is rational and orderly and that the period of time for which the assistantship is offered is unambiguous. Awards should be made as early as possible, but without undue haste. The students' qualifications should be reviewed carefully, and assignments should be within the capabilities of the assignee. Student workloads should not be too disparate, since student morale can suffer if some students feel that they are being required to work much harder than others. Low student morale can affect the mood of the whole department.

Students

Students are one of higher education's most important resources. Without them there would be no universities and no departments. Most institutions of higher learning depend on funds that are linked to the number of students enrolled. Those departments that experience sharp decreases in enrollment are understandably concerned about losing faculty positions and other resources. To ensure their ability to survive, some departments feel compelled to recruit large numbers of students to make up for the decreases. In so doing, they admit a greater number of marginally qualified students than they ordinarily would have.

The ideal situation, of course, is when a department attracts enough students of good quality to ensure adequate funding. How can a chairperson encourage good students to enroll and simultaneously foster programs that stimulate student interest and participation?

Students are attacted to institutions, programs, and departments that offer them the most in terms of quality of instruction, financial support, and other less tangible benefits. On the undergraduate level, students who are shopping for a major field of study are likely to be impressed with programs that spend time and effort making the introductory courses lively and interesting. The chairperson should, therefore, encourage the most outstanding, dynamic instructors to teach the lower-level courses. In addition, graduate teaching assistants who are given charge of sections should be carefully supervised. Students appreciate lectures that are well organized and well developed and grading policies that are fair rather than punitive. Unfortunately, many faculty members have never spent time thinking about teaching methods. They ought to be persuaded to do so.

The department should also encourage the creation of student advisory committees and help them find faculty sponsors. The chairperson should regularly meet with groups of students to obtain student reactions to department services and policies. A student committee might even be commissioned to assess student opinion about the department, the faculty, and course offerings.

The chairperson should also be alert to student complaints about poor teaching and inappropriate behavior of faculty members and be prepared to investigate recurring complaints. Often a prompt discussion with the faculty member may be in order. Occasionally, the chairperson may have to consult with the dean or academic officer about serious allegations.

Inquiries from current and prospective students should be answered promptly and courteously. In general, someone should be in the office at all times both to respond to student questions and to make needed referrals. Similarly, replies to correspondence, especially about admissions, should be made within two or three days, at most. The chairperson should periodically emphasize to the faculty and staff the importance of prompt responses. Faculty members should be urged to contact personally those applicants who seem to be well qualified. A caring attitude will impress potential students and can influence their choice of a university.

Another activity that may benefit the department is recommending students for honors, grants, awards, fellowships, and so forth. Individual faculty members, as well as committees, should be encouraged to name students who deserve recognition or rewards for their achievements. Recognition of student accomplishments is a sign that the department cares about its students; furthermore, publicity about outstanding students enhances the department's reputation.

Departments should also try to keep in contact with their graduates. Alumni are sometimes willing to make contributions to fellowship funds and library collections and can also help graduates obtain employment. Maintaining contact with alumni may allow a department to conduct follow-up surveys, which can be useful in times of self-study.

The chairperson may be called on to help students with problems encountered elsewhere in the college or university. The department staff can help develop a useful informal network of "problem solvers" throughout the university. Students who have encountered problems can be plugged into the network.

Occasionally, a chairperson must deal with students who exhibit aggressive, destructive, or violent behavior. Neither threats against faculty members nor threats of suicide should be taken lightly. The chairperson should be aware, before a crisis arises, of campus security procedures as well as the availability of medical services and psychological services. Many departments have developed, with the help of students, codes of student conduct. Other departments have used students to help resolve problems of cheating and vandalism.

Chairpersons should be aware of institutional policies and procedures concerning student misconduct and be prepared to use student advisory committees to manage student problems. Of course, chairpersons should also be cognizant of federal rules concerning privacy for student records.

Management of Other Resources

Expense, equipment, and temporary funds constitute the bulk of "other resources." Chairpersons require little guidance regarding the planned expenditures of these funds. Generally, funds are allocated in response to the greatest need. A research-oriented department that is competing nationally may rank travel among its primary needs. Another department—in a college of education, for example—may require extra expenditures for telephone service to expedite its involvement in the regional in-service teacher education process.

What a chairperson should consider, however, are functional alternatives, especially those that have the least negative effect on the department's morale. For example, placing restrictions on the quantity of pencils, pens, and paper available to faculty members can adversely affect their attitude. Perhaps doing away with one or two telephones within the department would provide resources needed to supply pencils and paper. The primary task, in regard to budget allocations, is determining possible alternatives and assessing them in terms of feasibility and potential benefit before deciding which course of action to take.

Another resource that must be managed carefully is space. Faculty and staff members get very territorial and possessive about their offices and laboratories. In modern buildings, an office with a window can become a prized status symbol. If the chairperson is able to foresee that a faculty member will have to share an office or laboratory with another person, this arrangement should be discussed with all concerned as soon as possible.

Some Typical Problem-Solving Situations

Following are four examples of problems that chairpersons have encountered when trying to decide how best to allocate department resources. Most discussions or problem-solving techniques contain essentially the same elements: alternative solutions to the difficulty and some method of evaluating or ranking the alternatives.

The chairperson of a geology department is faced with increasing demand for more frequent offerings of some of the more specialized petrology courses. He draws up a list of alternative solutions to the problem and evaluates each alternative using three criteria: (1) its potential for solving the problem; (2) its cost; and (3) its feasibility. These criteria are admittedly a bit fuzzy, but they have a certain logic. They allow the chairperson to determine what the chances are that the proposed solution, if implemented, will actually solve the problem; how much the proposed solution will cost; and what the chance is that it can be implemented. The chairperson considers five alternatives.

1. One possibility is to hire additional faculty members to meet the increased demand. More instructors would certainly solve the problem, but the cost would be high and the chances of getting new lines approved by the dean are not good.

2. A second alternative is to reduce the number of courses offered by the department to shift faculty members to the petrology courses. This approach would solve the immediate problem at practically no cost, but the faculty members whose courses would be dropped would surely object and the sequence of course requirements in other specialties would be disturbed. Therefore, the likelihood that this alternative could be implemented is only fair.

3. A third suggestion is to hire additional graduate teaching assistants to help teach the petrology courses. Unfortunately, the courses are too specialized to be taught by graduate assistants. Graduate students, however, might be used to teach other courses, especially basic courses, thereby freeing faculty mem-

bers to teach petrology. In this case, the potential for solving the problem is somewhat higher. Although the cost of employing additional graduate students would not be as prohibitive as hiring additional faculty members, obtaining funds for this purpose would not be easy.

4. A fourth alternative is to increase the use of instructional technology. Although programmed instruction is a viable technique, the faculty feels uncomfortable with it. It has the potential for partially solving the problem, but the effort involved in gearing up to use it would be fairly expensive, and the probability that the faculty could be motivated to develop such a system is not high.

5. A final alternative is to reduce the number of sections by increasing the number of students per section. With fewer sections to teach, the instructors would have time to devote to teaching petrology courses. The costs here would be negligible, and the proposed plan would be relatively easy to implement.

The chairperson draws up a list of these five alternatives. He then ranks each criterion on a three-point scale: "high," "medium," and "low" (see figure 13.1). Examination of the list reveals that the fifth alternative combines high potential and high feasibility with low cost. The chairperson, therefore, does select this alternative.

	Potential For Solutions	Cost	Feasibility
1. Additional faculty positions	High	High	Low
2. Reduction in course offerings	High	Low	Medium
3. Increase in graduate assistants	Low	Medium	Medium
4. Increased use of instruction technology	Medium	Medium	Medium
5. Reduction in sections per course	High	Low	High

Fig. 13.1. Ranking of alternatives to accommodate course demand

In many instances, however, the choice is not so easy. Two or more alternatives may be equally attractive. Approaching a problem in the manner suggested above can help eliminate some suggested solutions quickly and allow the department to concentrate its energies on deciding among the most feasible alternatives. Some chairpersons do not feel compelled to put all the alternatives in writing, preferring to debate the issue mentally. Whether the chairperson writes down the alternatives or not, the decision process is basically the same. The chairperson could also organize a group of faculty members to handle the task of listing alternatives and making rational choices.

Our second example of a resource allocation problem is much like the first, although more complicated. A department of interior design experiences a steady enrollment increase in a department subspecialty, nonresidential (industrial and institutional) space analysis and design. The courses in the subspecialty are taught by Faculty Member S and Faculty Member J and their graduate assistants. The two professors are nationally recognized as experts in the field. Conscientious and productive, they are trying to implement a design internship program that requires much travel and supervision. While capable of doing research, they have published nothing in the last two years because their teaching duties have been so time-consuming.

To allow themselves more time for research, Faculty Member S and Faculty Member J request that additional faculty members be assigned to help teach the nonresidential design courses. The chairperson, recognizing that productive research is indispensable to the faculty members' careers and the department's reputation, wants to do everything possible to provide the faculty members with research time.

| | —— FALL —— | | — WINTER — | | — SPRING— | | — SUMMER — | |
Course	Enroll-ment	Faculty Member	Enroll-ment	Faculty Member	Enroll-ment	Faculty Member	Enroll-ment	Faculty Member
IDE 4200	15	S	16	S	15	S	14	S
IDE 4220L	19	S	19	S	18	S	16	S
IDE 4240	23	S	25	S	29	S	20	S
IDE 4300	30	S	35	S	38	S	25	S
IDE 5943	28	J	26	J	20	J	22	J
IDE 5943r	12	J	14	J	18	J	16	J

Fig. 13.2. Instructional load, courses in nonresidential design subspecialty, department of interior design

A review of the course enrollments in the subspecialty shows that the two faculty members are, indeed, carrying heavy instruction loads (see figure 13.2). All the courses, with the exception of IDE 4220L, are 5-credit-hour lecture courses. The exception is a 3-credit-hour laboratory class that requires supervision. The institution is on a quarter calendar, and every course is taught every term. The faculty members' failure to carry out their research interests is understandable, for each course was offered four times a year.

The chairperson, when considering possible solutions, realizes that other department members will be unwilling to teach the nonresidential courses because they are not primarily interested in that aspect of interior design. Hiring new faculty members, on the other hand, is not at all feasible given the budgetary constraints at that time.

The chairperson then asks himself whether the classes could be offered less frequently without a decline in enrollment and whether the classes could be increased in size without a decline in quality. Discussions with faculty members and students indicate that the lecture courses could be taught just as effectively even if they were much larger and that they could be offered every second term without depriving students of the opportunity to complete their required courses within a normal time frame. The laboratory course would have to be taught each term because the number of student work stations is limited; no more than twenty students per term can be accommodated.

The first two examples present allocation problems that involve creating additional time for faculty members to conduct research or to teach new courses. The third example deals with the opposite type of situation. Because of circumstances beyond the department's control, certain of its activities have been reduced, leaving the faculty members with considerable time that is not fully occupied. The challenge is to create activities to replace those that have been curtailed.

The department of modern languages in a large urban university suffers a drastic decrease in enrollment when the undergraduate curriculum committee of the college of arts and sciences votes to abolish the foreign language requirement for the baccalaureate degree. Although the university is not absolutely devoted to funding departments on the basis of student credit hours taught, the situation in the modern languages department is very serious. The department is demoralized, the funding for graduate students is reduced dramatically, and even scholarly senior professors who do little undergraduate teaching seem to be affected.

The chairperson reviews the situation in her mind. From the outset, she realizes that the least desirable solution to the problem would be to dismiss nontenured faculty members and to abolish certain programs, but she also realizes that this possibility might become a reality in the absence of other viable solutions. Aware that the university will not reinstate the language requirement, she nevertheless decides to make contact with several other departments to emphasize the value of foreign languages at the undergraduate level. She considers several ideas, but before deciding on a course of action, she needs answers to the following questions:

- How many areas and programs would continue to encourage their undergraduates to take language courses as electives for cultural or practical reasons?
- Would it be profitable for the department to reschedule and restructure its undergraduate teaching to accommodate the university's urban environment?
- Might rescheduling some courses to the late afternoon or evening attract a new student clientele? If offered to the adult community as part of a continuing education program, would such courses find acceptance?
- How many secondary school foreign language teachers might be interested in attending in-service courses designed especially for them?
- Would the department faculty cooperate with other departments to develop interdisciplinary programs of a cultural nature?
- Could special foreign language courses be designed to serve business needs? Foreign manufacturers need instruction manuals translated into colloquial English. Similarly, American manufacturing companies with a large export market need staff to translate instruction, repair, and service manuals from English into foreign languages.
- Could special training be provided for persons who want to develop competencies in translating such manuals?

Some of these ideas are good ones; some are not. The chairperson must try to assess the potential benefit and the feasibility of each alternative. Perhaps all the alternatives taken together may not be able to reestablish lost enrollment. The department's survival at its present size may well depend on its importance to the university's overall mission. If that is the case, a written report justifying the retention of the current faculty members may become necessary. The chairperson should anticipate the possible need for such a document and involve the faculty in preparing it even before a request is received from the dean or vice president.

In our fourth example, the chairperson of the department of urban and regional studies in a medium-sized university receives a memo from his dean, who has just returned from a conference in Washington. The dean has learned that a certain federal agency is about to initiate a new program for funding university projects in community development. In the memo, he suggests that the department consider submitting a proposal for a grant to fund a three-year project at $100,000 per year. In a subsequent telephone call, the dean again raises the subject of the desirability of the department's pursuing a federal grant in community development as described in his memo.

Before making any commitment, however, the chairperson wants to satisfy himself that a project funded by this particular federal agency would benefit the department; that faculty endorsement and support could be obtained; that certain department members have the competency to write a persuasive proposal; that sufficient department resources could be made available to those writing the proposal; and that the department would be able to carry out the proposed project successfully should it be approved.

Let us review the questions that go through the chairperson's mind: Can a project be developed that meets the goals of both the agency and the department? How will the project benefit the department and its faculty members? If the project does not contribute to the department's goals or the faculty's benefit, it should not be pursued.

Let us assume that in this case the chairperson has positive feelings about the dean's suggestion and believes that the project would be a good one for the department. His feelings are buttressed by several sound reasons: some faculty members have the necessary competencies; the project would give visibility to the department and the university; the project would provide hard data for valuable publications by faculty members; and, last but not least, funds would be available for graduate assistantships and salaries for summer faculty members.

The next step is to determine the best way to get faculty support. The chairperson remembers full well the circumstances when he tried to obtain support for an idea by presenting it for the first time to the whole faculty during one of its meetings. To overcome the department's initial negative reaction took several months of difficult lobbying. He later learned from a friend who was a seasoned administrator that a group will usually have a negative reaction to any idea that is presented for the first time to the group as a whole. Therefore, he decides to discuss the idea individually with some department members, especially those who are faculty leaders. If they cannot see the advantages to the department and their support is not forthcoming, the idea should be dropped, at least for the time being.

Once the support of key faculty members is obtained, the chairperson must think about the best time for placing the matter on the agendum of a full department meeting. At the meeting, all faculty members will have an opportunity to express themselves, and those colleagues with whom he has spoken earlier can be counted on to support the idea and emphasize its potential advantages to the department.

After satisfying himself and his faculty that the department should prepare a proposal, the chairperson must make decisions about who should write the proposal and what resources can be made available for the effort. He reviews in his mind all the department members and their respective workloads. The faculty consists of three full professors (including the chairperson), four associate professors, and three assistant professors. Among the faculty members are experts in the areas of transportation planning, housing and community development, health planning, and environmental planning.

Two faculty members, Smith and Jones, are recognized experts in community development and are especially suited to the task. The chairperson wonders whether the task of writing the proposal could be added to the existing assignment of either or both professors, whether a workload must be reduced in order to make time available, and who will assume the excused duties in the event a person's workload is reduced.

The chairperson now examines the existing workloads of Smith and Jones in terms of the number of courses each teaches, the number of students in each course, the time required for preparation of lectures, research involvement, committee assignments, and so forth. He finds that the workloads of both professors are approximately equal.

Smith indicates that he is willing to be the principal writer if he is given a reduced workload. When he is asked what part of his assignment he would prefer to relinquish, however, Smith produces a list of his reasons for not giving anything up. He volunteers some personal time for the assignment. Jones is also willing to write the proposal, but he is not very enthusiastic about it because much of his personal time is taken up with outside consulting activities and he depends on the income the consulting produces. In order for Jones to write the proposal, he would have to curtail his consultations.

The chairperson assigns Smith to be the writer and suggests that for the coming term Smith either cancel one undergraduate course or turn it over to a well-qualified graduate student to teach under Smith's supervision. In either case, the time saved would not be enough to carry out the entire task, so Smith will have to devote some of his personal time to the activity. Smith agrees to accept the responsibility for writing the proposal and selects one of his best graduate students to teach the undergraduate course.

The chairperson also considers the costs of writing the proposal in terms of staff time and department money. The secretarial staff consists of two full-time secretaries and a half-time typist. The chairperson must decide whether the staff can provide the necessary help to the proposal writer. If not, can expense dollars be used to hire a temporary typist for the final draft? What would have to be cut from the expense budget in order to hire the typist? Expense dollars usually pay for items such as travel, duplicating, telephone, and office supplies. A reduction in any of these categories could involve some changes in department operation. For example, what would be the effects of cuts in travel money? How would the faculty react if travel money that had already been committed could not be delivered? Might the dean be willing to provide either money or secretarial time for so worthy a project?

Finally, the chairperson ponders the personal costs of pursuing and administering the grant. How much time will he have to spend supervising the preparation of the proposal? How much time will be spent supervising the activities of faculty members who will be involved in implementing the project? The chairperson must consider the effects of any ambitious undertaking on himself as well as the department as a whole.

When resources are shifted to accommodate an added activity, the department equilibrium becomes upset. Some faculty members may feel that they are being asked to sacrifice too much for an undertaking that does not seem to benefit them personally, and the chairperson must be prepared to soothe them.

Whenever a department considers taking on some significant,

previously unanticipated activity, all the variables of department operation must be carefully examined. Important decisions should be made on the basis of available data. Some of the data is to be found in department records, and some may be obtained from the office of institutional research. Chairpersons should learn about the kinds of data that are available in a college or university office of institutional research, how to obtain such data, and how to use it to the department's advantage.

Questions and Exercises

1. Think of a problem involving the management of department resources—time, people, or expense money—that your department or some other department has encountered during the past two or three years and that was resolved satisfactorily. Make a list of the steps taken to resolve the problem, using the procedures described in the chapter. What circumstances led up to the problem? What alternative courses of action could have been taken?
2. Think of a problem involving department resources that is currently being encountered in your department or some other department and that is as yet unresolved. What circumstances led up to it? What alternative courses of action might be taken? Which course of action seems to be best?

References

Blackburn, Robert, et al. *Changing Practices in Undergraduate Education.* Berkeley: Carnegie Council on Policy Studies in Higher Education, 1976.

Bowen, Howard R., and Douglas, G. K. *Efficiency in Liberal Education: A Study of Comparative Instructional Costs and Different Ways of Organizing Teacher-Learning in a Liberal Arts College.* New York: McGraw-Hill, 1971.

The Carnegie Foundation for the Advancement of Teaching. *Missions of the College Curriculum: A Contemporary Review with Suggestions.* San Francisco: Jossey-Bass, 1977.

Dressel, Paul L. *College and University Curriculum.* Berkeley: McCutchan, 1971.

————. *Handbook of Academic Evaluation: Assessing Instructional Effectiveness, Student Progress, and Professional Performance for Decision Making in Higher Education.* San Francisco: Jossey-Bass, 1976.

Mayhew, Lewis B. "Curricular Reform and Faculty Well-Being." *Educational Record,* January 1963, pp. 53–61.

————. "Curriculum Construction and Planning." *Handbook of College and University Administration,* edited by A. S. Knowles. 2 vols. New York: McGraw-Hill, 1970.

14

Faculty Views about "Management"

The term *management,* when used in connection with the operation of a college or university, tends to create uneasiness among some faculty members. They view management as a process primarily associated with business organizations and reject the idea that the same management process is appropriate for institutions of higher education. Consequently, faculty members react negatively to terminology used by management specialists and are skeptical of programs designed to enhance the management skills of their department chairpersons.

Although the term *management* can be defined in many ways, most definitions reflect the concern for accomplishing organizational goals and objectives by working with and through individuals and groups. In attempting to achieve organizational goals, the manager must perform such functions as planning, organizing, motivating, and controlling.

The principles and processes of management, according to many writers, are applicable to all types of organizations, including educational institutions. The concern for accomplishing goals and objectives is just as important for colleges and universities as for hospitals, government agencies, and industrial corporations. Moreover, the same management functions are performed in colleges and universities as in other organizations, but the individuals or groups of individuals who perform these activities in educational institutions are not generally called managers.

Regardless of whether or not they are called managers, however, the persons responsible for carrying out the basic functions of management must have a complete understanding of management functions as well as certain interpersonal skills. Business executives, government agency heads, and department chairpersons all require the same interpersonal skills if their organizations are to be managed effectively.

Many chairpersons have difficulty perceiving themselves as managers or administrators. Some prefer to think of themselves as facilitators, even though they perform functions that come under the heading of management. Their preference for the term *facilitator* may be a response to department members' negative attitude toward the term *manager*. Also, the use of *manager* implies a supervisor-subordinate relationship. Even though department chairpersons are expected to provide their faculty members with some "guidance" (a euphemism for *supervision*, perhaps?), faculty members consider themselves colleagues and peers of the chairperson, not subordinates.

Some writers classify academic department chairpersons as "middle management" in educational institutions. Although this classification may be correct from the standpoint of an organizational chart, the reaction of chairpersons to this classification ranges from amusement to irritation. After all, chairpersons are faculty members who have been chosen to assume the additional responsibility of providing leadership for their colleagues. How dare anyone call them "middle managers"!

Since most chairpersons retain their faculty status and continue to perform faculty duties even while serving as chairperson, they are able to reflect the concerns of their fellow faculty members about the management process. Faculty members fear that close supervision might stifle their creativity, that management by objectives might eliminate the flexibility they feel professional academicians need. Being required to provide a detailed statement of their objectives for the next one or two years is a new experience for most faculty members. They are concerned about the consequences of not being able to meet all their stated objectives. They fear that they will no longer be able to add new objectives or drop old ones in the middle of the year, as they have been able to do in the past. They worry that the quantitative types of performance evaluation used in industry to measure "output" will not adequately evaluate the quality of performance in the areas of teaching and research and that, hence, a faculty member's value to the department might not be properly recognized and rewarded.

The truth of the matter is that the principles and processes of management can be adapted for use in academic departments in a manner that is nonthreatening to the faculty. In adapting these principles, the chairperson must take into account the concerns and sensitivities of the faculty members in his or her department and assure them that most of their concerns are unwarranted.

Despite their claims to the contrary, most chairpersons receive enough satisfaction from being chairpersons to want to continue in the position for as long as possible. One young chairperson of a sociology department stated, only somewhat facetiously, that the only thing worse than being chairperson of the sociology department is not being chairperson of the sociology department. Despite complaints about paperwork and other so-called unpleasant duties, 90 percent of chairpersons serving three-year terms said that they would seriously consider serving an additional term if invited to do so.[1] Many of these chairpersons want to enhance their administrative effectiveness and could do so by learning more about management processes and developing whatever additional interpersonal skills are necessary to implement these processes.

Many books written about management are organized around a series of management processes. Each process is defined and described in some detail without reference to any particular level of management or type of organization. Examples are given of situations in which the process can be used to help resolve a problem. Readers of these books are expected to select the processes that are pertinent to their organizations and to adapt them to their own situations. Although such books may be useful to many different types of managers or would-be managers, they are rarely used by department chairpersons who are looking for solutions to their problems.

The present book is organized around selected major problems, issues, and concerns that confront most departments. The problems are described in some detail and several suggestions are offered that might help resolve a problem. These suggestions are not identified as management processes, although that is what they are. Descriptions of management processes, therefore, are included in the book but only as they apply to selected department problems.

The text avoids much of the management terminology and nomenclature that intimidate the academic community. It emphasizes, however, the value of applying sound management procedures to all administrative levels in colleges and universities. The book is directed specifically to chairpersons' concerns about the use of the management process in seeking solutions to department problems.

---

1. Survey conducted in 1977 by Allan Tucker, unpublished.